50

The Textile Book

The Textile Book

Colin Gale and Jasbir Kaur

Oxford • New York

First published in 2002 by
Berg
Editorial offices:
150 Cowley Road, Oxford, OX4 1JJ, UK
838 Broadway, Third Floor, New York, NY 10003-4812, USA

Berg is an imprint of Oxford International Publishers Ltd.

Library of Congress Cataloging-in-Publication Data
Gale, Colin.
    The textile book / Colin Gale, Jasbir Kaur.
        p. cm.
Includes bibliographical references and index.
    ISBN 1-85973-507-X -- ISBN 1-85973-512-6 (pbk.)
  1. Textile industry. I. Title.
    HD9850.5.G35 2002
    338.4'7677--dc21

                                                        2001007579

British Library Cataloguing-in-Publication Data
A catalogue record for this book is available from the British Library.

ISBN 1 85973 507 X (Cloth)
       1 85973 512 6 (Paper)

Typeset by JS Typesetting, Wellingborough, Northants
Printed in the United Kingdom by Biddles Ltd, Guildford and King's Lynn

For Our Families and Friends

Contents

Contents

Preface

Textiles is a broad discipline and for most people who work in the subject it is a very practical discipline too. The breadth of the subject and its straightforward place in the world has in many ways proved to be its academic undoing. There are so many facets, so many stories and examples, that the subject pretty much defies attempts to sum it up. Anyone who has taught textiles or has been asked 'what is textiles?' will know the impossibility of trying to explain something that can be science or art, business or hobby, and even worse of attempting to answer the question 'what kinds of job are there in textiles?' This difficulty is probably not a result of communication problems, since there is much excellent writing about textiles: books on special aspects, magazines, journals and websites. The difficulty lies more likely in the variety of issues needing explanation: how, for example, could someone starting a career in textiles comprehend how chemistry, history, a scarf, politics and economics might all intertwine? The classic answer, of course, is 'only with a great deal of effort and good advice'. Most textile professionals acquire the complex range of knowledge and skills appropriate to their sector, piece by piece, building their expertise over years; few would claim to understand the full diversity of the textile world and its history.

Textiles and its associated industries constitute one of the largest sources of employment in the world. Consequently there are a myriad of educational courses in schools, colleges and universities specifically dedicated to the study or practice of textiles. For such courses, as far as we know, there are no textbooks that attempt to tackle the initial problem of explaining the diversity and complexity of the textile world. Partly this is for the reasons already given but partly also, we suspect, because it wasn't possible before now. The advent of modern communications and the internet has proved a significant boon to those who want to develop an overview of contemporary textile practice and industry. It is in the nature of textiles to be a part of its time, to be current, and even textile history plays an active role in the modern world. It is also in the nature of textiles to be where it is needed. With this field being so tied to geography and time, we suggest that without the internet, for example, it would have been almost impossible for someone to have written this book twenty years ago.

Conscious of the fact that most other subjects offer textbooks designed to introduce students to a variety of perspectives appropriate to their study, we set about building on this standard academic practice. The concept for this book was some five years in its gestation, and its final form (compiled rather more quickly) is very much a result of the dialogue between ourselves. It has also benefited from the mutual experience we have, teaching students with highly individual approaches to textiles. It is in the structure of the book that perhaps its creativity lies. While writing it, we have been very conscious that there is far more information (and probably better information) about textiles than we have managed to include. No doubt as well, we will offend many by our omissions of what others deem to be more important or more accurate. Finally, it has been hard to attempt to sustain a global view. Whatever the failings, we feel confident that the condensing of the subject into one useful set of references will provide something that has not been available before. Probably more a book to dip into than one to read end-to-end, we hope also that the diversity of materials will prove both stimulating and informative, allowing readers to draw their own conclusions and make their own connections. For the enquiring new student or the seasoned professional, the text is scattered with leads, many of which should cut down on wearisome surftime.

Acknowledgements are particularly due to the following for their contributions and assistance: for talking to us and sharing their experience – Peta-Gene Goodman of Agal Ltd, Johan Verbruggen of Liberty's, Donna Warner of *Metropolitan Home* and designers Lindsay Bloxam and Liz Marchetti. For contributing written materials and thoughts especially for the book – Lesley Millar, Curator of Textural Space and textile artist and craftsperson Valerie Kirk. For assisting us with visuals – Mercedes Renjel of Asur, Gill Poulter and the Dundee Heritage Trust, Verdant Works, Tony Jordan of DuPont UK, Sanderson, Kandola. For the willingness of the artists, designers and craftspeople to allow us to use their work in the book – Sophie Roet, Isabel Dodd, Sarah Taylor, Janet Emmanuel, Kei Ito, Miglena Kazaski, Anne Belgrave, Asako Ishizaki and Chiyoka Tanaka (courtesy of Textural Space), Bullen Pijja Design, Sharon Ting and Victoria Richards. We would also like to thank in general those from the world of textiles who have been so supportive in their comments and assistance, and to thank specifically Kathryn Earle, Sara Everett, the staff at Berg, and George Pitcher our copy-editor, for making this project a reality.

As well as our thanks and acknowledgements to the many whose works and thoughts are included in this book, we would like to thank our families and friends for their forbearance during our period of hibernation. Particularly those most affected, Jill, Amy, Frank, William and Matthew, and Satpal, Jaswant, Manjit and Jaspal.

Colin Gale and Jasbir Kaur

Part I
Overviews

What is Textiles?

Whenever we talk about what makes our species unique and different from all others on the planet, two abilities are raised as evidence – language and the power of invention. There are perhaps a handful of inventions so central to our being and our ordinary lives that we have almost forgotten how remarkable they are. Cloth is one of these; like basic mathematics we find its nature so obvious and its presence so universal that we often overlook the genius of its invention. In considering what textiles is, we must remember that the origin of the earliest and humblest cloth is lost to us; it pre-dates our recorded history, it precedes the age of metals and the invention of the wheel. As our civilizations have grown, so has fabric developed with us, an integral part of every cultural nuance, a resource in every struggle, a comfort in the most personal and domestic spheres of our lives. Each of us has a relationship with fabric from cradle to grave. Cloth has also become the basis of a vast textile industry. Like electricity, a much newer arrival, textiles is an industry which is part of the very rhythm and pulse of humanity. We can barely conceive of how different it makes our lives.

There is a famous model of human motivation, called Maslow's Hierarchy of Needs (Maslow, 1970); like all ideas it has its critics, but it is a useful way to measure and compare the importance of the things we do and the things we have. Among the seven categories of human need that Maslow identifies, textiles could be deemed to have a role in each one. Few other 'arts', except perhaps for architecture and clothing, have a place in fulfilling every human need, from basic survival to spiritual development. Textiles provide fundamentals such as warmth and protection; they help us to identify with one another and can signal social status and role. For those who work in textiles, it is possible to develop pride in one's craft and to explore a world of endless material opportunities, to create something of stunning beauty. Finally, for textiles professionals their work can become their vocation, their identity inseparable from their practice.

In this book the intention is to map out a subject and practice so great that none seem to have attempted it, in its entirety, before. Textiles leaves a huge trace in its wake and busies itself only with the current and the future; few lift their head up to survey the endless vista that it constitutes. Within textiles is art and science, craft, technology and design, industry, history, culture and politics. For humanity itself, textiles has been both an enemy and a companion, it has made and broken communities. A shrinking world, the speed of modern finance, the miasma of contemporary culture now accelerate the pace of a global industry. The epic story of how, throughout history, billions of people have been involved with textiles is something that cannot be recounted. Instead perhaps, as we enter a new electronic age, something of the overall structure can be glimpsed for the first time. For textile professionals of the future such an overview may prove central to their survival.

The dissection – or perhaps construction – of textiles as a subject is tricky. Each audience and each reader will have its own sense of priorities and its own list of essential facts for inclusion. Each interest group and discipline already has its own specialist publications. Textiles is not a single subject in the classical sense, it is a collection of many that spin around the presence of cloth; its making, its analysis, its sale and its use and even its demise and disappearance. Many sectors and individuals believe they 'own' or are the guardians of some special 'spirit' of textiles, but textiles is greater than any one group or person and reflects the broad diversity of humanity. Because of this, any book attempting to define textiles as a single subject or subject grouping is doomed to criticism and lost to rationality. There remains only common sense and intuition to identify what might be of general interest and use to the reader.

This Book

This book is divided into four sections; **Overviews, The Creative, The Social and Industrial Context, Related Disciplines and Studies**. In Part I, Chapter 2 'The Cultural Place of Textiles' attempts to bring together some of the social effects, influences and categories that shape textiles and which it, in turn, has shaped. In the very broadest interpretations of our cultural histories and institutions it can be seen that textiles has influenced fundamental features of modern life. Things that we take for granted but would not begin to associate with what we wear on our backs or decorate our houses with. Things like the identities of women, spirituality, money, capitalism, communism and shopping. Textiles is in the very grain of what we are – as we respond so it responds, as we change so it changes. Sometimes, because textiles is so implicated in what we are, as an industry or culture it has had the power to influence human destiny, influencing social and political structures.

Chapter 3 'Perceptions of Fabric' portrays some of the difficulties in assessing exactly what textiles is, what its traditions are, whether there are natural divisions within it. The past of textiles is so rich and the present of it so dynamic, analyses often swiftly reduce to some simple and readily comprehendible subject or explanation. While the practical advantages of this function are clear, it does little to convey the nature of modern textile practices. Equally it is often hard to understand that no sphere of textiles stands perpetual and isolated; changes in design culture, technology, business or education all influence what textiles will become.

Part II looks at four contemporary 'types', whose vocation is to create new fabrics or textile products. Between them Chapters 4 'The Textile Designer', 5 'The Designer-Maker', 6 'The Craftsperson' and 7 'The Textile Artist' cover the broad range of career opportunities and practices at the creative end of the textile industry. Among the various art and design disciplines, textiles has the rare luxury that it can be put to almost any cultural or practical use. Consequently a range of professional skills and expertises are required. This section looks only to the art and design sector, though it might equally have looked to the engineer or the scientist. Of the four disciplines portrayed, none is perhaps so clear in real life. People change their jobs, they change their perception of textiles, their interest in the subject may come and go. However, the four 'types' discussed in these four chapters and the descriptions of their sectors help to show how wide the approach to textiles can be. It also shows how varied the nature of personal attachment to the subject can be. Even though all of those whose names appear identify very strongly with the subject, the nature of their practice and their attachment to textiles differ widely.

Part III, The Social and Industrial Context, looks at the textile world and starts to consider its implication in human affairs. For thousands of years textiles has been a cause of trade, and the demand for clothing and fabric has stimulated travel, barter and exchanges of industrial and craft knowledge. Chapter 8 'Global Textile Traditions' looks at the history of textile cultures around the world and how trade disseminated them, carrying motifs, sensibilities and sensuality far and wide. Epic themes, both good and bad, are dealt with in Chapters 9 'Ecology' and 10 'Industry'. As a basis of employment, a feature of industrialization or creating wealth, textiles has few peers either now or in the past. As much as textiles has brought advances and joy and hope, for some it has brought hell on earth, ruining lives, ruining environments, breaking hearts. Sometimes the very personal benign relationship we have with fabric makes us forget that textiles can exact a price on us too. In a lighter vein, most of the time we are content to enjoy and take pleasure in the colourful and subtle changes in our working environment, the fashions and styles, the games of identity that textiles allows us to play. Throughout the world the daily nature and substance of what we are depends on how we look, the money we have, where we can go and what we can see. Textiles has underpinned many of these features of our lives and is likely to go on doing so. At a commercial level, knowledge of present and future tastes is fundamental to business success. Chapter 11 'The Role of Trends and Forecasting' looks at the agencies and individuals who influence the direction and future of textiles.

Whatever your professional relationship with textiles, there will always be people doing a job that you don't quite perceive as being 'textiles'. They may be research scientists, they may be financiers, they may be politicians. The relationship these people have with textiles is just as real and important as that of a designer, or an artist or a manufacturer. The degree of their specialist knowledge and how it can be applied to textiles will be no less than that of any other professional. Part IV of this book, Related Disciplines and Studies, clearly establishes the role of other disciplines and professions and the part they have to play. As a major cultural force and industry, textiles has need of most professions; lawyers, managers, communicators, technologists. While some professions have only a fleeting involvement with textiles, some stand in special relationship to the subject. Often careers are to be had combining a knowledge of textiles with that of another discipline or subject. A sample of these disciplines and careers is portrayed in Chapters 12 'The Buyer', 13 'Journalism', 14 'Science', and 15 'Research'. Buyers and journalists play key roles in the day-to-day operations and successes of the textiles sector, while science and research underpin what has been, what is current and what is to come.

There is a saying 'you can't see the wood for the trees': a similar phrase might be developed for textiles. To say what it is, is very hard, but as soon as an explanation is begun it seems to never end. Textiles is so many things that it might best be understood through experience, gradually, approached with an open mind. Each person comes to his or her own understanding of what textiles is and in this lies its charm and its power. At the simplest level it is no more than a piece of cloth and perhaps that is where everybody must begin. We have tried in this book to provide a broad picture, one which many in the past would have appreciated during their studies. We don't fully answer what textiles is, but our book at least starts to paint the picture.

2

The Cultural Place of Textiles

It is interesting to reflect on how textiles has affected civilization and culture, although it is improbable we could adequately measure its influence. The story of textiles begins before the recording of human culture. With regard to the earliest civilizations, we have little idea what the psychological, spiritual or social impact of fabric was. We know that textiles found a place in every society around the world and that textile skills must have been widely communicated. We also know that textiles must have been one of the very earliest of tradable commodities. By its ubiquitous nature textiles has touched the lives of millions of individuals, shaping their experiences, their hearts and their minds. Because textiles has been a part of so many different cultures and lives, it is difficult to suggest that there would be some common and universal experience of it. However it is worth attempting to portray some of the starting points of a cultural analysis; how textiles has been involved in the best and the worst of human endeavours; how it has been central in the development of modern society; how it touches the human psyche. In this chapter a few analyses and examples are brought together to portray the scope and complexity of textiles' cultural influence, but they are not definitive. Each reader will be able to find examples and analyses more pertinent to his or her own culture and interests. The examples touch on a few standard issues of culture – gender, identity, politics and modern life.

Gentility and Gender

One common perception of textiles is that it is a feminine art. There have been enough male weavers throughout history to dispel that belief but in many circles the perception persists and it is revealing that it should. It is also true to say that the majority of textile design courses throughout the world are populated largely by women. In terms of practicality, realistically it seems a little unlikely to presume that all women have some special predisposition, some sense of elegance or sensitivity, that provides them an exclusive relationship with fabric. Far more likely, the somewhat demeaning observation that small hands and little fingers facilitate the execution of fiddly work, as is often the case in electronic component assembly. However the true reasons underlying the special relationship with textiles are really sourceable elsewhere, to the social relationships between men and women, between women and women and between men and men. Beyond the perfunctory analyses of feminism, the two main likely causes are romanticism and the division of labour between the sexes.

It is possible to glean the impression that in many civilizations, the wealthy and the powerful had a particular relationship to work and labour – they developed poetic constructions about the relationship between men and women, they put the two together and found embroidery as something for privileged women to do. Certainly the European model of this explanation stretches back beyond the days of chivalry. Embroidery is potentially one of the more lavish and expressive forms of textiles. As a handcraft, concerned almost exclusively with embellishment rather than functionality, it lends itself to the world of wealth and status; it is not cheap to do. It is not heavy or messy work, like hand weaving or printing can be. The result is an embroidery tradition (with some variations) pursued by aristocratic and privileged women over a thousand years:

> In the evening went to a concert at the reigning Duchess's. I do not find an atom of that form I was taught to expect in all German Courts. Not only the Duchess, but the ladies who played raco with her, worked in the intervals of the game. At another table there was a large party employed in knotting, netting, embroidery, and even the homely occupation of knitting stockings; while the Hereditary Princess and those idlers who had no regular work, were busy making lint for the hospital. (Chenevix, 1799)

While this is not the same as the commercial hand embroidery traditions undertaken by ordinary people, it is significant insofar as the most socially influential groups in European history, the educated and the powerful, established a consistent view about the relationship between women and needlework. The most authoritative voices propagated philosophies regarding women's education, etiquette and behaviour. As a result of colonization and emigration these views were spread far and wide. The pursuit of embroidery or tapestry was seen to be 'ladylike', dignified and a sign of virtuous womanhood. It established an aesthetic lexicon about prettiness, subject matter and technical finesse. These sentiments carried well into the twentieth century and persist to this day:

> The ladies of the Royal Family are indefatigable needlewomen, and they are carrying on the fine tradition of the Queens and Princesses of Tudor and Stuart England, in whose day English embroidery work was famous throughout Europe. And they do not idly take up pieces of useless embroidery with nothing but attractiveness of appearance to recommend them. H.M. the Queen has set an example in real industry for a useful purpose, and the Princess Royal, both the Duke and Duchess of York, H.H. Princess Marie Louise, the Queen of Spain, and others, have followed her with enthusiasm.
>
> (*The Queen*, 1935)

Whether there is such a thing as a woman's approach or a woman's style depends on your point of view. Nonetheless, after feminism, many women see the idea of gender-specific traits as an insult and injury. Such feelings are reinforced by their witness of how, throughout history, the creative stature of women has often been ignored or diminished. Often within feminist criticism, decorative textiles are either valorized or dismissed; on occasion it is possible to suspect less than respect for decorative arts and crafts and, by default, a reassertion of elitist ideals of cultural rank in the arts:

> Women are considered to possess sex-specific skills that determine their design abilities; they are apparently dexterous, decorative and meticulous. These skills mean that women are considered to be naturally suited to certain areas of design production, namely, the so-called decorative arts, including such work as jewelry, embroidery, graphic illustration, weaving, knitting, and dressmaking. (Buckley, 1989)

Perhaps the most outstanding feminist tract on the status of women, textile crafts and the issue of gender is that provided by Rozsika Parker and Griselda Pollock, which the interested reader would do well to seek out (Parker and Pollock, 1981: 50–81). Regardless, history has proved that men can be as much enamoured of fabric and decoration as women, and also that the pleasure men can take is not necessarily dictated by assertions of power and wealth, by patriarchal inclinations, or even social and industrial necessities, but instead by more human traits of vanity, fashionability and joy:

> What should I say of their doublets with pendant bags on the breast full of jags and cuts, and sleeves of sundry colours: their galligascons to make their attire to sit plum round (as they term it) about them, their fardingals, and diversely coloured nether stocks of silk, yardsey and suchlike, whereby their bodies are rather deformed than commended. I have met with some of these in London so disguised that it hath passed my skill to discern whether they were men or women. (Holinshed, 1577)

There are more prosaic explanations of why women are associated with textiles, a prime example being that women, through childbirth and childcare, develop a role in and around the home, thereby taking up categories of work appropriate to the domestic environment. Such arguments are often developed further to suggest that through their industry, women establish the nature of community; textiles manufacture generally requiring a fixed location and a variety of activities. Men on the other hand, by implication, take on more mobile or physically heavier work such as hunting, farming or animal husbandry. This particular explanation, based on the principle of a division of labour and gender aptitude, is rather tied in to a pre-industrial model of textile production and even then seems an unlikely generalization

> In the times of Ancient Britons, Romans and Saxons and ever since, the spare moments of the housewife, her maids and daughters had been devoted to spinning ... equally from the earliest times the more difficult art of weaving had been practised by men specially trained as websters, sitting all day each at the loom in his own cottage, to provide the coarse clothes of the local peasantry.
>
> (Trevelyan, 1942: 35)

The explanation of why, in many developed modern societies, more women than men undertake textile education is not straightforward; certainly there is no universal indication of preference based on gender, so we must presume it is a social construction, a familiar and accepted belief. We might equally presume that men have been encouraged to have negative perceptions about the practice of textiles. Economics can also play a role; if more women work in the textiles industry, then it is most likely on the exploitative basis that they can be paid less. There are undoubtedly a range of primarily sociological and feminist answers to this subject and gender divide. There remain, though, some more difficult questions and intuitions about textile psychology, not so much about women and textiles, but issues such as 'femininity' and textiles, perhaps even 'masculinity' and textiles, matters which by and large remain unstudied to this day.

The Inner Spirit

We all come into contact with cloth. Consequently we all have an ordinary and familiar relationship with it. Over thousands of years, hundreds of millions of people have had an even more direct relationship with textiles, through business, pastime, ritual or necessity. Textiles reach the senses, they provoke and draw on memories, they can become familiar friends, they have even been a sign of terror. The steady unrelenting nature of textile production, whether producing raw materials, yarn or fabric, has been a cause of satisfaction to some and a humiliating, backbreaking experience for others. Being so close to us, textiles can become part of our innermost identity. Being so much a part of the world, textiles can also ruin or make lives. The range of personal associations that people have had with textiles is as diverse as the people themselves and their changing circumstances. Sometimes in looking at the broad social sweep of textiles and its history it is easy to forget that the story of each individual involved is different and personal.

For many, regardless of gender, an inner psychological or spiritual experience of textile craft is common. Not all textile production takes place in a difficult context. Textiles are often produced for pleasure, as a hobby or as personal expression, some people may also be lucky enough to combine work and pleasure. In these situations, there is often an experience of an inner quiet, of reflection. Perhaps this is not much more than honest labour, but in combination the self-

Figure 1. Retting and stripping jute. Courtesy of Dundee Heritage Trust, Verdant Works.

control, precision and sensuality of sewing, weaving and so on will often create a meditative reverie. In a charming piece of writing, *The Sempstress*, the French novelist Colette tells of her nine-year-old daughter Bel-Gazou in 1922 as they spend a hot, languid summer together by the sea. After considering the effect that reading has on her daughter she moves on to drawing and sewing

> If she draws, or colours pictures, a semi-articulate song issues from her, unceasing as the hum of bees around the privet. It is the same as the buzzing of flies as they work, the slow waltz of the house painter, the refrain of the spinner at the wheel. But Bel-Gazou is silent when she sews, silent for hours on end, with her mouth firmly closed, concealing her large, new-cut incisors that bite into the moist heart of a fruit like saw-edged blades. She is silent, and she – why not write down the word that frightens me – she is thinking.
>
> (Colette, 1974)

The sensation will be familiar to many who undertake creative disciplines which involve a craft element, as if the 'speaking' part of our mind for a while has no useful role, and wanders unhindered yet in parallel, measuring, fretting, musing or calm.

For others, textiles has been a curse: perhaps their social position or circumstances meant their lives would not have been markedly different anyway, but for those who had to work in the gruelling environment of industrial textiles, life could hardly have been any worse. In 1916 the cotton mills of Shanghai ran twenty-four hours a day, with spinning all the time and weaving for perhaps fourteen of those hours. Apprentices could do up to eighteen hours per shift. Most mills granted no rest, nor any break for food. At one time mothers would bring their nursing babies and lay them at their feet while they worked. The vast majority of workers in these factories were desperately poor and would often have to make their way to work through harsh conditions before their ordeal began:

> But what of the chill days in winter, with a bleak wind blowing, rain falling, and roads treacherously slippery with mud? It is hardest for the women who have bound feet, women too poor to pay for a seat on a wheelbarrow with five or six others. Yonder comes a group uncertainly picking their way along in the blinding mist. One poor soul at last reaches the gate of the mill and drops all in a heap on the cold wet ground to wait for the blowing of the whistle. 'Have you come far?' is asked of her pityingly. Half fearfully, half defiantly, as if braced for a reprimand, she struggles to her feet and answers, 'From Honkew,' a distance of nearly three miles. (Gamewell, 1916)

The woman would shortly be faced with twelve hours of continuous work; if she was lucky and worked at a loom she would at least get to sit on a bench, but if she was a spindle-watcher she would stand her entire shift. Against this kind of background the political upheavals of the twentieth century seem more than predictable and we should perhaps remember that for many, suffering of one kind or another in the name of industry still continues. To survive such ordeals, there must be a fight of spirit over body, every day. This has been the lot of millions of people.

Capitalism and Communism

In *The Communist Manifesto*, Marx and Engels provided an analysis of social change, of how over seven or eight hundred years there had been an inexorable move to a state of affairs they believed to be profoundly unjust:

> The feudal system of industry, under which industrial production was monopolized by closed guilds, now no longer sufficed for the growing wants of the new markets. The manufacturing system took its place. The guild masters were pushed on one side by the manufacturing middle class: division of labour between the different corporate guilds vanished in the face of division of labour in each single workshop.
>
> Meantime the markets kept ever growing, the demand ever rising. Even manufacture no longer sufficed. Thereupon, steam and machinery revolutionized industrial production. The place of manufacture was taken by the giant, Modern Industry, the place of the industrial middle class, by industrial millionaires, the leaders of the whole industrial armies, the modern bourgeois.
>
> (Marx and Engels, 1888)

What Marx and Engels fail to mention in the immediate context of these passages is how the *wool* industry did more than any other to create the structures and processes of capitalism, while the *cotton* industry probably did more than any other to create 'Modern Industry'. This may seem an ambitious claim for textiles but it is important to remember that after food and water there is no other commodity so universally required as cloth. Consequently the scale of the historical textile trade was always immense and, in comparison to that of the food industry, became international in dimension. The very size of the textile trade was key to its economic and social influence. Textiles changed the way we live, the way we do business and how we create goods. In effect, in the space of less than a thousand years, the growing infrastructures of the wool and cotton industries changed the world.

At the beginning of the fourteenth century, England exported 30,000 sacks of wool a year and about 5000 cloths. Over two hundred years later raw wool export had dropped to 4000 sacks while more than 100,000 cloths were sold abroad. England came to dominate the wool trade in Europe and during this period the basic structures of modern capitalism and finance emerged. The financing of the state became increasingly dependent on the taxation of wool. Increasing business activity required loan facilities:

> The great breeding season of English capitalism; in the early phases of the Hundred Years War, the time when the exigencies of Royal finance, new experiments in taxation, speculative ventures with wool, the collapse of Italian finance and the beginning of the new cloth industry, all combined to bring into existence a new race of war financiers and commercial speculators, army purveyors and wool monopolists. (Postan, 1939)

The increasing demand for cloth had also played a part in shifting fabric production from towns to the countryside to exploit water power, a thirteenth-century version of the Industrial Revolution. The period of the wool trade marked a shift throughout much of Europe, from a medieval and feudal society to a more modern one. It was the first step in a two-phase process toward creating our modern society. The mercantile and financial framework it established was to be the seedbed in which the Industrial Revolution grew some three to five hundred years later:

> Capitalism as the organizer of industry is first clearly visible in the cloth trade. Already in the lifetime of Chaucer, the capitalist clothier could be found, employing many different people in many different places. He was a social type more modern than mediaeval, and quite different from the master craftsman labouring at the bench with his apprentices and journeyman. (Trevelyan, 1942: 37)

By the early eighteenth century the cloth trade had become both international in dimension and well ordered. The trade provided (war forbidding) clear patterns of communication, transportation, economic exchange and finance throughout Europe, the Americas and elsewhere. Daniel Defoe, better known as the author of *Robinson Crusoe*, also wrote one of the best accounts of life in England at this time; the following is an extract from his fascinating account of the cloth market at Leeds, which took place twice a week. It provides some insight into the new 'social type' of which Trevelyan speaks. The clothiers swiftly and quietly laid out their wares 'as close to one another as the Pieces can lie longways', and formed a double line of trestle stalls to create, as Defoe calls it, a 'Mercantile Regiment'. We are then treated to an early account of the life of fabric buyers:

> As soon as the Bell has ceased ringing, the Factors and Buyers of all sorts enter the Market, and walk up and down between the rows, as their Occasions direct. Some of them have their foreign Letters of Orders, with Patterns sealed on them, in their Hands; the Colours of which they match, by holding them to the Cloths they think they agree to. When they have pitched upon their Cloth, they lean over to the Clothier, and, by a Whisper, in the fewest Words imaginable, the Price is stated; one asks, the other bids; and they agree or disagree in a Moment. (Defoe, 1725)

Just as one great textile industry, that of wool, was to establish modern economics, so another, that of cotton, was to drive the creation of modern industry, to spread the factory system throughout the world. Along the way cotton would first replace wool as the fabric of choice:

> In a pamphlet of 1782 we read: 'As for the ladies, they wear scarcely anything now but cotton, calicoes, muslin, or silks, and think no more of woollen stuffs than we think of an old almanac. We have scarcely any woollens now about our beds but blankets, and they would most likely be thrown aside, could we keep our bodies warm without them.' (Trevelyan, 1942: 389)

The history of the cotton industry and its role in the industrial revolution is well recorded. Various things may be accredited to the cotton industry, not least the disgraces and suffering of the slave trade (Walvin, 1993; Olmsted, 1996). The cotton industry was also to play a part in a great change: that point at which Capitalism nurtured its antithesis – Communism. While political upheaval and revolutionary ideas had existed for centuries, it is interesting that Communism would take seed in countries faced with huge difficulties implementing industrialization and economic modernization, the two great gifts of cotton and wool.

During the seventeenth and eighteenth centuries the main British export to Russia was cloth for the military. This had led Peter the Great to attempt to modernize the textile industry, most other industry being technically backward and based on handicrafts and domestic industry. Russia had not been self-sufficient in cloth production even though its capacity for producing raw materials was substantial. (At one time Russia closely followed India, ranking third in the world for raw cotton production.)

> The first half of the nineteenth century saw the expansion of the cotton textile industry, mainly concentrated in and near Moscow . . . Between 1820 and 1860 raw cotton imports (entering free of duty from the United States via England) increased over thirtyfold by weight, and the workers in the cotton mills were much the largest group of factory operatives. English machinery was used in some factories, but cheap English yarn was imported in increasing quantities down to 1842. In that year Great Britain repealed the prohibition on the export of machinery. As a result the Russian cotton-spinning industry began rapidly to be mechanized, and, much more slowly, the weaving industry followed suit.
>
> (Sumner, 1966: 320)

During the latter half of the nineteenth century, faced with a largely feudal system, a primarily peasant population, a failing financial system, poor transport and communications, Russia was to make a momentous change. This would be in sharp comparison to Western Europe and the Americas where, over centuries, there had been a gradual (though sometimes turbulent) adoption of new economics and more democratic social orders. In the West the populations had changed and adapted to new industry. Industrialization itself took place over a century or more. This was not to be the Russian experience: Russia would attempt to catch up in the space of fifty years. Prior to the Crimean War industrial development along the lines of the West had largely been dismissed by the Russian Government; now, Russia became the biggest borrower of foreign money and a significant importer of goods. Productivity outstripped that of all other modernized nations, although actual production was lesser in volume. By 1905 the scene had drastically changed; there were new centres of industrial activity and a growing divide between town and country. There was a new and politically active proletariat, factory workers. While many other Russian industries made substantial growth, almost half of all those classed as factory workers were in fact textile workers. Collectively they formed the largest group of the proletarian 'vanguard' which was to precipitate the Revolution of 1917. Undoubtedly the huge social upheavals Russia was going through and the First World War played a part in the Revolution. However, perhaps a new urban class, experiencing textile-factory work, did much to agitate discontent and demand change.

The volatile circumstances surrounding the Russian Revolution were an inevitable consequence of modernizing from an almost medieval society. The problems of capital, business, communication and war are close to those that faced China in 1932, where once again the textile industry featured, and once again the largest factory workforce were textile workers; also once again, no doubt they played a significant part in social change:

Among the factors retarding the development of China's cotton industry, the most important is undoubtedly the chaotic political conditions that prevail today. The recurrence of civil war entails an increasing burden of taxation, gives rise to the uncertainty of transport, reduces the area of cotton production, and shuts off the market within the war area. It interrupts normal operation and saps the vitality of almost every industry . . . Other factors, mainly economic, are more or less inherent in the transition of China from a medieval to a modern economic order . . . In China's cotton industry, the largest factory industry today, the economic factors are at work everywhere. (Fong, 1932)

The textile industry has played a fundamental role in defining the political and social landscape of our times, perhaps more so than has any other industrial sector. Through textile production and trade, millions of people shared the experience of an emergent new world order, both the good and the bad of it. On the basis of this they established philosophies and practices by which we all now live.

Lifestyle

One area that concerns all industries and nations is that of the changing patterns of consumer wealth and what motivates people to spend. In the second half of the twentieth century the phrase 'alternative lifestyle' came into common use to describe the way various sub-cultures chose to live, including what they wore, their eating habits, their attitudes, rituals and so on. From this origin, the term 'lifestyle' seems to have evolved and become a central concept for all who have a vested interest in consumer habits, including the consumers themselves. Lifestyle is now a term accepted around the world and used by a wide variety of government and industry analysts. Lifestyle analyses generally dwell on the four categories of home, work, leisure and fashion. The interrelationships between these categories are a key feature of modern lifestyle analysis.

Social and industrial evolution contributed to definitions of home, work, leisure and fashion. Argyle comments on how in Britain the Industrial Revolution clearly defined the world of work, how clothing and possessions in the nineteenth century defined wealth and status, and how free time gradually increased in the twentieth century (Argyle, 1996: 20–8). Forty remarks on the role of the Industrial Revolution in defining the home, stating that, previously, much work had been carried on in the homes of craftsmen. He also presses the case that the home became some kind of fiction, an escape from the 'brutal and deceitful' world of work:

The home, therefore came to be regarded as a repository of the virtues that were lost or denied in the world outside. To the middle classes in the nineteenth century, the home stood for feeling, for sincerity, honesty, truth and love. (Forty, 1986: 100–1)

Home ownership is now a typical aspiration of modern consumers, central to their ability to create a private or 'different' space. In China, according to the National Bureau of Statistics, approximately 70 per cent of people plan on buying a home, although the costs remain high (*People's Daily*, 2000). While in Japan the size of living accommodation is having a direct effect on consumer purchasing with smaller wardrobes and more prestige-status goods in the home (TCFoz, 2000). Also the number of young Japanese sleeping in beds rather than on futons has been increasing and there are more Western-style rooms in new houses (Tradepartners UK, 2001b). The home furnishings market is becoming increasingly fashion conscious:

> The home has become the most desired status symbol for Americans, and as such, a growing portion of the American families' discretionary spending is budgeted for the home . . . the home market has been transformed from a largely functional to a fashion business, thus allowing consumers to dress and decorate their houses like they dress and accessorize themselves.
>
> (Danziger, 2001)

There can of course be winners and losers in this scenario and, for some time, a typical story in many industry reports is how consumers are spending more on home furnishings than on clothes:

> Consumers are shifting their spending habits . . . 'The same consumers who might have bought expensive designer clothes now stay home a lot more than they used to,' explains Kurt Barnard . . . 'Their priorities have changed. They no longer need as much in the way of clothing . . . Proportionately, more of their income is going towards home enhancement merchandise.'
>
> (Cotton Incorporated, 2001a)

One of the most recent developments within the lifestyle arena is the impact of globalization. Consumer trends, aspirations and products are becoming increasingly similar around the world. This echoes the influence of the International Style during the twentieth century. Although it represented the 'modern' it was also criticized for its anonymity and uniformity (Woodham, 1997: 35). In the twenty-first century it seems that a new kind of uniformity is emerging, but for different reasons:

> For the first time now the home textile market is approaching a global dimension. Much more than in clothing, consumer tastes in home textiles have always had strong national and regional connotations, and now they are starting to bear a closer resemblance to each other, within Europe and on both sides of the Atlantic. The strengthening of the large international retailers is not foreign to this phenomenon: they are offering increasingly similar goods on the various markets – they are global products even from the

manufacturing standpoint since they are made in every corner of the world. (Hermes Lab and Associazione Tessile Italiana, 2000)

Underlying this convergence of style and product are the common experiences of modern consumers. In the clothing sector, these are identifiable as

- less personal or free time – creates a demand for convenience and easy-care goods
- less formality in society – creates a need for casual but smart clothes
- dividing time between work, home or leisure – need for versatile and comfortable clothing
- educated consumer – demands value and quality for money

While there are some exceptions to these rules, notably between Asia and the rest of the world (for example Japan still adheres to a greater formality at work), they are found to apply to most of the world's consumers. Consequently industry is making strategic responses to global lifestyle trends. The Woolmark Company has identified potential opportunities in the areas of elegant casual clothing for various occasions (what it calls the 'third wardrobe'), leisurewear, and technical innovations to enhance wool's performance. It has also identified the United States as the style leader in sports clothing and leisure wear, Italy as the style leader in 'smart casual' and Japan as the source of technical innovation. The Woolmark Company has now targeted the textile industries in these countries as partners for collaborative innovations in wool (The Woolmark Company, 1999).

The basis of industrial competition has changed and so has the nature of shopping. It is reported that in the United States 37 per cent of women say they don't have time for clothes shopping, and that 25 per cent spend less than an hour per visit among the clothing racks. This is resulting in attempts to make the shopping experience more personalized and efficient (Cotton Incorporated, 2001b). Similar phenomena in the competitive German clothing market (the largest in Europe) have had an impact on suppliers to the retail sector:

> . . . focus is no longer confined to the actual garment offer as such. The main focus has now switched to the ADDED VALUE attributes of potential trading partnerships such as marketing concepts and skills, flexibility, quick response and customer service.
>
> (Tradepartners UK, 2001a)

The effect of lifestyle changes are such that manufacturers and retailers find themselves under new pressures and have to deal with problems not previously encountered in their industries:

Players in the consumer apparel market are now no longer competing among themselves. They are competing against alternative lifestyle, recreation and entertainment choices available to consumers. And when consumers do purchase clothing and apparel they do so within increasing requirements in regard to performance, convenience, adaptability and style. (TCFoz, 2000)

Textiles and its dependent industries must survive in the new context of the lifestyle marketplace, which has particular qualities: our lives and relationships are increasingly mediated by systems of communication, and industries that revolve around pleasure and well-being are central to modern culture. We face a future that, for the moment, makes a great deal of shopping, of watching films, of eating out and travel. There is a new symbiosis between the market and the media which results in the promotion of a desire and the sale of whatever fulfils that desire, and which also stimulates activity within textiles in a variety of ways. One way is an acceleration and diversification of styles that match the seasonal or marketing need for new products. This tends to create a synchronization of the supply chain and the retail outlet. Another side effect is that stories need to be developed and told – there is a journalistic requirement to identify an explainable or identifiable phenomenon, whether it is cast as the future trend or as a stylish subculture; there must also be a perpetual supply of the 'new'. We get used to looking for something new, we always want something new, somebody is always telling us about something new.

The concept of lifestyle now forms the basis of a synergistic approach prevalent in modern retail, marketing and journalism, an approach which looks for and uses the idea of a coherent design theme or story that is linked to consumer fashion and taste. These stories or stylings can link most products such as clothes, ceramics, furniture and textiles. While the approach is not new, the comprehensive and very conscious use of associations, stories and ideals has become a standard methodology as important for the designer and manufacturer to be aware of as for the marketeer. As retailing practices and markets have grown more complex, so too have the number and diversity of lifestyle images and symbols. In the twentieth century, the academic world was dominated by theories about language, sign and symbol. This may seem a little remote from buying a nice embroidered scarf to match your coat or cushion to match your sofa, yet a study of the work in computing (Negroponte, 1990), semiotics (Barthes, 1983; Baudrillard, 1994) and communication theory (McCluhan and Fiore, 2001) provides us with many insights into our daily experience of the world, as shoppers, magazine readers or internet browsers. Just as interesting are some of the signs and symbols of textiles' communication, its celebrities, politics, fantasies and mythologies. Through the language of 'lifestyle', textiles keeps pace with contemporary culture. To stay competitive, textile professionals need to be alert to the changing cultural nature of work, the home, leisure and fashion.

3

Perceptions of Fabric

In recent years there has been a dynamic shift in attitudes toward textiles, and a new type of textile designer has challenged traditional forms of construction and content. As a result of a broadening vocabulary of materials, processes and techniques, textile designers are faced with more creative choice than ever before. New sensitivities and responses are also called for. On another level, attitudes and activities within the practice now mirror all facets of contemporary life; textile designers can be radical, funky, technical, conservative or serene; tradition has loosened. Many of the exciting changes that have happened in fabric in recent years have acted as a creative stimulus for other design disciplines. This versatile medium now supplies the worlds of fashion and interiors with an increasing and sometimes challenging range of materials and products. The fashion designer now constantly looks for original, innovative materials to work with, making fabric a fundamental part of contemporary fashion statements. For the interior designer or architect, new textiles offer everything from the complete co-ordinated chilled look to eclectic zany mixes. Whether they are looking for harmony, drama or functionality there is always one or more of these on offer, and quite often all three of them at the same time.

An increasingly diverse and sophisticated consumer market has witnessed innovations in fabric blends, the use of new technologies and the amazing march of synthetics. The effect of this combination has been the ability to explore new surface qualities of matt and shine as well as new combinations of weight and performance, and to reinvigorate old yarns and traditional fabric patterns. The look, the feel and the drape of fabric has entered a new era. No longer is the use of materials restricted to a perennial function: sportswear enters streetwear, safety and protective clothing can influence couture. These dynamic fusions in their own way stimulate further opportunities – there are new surfaces to print on, and fabric development starts to play with surface qualities as variable as the difference between paper and rubber, between moss and cellophane.

New Fabrics, New Aesthetics

The fusion of technology and tradition has revealed itself in a diverse assortment of new fabrics and materials, impeccably mirroring changes in lifestyle and the way we embrace modernity and progress in the twenty-first century. Increasingly the gap between the producer of textiles and the consumer is shrinking, enforcing the demand for innovation. The merger of tradition and technology applies to almost every aspect of the textiles world; from designers to craftspeople to artists and industry. Lifestyle culture has also been responsible for blurring the relationship between these disciplines and creating new intermediate markets and opportunities. Similar changes in the world of fashion create even more hybrid designers and virtuoso applications of fabric. Consequently, during the last decade of the twentieth century, a new breed of designers came to the forefront of textiles, and their work sits as comfortably in a gallery as it does on the shelf in Barneys, Liberty, Bergdorf Goodman or Harvey Nichols. The 'new' textile professional has foresight and employs intuition, working in a space where there are no limitations or restrictions.

Advances in textile design have had a remarkable effect on fashion. In addition to exploring issues of silhouette, the fashion designer envisages material innovation as an important motivating factor in his or her creative process. On occasion the material itself may well inspire silhouette. The creative collaboration between the fashion designer Issey Miyake and Makiko Minagawa, the textile director of Miyake Design Studio, illustrates this. Today's textile designer is resourceful and multi-talented, and can be found either in a laboratory breaking new ground through developing hi-tech materials, or leading the way by broadening the vocabulary of advanced decorative effects. This is often achieved by means of investigating processes and treatments such as moulding, embossing, heat-bonding and sculpting as practiced by Sophie Roet (Mahoney, 2000b) and Nigel Atkinson. Material innovation in textiles involves surface exploration which can now result in novel, sometimes curious and extraordinary fabrics. These are attained by way of combining various methods of production and finishing. Outcomes can be exciting but poised carefully between the worlds of commercialism and discovery.

More unconventional approaches to making and designing are often stimulated by developments in yarn and fibre technology. These constantly enhance the creativity of the textile designer, as do innovations in textile processes which direct us away from traditional notions about the subject. Yarn innovation has led to avant-garde mixtures of fibres, including the silk and aluminium 'Inox' yarn (Jones, B., 2000a: 48–50) and the wool and stainless steel blend from 'Bekintex'. These blends not only boost the properties of natural fibres but also usually offer additional qualities such as reducing static. Besides possessing performance-enhancing benefits, yarns are also developed for aesthetic reasons in order to achieve specific visual or textural effects. Synthetic fibres are often treated to mimic the intrinsic qualities of natural fibres or to create unusual, quirky finishes such as crunchy, glassy, clear nylon or novelty rubberized wool that feels like paper and looks like bark.

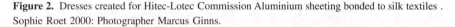

Figure 2. Dresses created for Hitec-Lotec Commission Aluminium sheeting bonded to silk textiles . Sophie Roet 2000: Photographer Marcus Ginns.

The recent technical and aesthetic progress in textiles deserves wider recognition. Today, the subject includes remarkable fabrics, distinctive furnishings, fascinating artworks and spectacular fashion. We are witnessing an era that is historically unmatched in terms of invention and experimentation in the field of textiles. An increasing number of designers are revealing the scope of the subject and the versatility of textiles as a creative medium. Through its major trade fairs, scattered across every continent, textiles now manages to disseminate these innovations rapidly across the globe.

Fundamental Skills and the Evolution of Textile Practice

Conventionally, textile designers will have a strong grounding in one or perhaps two of the traditional specialisms of woven, printed, knitted and embroidered textiles, and these are still considered fundamental skills in textile practice. However, now is perhaps the right time to question and dispute these traditional categorizations of fabric. After all, current material experimentation within the discipline takes the subject beyond the realm of the yarn and the cloth. Technological advances, sophisticated consumerism, changes in society and lifestyles, diverse innovative thinking and media and communication touch not only textiles practice and philosophy but also the wider sphere of design disciplines in general. Textiles is closely implicated in disciplines as diverse as fashion, visual communications, product design and interior design. Attempting to maintain the separate quality of traditional textile practices has proved difficult: as the subject has evolved, there has often been contention over the value and purpose of maintaining the purity of techniques and approaches; calls for change, and calls against it, immediately face an onslaught of criticisms. Textiles is now obviously something greater than the craft disciplines it has grown from. Given this, these elementary skills still remain the foundational experience of textile practice, and they provide the textile professional with an initial framework. However, what follows the acquisition of those first skills is rather more complicated to describe or constrain. Simply describing textiles as printed, constructed or embroidered is not adequate. Crossovers occur continually, and they are not only within the disciplines mentioned here: textile designers dabble in history, culture, industry and science. The language of textiles has thus expanded through the absorption of technical knowledge or artistic ambition drawn from other subjects. With inventiveness and vision, new dimensions have been applied to time-honoured skills and materials and a case can now be made for the redefinition of textile practice.

Figure 3. Printed PVC. Isabel Dodd 1997.

Isabel Dodd is one of the new generation of designers whose alternative approach to textile design securely positions her in the future. Working with the most modern of synthetic materials, her printing process causes the surface of stretch jersey and velour to crinkle and pucker, producing marks similar to those formed through embroidery. We could loosely categorize her as a printer, simply because she uses a print screen. However, she is actually a typical example of individual textile designers who transcend their original formal training (Dodd's was embroidery) in order to interpret and communicate new creative ideas. We may think that jumping from one specialist practice to another is daunting, yet many contemporary textile designers use whichever methodology is most appropriate for them to realize their conceptual ideas. In many ways this method of working is far from being a hindrance – in fact, a greater knowledge of process, by and large, enhances creative aptitude. Dodd's fabrics have been described as unusual, curious, avant-garde and sculptural, but whichever way they are explained, they are not what we traditionally associate with the conventional tools she uses (*International Textiles*, 1997b: 30–1).

The Influence of Skill

Fusions of traditional skills and new technology question whether textiles practice sits more comfortably in the scientific and industrial arena or whether it is essentially hands-on and skills-based. The introduction of new technology raises the question as to whether the practice could be branded as either purely scientific or, more traditionally, as an expression of an aptitude with material. The new concerns within textile practice have encouraged a fresh approach to a traditional discipline; one that is now in transition and appeals for re-evaluation as amply demonstrated by the recent 'A Twist in the Yarn' conference organized by Alan Holmes at Manchester Metropolitan University (www.artdes.mmu.ac.uk/tfg). There is currently much research taking place in the textile world, exploring technologies related to textile production, and design issues involving the relationship between surface and structure. There are also a number of textile professionals involved in material development and research who would challenge any predetermined views of what textiles constitutes. Sarah Taylor, Janet Stoyel and Janet Emmanuel are among those who are revolutionizing our perceptions of fabric.

Sarah Taylor has become somewhat of a pioneer in the field of weaving, having worked in collaboration with the Japanese company Mitsubishi Rayon. Her research centres on developing light-emitting fabrics through the use of fibre optics. The close supportive relationship she has with industry is vital in the development of her technologically advanced woven fabrics. Despite the craft origins of Taylor's work, perhaps industry on more than one level has historical sympathies with her

Figure 4. Woven fibre optics. Sarah Taylor.

practice – after all, the implicit data at the heart of weaving is easily convertible for mass production in industry:

> There is a fluidity in the practice, design and art of woven textiles that enables textiles to fit easily with contemporary technology. A textile maker or designer who works at a small craft-shop level producing one-off pieces can, from the same conceptual base and using the same equipment, produce samples that industry can convert without any fuss for factory production.
>
> (Dormer 1997: 168)

Fibre optics have been used in protective clothing for military use, but Taylor has been investigating their possible applications within interiors, perhaps as multifunctional mood-enhancing design pieces. Through controlling the colour of the light released from the fibres, Taylor proposes that it would be possible to agitate or calm the environment (Jones, B., 1999b: V–VII). Cheryl Adnitt is also developing methods of incorporating light within her fabrics. Her approach differs from Taylor's in that she uses either translucent monofilament which glows when exposed to ultraviolet light, or weaves conductive wire and LEDs into her fabrics, which illuminate when connected to a power source (Cassalle, 2000: 46–7). The latter part of the twentieth century witnessed a definite move in the direction of a rather more scientific, technological and laboratory-based approach to textiles. This combination of chemistry, physics, textiles and design has conjured up numerous ground-breaking fabrics.

Janet Stoyel's work fits into this new category of practice, and she would no doubt agree that industrial liaison is advantageous and sometimes essential when working on developing hi-tech processes through innovative design. Stoyel is recognized as leading the way in the use of lasers for producing textile designs. Conventionally, ultrasonic technology has been employed for various purposes in the medical and industrial worlds. On the whole, within the textile industry, it is a relatively new discovery, first appearing on the scene in the early 1970s. For Stoyel to practice her design skills, it was crucial that she should be able to demonstrate proficiencies in areas other than textiles. There was a significant learning curve before she was able to operate the sophisticated machinery she needed in order to create the sculptural pieces she envisaged. Stoyel's range of skills can be compared to that of other textile designers such as Dodd and Taylor, already mentioned. Much of Stoyel's material explorations conform to her unorthodox rules in that she blends synthetic metal and polymer textiles with such natural materials as silk and paper. The UK Ministry of Defence assisted Stoyel in her efforts to unify textile design and technology. Through utilizing their expertise she was able to establish her process of cutting using lasers and welding with ultrasound in order to create three-dimensional constructions (Jones, B., 1999d: XXXIII–XXXV).

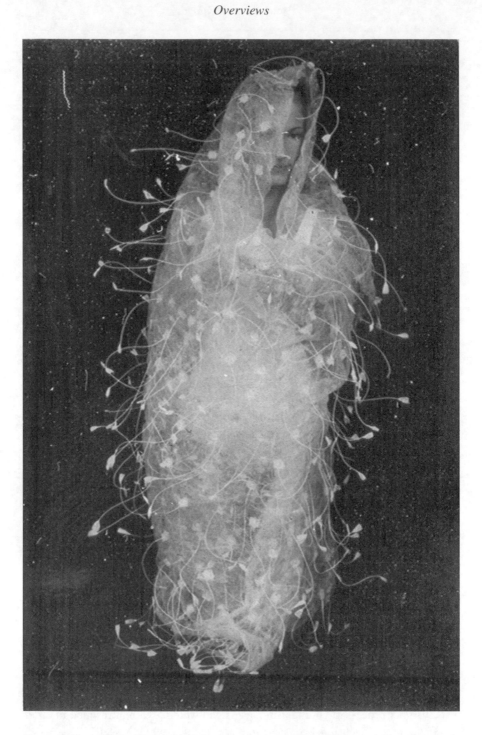

Figure 5. 'Acoustic Shadows'. Industrial nonwoven, paper, string and ultrasound. Janet Emmanuel.

Following in Stoyel's footsteps is Janet Emmanuel; although they share common ground in the equipment they use, their reasoning for making and the culmination of their efforts is quite different. Emmanuel's initial interest in technology can be narrowed down to a period at the end of the twentieth century when creative professionals from all design disciplines began to exploit new methodologies and materials. Her preliminary studies within the subject focused on origami techniques, initially in silk organza and then in synthetics: these evolved into pleating ideas which were explored through traditional and industrial means, the goal being for the forms to become permanent. Some may feel her personal inspiration is somewhat obscure, but the driving force behind her research was to explore sound. In contrast to twentieth-century artists such as Kandinsky and Yves Klein who were fascinated with the visualization of sound (interpreting the relationship between colour, music and mark), Emmanuel opted to translate and examine what she calls silent sound, manifesting this through material manipulation (Emmanuel, 2000: 163–5).

The Influence of Science and Engineering

It is very difficult to escape the fact that science and engineering play a huge part in textile industries; much of the textile 'engineering' that occurs is usually intended for the manufacturing sector, but can also greatly influence design. An observation of history reveals that there have been major technical advances which in time have proven to be revolutionary for designers. Among these have been man-made regenerated fibres, synthetics and more recently smart or intelligent fibres. One reason behind the original development of materials that mimicked natural qualities was to provide the consumer with an alternative to natural fibre at a fraction of the cost. The purpose for developing these materials, which would act as a substitute for the authentic article, was at some point superseded by the idea that we developed fabric just because we could. The scientists and engineers were 'able to' enhance, improve on and surpass the previous advances . . . so they did. Issues like fabric performance were stimulated by specialist sectors such as the sportswear industry; coupled with increasingly sophisticated consumer requirements, conditions were perfect for developments to continue.

The first 'engineered' fibres were generated from organic material and were developed to mimic the qualities of natural yarns, enabling the production of artificial silk and wool fibres. Developed in the second half of the nineteenth century, these cellulose-based fibres, constituted from wood pulp, were chemically altered so as to compose yarn. Following this development many years later, under the influence of environmental pressures, a 'green' recyclable artificial fibre was launched, again based on wood pulp. Apart from the introduction of microfibres (very thin, fine versions of synthetic fibres), Tencel is the first new man-made fibre to have been introduced since Polyolefin in the 1960s. It is renowned in the industry for being the 'chameleon' of fibres as it is able to completely imitate the qualities of other fibres, at the same time enhancing their strength.

Synthetics on the other hand were developed in science labs from such substances as coal, oil, other minerals, glass and carbon, after the discovery of regenerated fibres. There are two prominent established players in the world of synthetics, which have now become household names, Du Pont and ICI. Much of the initial research underlying the development of synthetic materials took place in the 1930s, while manufacturing became firmly established in the 1950s. Many synthetic fibres such as nylon, acrylic and DuPont's famous brand Lycra are household names. Polyester is now combined with its many natural counterparts, and is the most commonly used synthetic fibre, recyclable from clear plastic bottles. Synthetics have become infinitely sophisticated since their introduction – microfibres and elastanes have been developed which possess virtues of high-performance and handle that natural fibres would find difficult to match.

In comparison to the innovations already mentioned, smart fabrics are in a league of their own. The sportswear industries drive the textile researchers, designers and technologists to create increasingly sophisticated materials to meet their demands. On first impression the needs and desires of the end user in this sphere could quite easily be confused with the stuff of a science-fiction novel. Materials that react to the body's needs are of the utmost importance in the sports world. More often than not, these materials are developed to enhance performance as in the case of the Sydney 2000 Olympic gold medal winner, Ian 'Thorpedo' Thorpe, who hit international headlines when he wore the Adidas hydro-dynamically styled 'Fastskin' swimsuit. This concept was actually originated by the Britain-based Speedo swimwear company to reduce drag in the water. They state that the conceptual basis for their material was sharkskin, and that 'Fastskin' was designed to imitate the way in which a shark's scales enable it to glide smoothly through the water (BBC, 2000). The theory of copying naturally occurring phenomena like this is not new and, as engineering skills increase, such copying is likely to happen more often.

An increasing trend is that fabrics and yarns developed for a specific application or industry are used by other product sectors. For example, fabric technologies originally intended for industrial use or medicine can now form a central part of sport or fashion. Both of these worlds are colossal industries in their own rights and it is difficult to ignore the volume of the textile components used within each of them. In order to indicate the scale of the industries we are examining, a recent study by the American Georgia Institute of Technology, revealed that sport alone is a bigger industry than a combination of the television, radio, motion picture and educational service industries. Dr Isa Hoffman, Project Manager at Interstoff, Frankfurt, Germany, sums up current opinion on smart materials:

It is the fabric that makes the trend. Garment physiology and environmental behaviour, comfort and lifestyle have become the components of modern fabric creations and turned them into high-fashion, high-tech products . . . Words such as 'intelligent' or 'electro-textiles', 'anti-bacterial' or 'biomimetic' could well come from a computer dictionary. Today's fabrics are 'programmable'.

(*International Textiles*, 1999b, 805: 24–8)

In beginning to reappraise the current condition of the textile world, we note that the 'future model' of the material supplier may also be transformed. As the definitions within textile practice begin overflowing into the worlds of science, engineering and technology, the fashion designer, product designer or architect that seeks innovative, original and new materials will inevitably search for a source other than that of the conventional fabric fair.

One such 'future model' of the fabric and materials supplier is George M. Beylerian, founder of Material ConneXion (www.materialconnexion.com). He offers the facility to track down the most advanced materials and their suppliers from all over the world through his resource exchange. Additionally, he provides the expertise to assist with market research, design sourcing and product develop-ment; in doing so, he connects the design community with its technological counterpart. Within this model, Beylerian is keen to work with material crafts-persons, believing their role to be that of creative philosophers, and using their various skills and methodologies to manipulate and control new materials. It is envisaged that the exploration and assessment of the intrinsic properties of these materials will reveal the scope and manner of their application. This knowledge would lead to further material evolution. The role of the material supplier, as Beylerian himself puts it, may well be as 'an intelligence bank for the future' (Black, C., 2000a: 83).

Re-evaluation

Definitions within contemporary textile practice are now open to debate, and traditional boundaries between sub-disciplines have become blurred. No longer does a weaver just sit at a loom, or an embroiderer at a sewing machine. Today, such persons, while engaged in their creative process, are to be found in front of computer screens, in science labs or engineering departments, or working alongside specialists from other disciplines. The creative processes now found in textiles defy the historical divisions and definitions applied to it. Currently, many practitioners who consider themselves textile specialists are occupied with roles and tasks not conventionally linked to the textile world. Textiles is full of contradictions which actually contribute to the innate nature of the subject, and simultaneously slants towards craft and towards technology. Complications and

Figure 6. 'Two White'. Front: hand stitched viscose, back: interfacing. Kei Ito.

confusions can also arise in its literature: we find printed textiles and felt-making featured in embroidery journals, craft periodicals don't have a problem with presenting textile art, and pieces on embroidery are included in felt-making publications. Since much textiles practice fuses invention, design, craft and technical skill, each discipline within the textile arena seems to fit snugly into another. This fusion is not some abstract theoretical hope – it is a self-evident reality, populated by real textile people. Among the many designers that fit into this rather blurred new categorization of 'designer/artist/textile professional' is Kei Ito. She investigates materials, amalgamating organic structures with ultra-modern fabrics, manipulating them to form clever, complicated outcomes. Ambiguities arise when an attempt is made to categorize the work, which sits easily between textiles, craft and fashion art (Jones, B., 2000b: I–III).

With the new approach to textile making come new approaches to evaluating the practice and the medium. Freddie Robbins attempts to intellectualize the physical realm of knitting and compares it to current technology, making observations about our perceptions

> There are many similarities between knitting and the internet. They are both physically solitary processes. Both are making sense of, translating and communicating information. Computers and knitting patterns use grids, with coloured squares to relay visual information. With both mediums it is easy to 'undo' or 'unravel' your work. However, knitting is an 'everyday skill' of the future which crosses social, cultural and geographic boundaries.
>
> (Robbins, 1999: 21)

The reappraisal of textiles has repercussions in education and in the definition of the textile industries in general. Over the last few decades of the twentieth century textiles gradually reformulated itself, perhaps not intentionally, but nevertheless it is now not what it used to be. This evolution is attributable to a new generation of inquisitive designers and the ready availability of exciting, versatile and innovative raw materials. All this makes the terms print, weave, knit and embroidery suddenly quite archaic, and one could almost say obsolete, as the divisions between them are eradicated. We are truly at a point in time where re-evaluation is needed; this is even reflected in the nature of the student experience within the subject, many no longer desiring pure and simple textile design. There is a craving for something altogether more definitive of the twenty-first century, textiles of the future. As a result of the perpetual changes in textiles technology and culture the impetus to redefine textiles will undoubtedly grow.

Part II
The Creative

–4–

The Textile Designer

The term 'textile designer' no longer has a simple definition – the role comprises a myriad of descriptions, including: engineer, inventor, scientist, designer and creative. Textile designers have to comprehend the requirements of the textile manufacturer and the intricacies of the marketplace. Starting with a consideration of the eventual use of a fabric, they develop ideas and realize their concepts. Marketable fabrics are created on the basis of informed decisions about colour, construction, composition, surface, pattern and yarn structure. Depending on the textile designer's area of expertise, be it creative or scientific, design outcomes can range from fabrics for use in fashion and interiors to highly complex, technologically advanced, performance materials. Areas of application range from aerospace to the world of sports. A textile designer has to find the right balance between creativity, innovation and commercialism.

Career options in textile design vary around the world but they can include selling designs directly to companies or other types of designer; selling through textile agents; working in a company that specializes in textile design; working in a special design section of a product manufacturer. Company environments are typically described as a 'design studio'. Designers who sell directly, sell through agents or have no fixed employment would generally be classified as 'freelance designers'. Categories or types of textile designer within the fashion and interior worlds range from the conceptual to the commercial and the chemical to the creative. Each is found in a variety of environments, working from home, in a studio or agency, in industry or a laboratory, linking them to parallel worlds of arts, culture, industry, science and commerce. In a country like the UK a large number of textile design graduates seek to establish themselves as freelance designers, many within a year of leaving higher education. This vocation always proves to be a popular choice and is seen as a flexible and glamorous career option: possibly the potential reward of fame and recognition among peers is the driving force behind decisions to enter this type of employment.

There are various levels of entry into the world of textile design, and the idea of market segmentation, of a high, middle and low, is shared with other sectors of the textile industry. Distinctions between these levels are based on issues of creative quality, exclusivity and costs. The status and recognition, which is associated with entry at the higher level, is probably that most desired by design graduates. This is further reinforced by the fact that there is a degree of elitism among those who design for the cutting-edge, avant-garde sector as opposed to those who design for the commercial mass market. Whether this superiority or snobbery is self-professed or bestowed by the media is a matter open to debate. There can also arise the assumption that the cheaper end of the market necessarily equates with 'poor' design.

It is standard practice for designers to initially produce a portfolio of designs which is usually exploratory and subjectively based on the designers' sense of market directions or exhibits a personal style. The contents of the portfolio and the way in which it is organized are appropriate to the market for which it is intended. Considerations such as its size, whether it is paper- or swatch-based and whether it is for fashion or interiors will dictate the style of representation chosen by the designer. Whatever guise it takes, a portfolio is considered a prerequisite for the designer seeking employment. On entering the textile industry, it becomes apparent that there are specific 'rules' regulating the production of particular sorts of design. For instance, it is usually required that print designs for interiors are presented in a repeat format and to fairly large dimensions, as opposed to designs for fashion which can be much more flexible in size and format. Trends and colour prediction can also have a significant influence, informing textile designers of variations in the market.

Traditionally, the role of the textile designer has involved the design and production of original woven, knitted or printed fabrics in the form of either flat paper designs or fabric swatches. Typically designers will use suggested colours, sketch initial concepts, formulate designs (perhaps in repeat format) and work with a variety of yarns and fabrics. They develop visual and tactile ideas, referring to a specific 'design-brief' which provides guidelines about what the designs should entail or what they are for. These activities are then combined with their technical and practical knowledge of fabrics and processes in order to produce designs. Through the process of original invention and renewing and revamping patterns, materials and motifs from the past, the designer is constantly able to create new textile designs. The textile-design industry is shifting constantly as design methodologies broaden, a scenario not exclusive to just the world of textiles but true of most contemporary design disciplines. Textile designers employ diverse approaches to their discipline; current and emerging textile designers are constantly adapting their skills and acquiring radical processes in order to produce readily a competitive portfolio of designs (Hoggard, 2000: 31–3).

Much design involves experimentation with the basic elements of textiles – cloth, dyes, yarn and image – but there can also be a focus on the ingenious use of finishing and surface treatments or new techniques. The broader repertoire of design can include processes such as pleating, coating, bonding, lamination, laser-cutting, burn-out and resist methods. The potential diversity in textile design is now immense and consequently many designers seek out interesting or unusual combinations of technique and material. The subject was once enjoyed as a simple exploration of fabric construction and image manipulation within clearly defined constraints; it has now transformed itself to provide immeasurable solutions for a field whose boundaries have become unclear. Also, as a result of the worldwide textile community sharing knowledge, process, skills and traditions, the capacity for invention has multiplied within the subject, making it more wide-ranging and sophisticated. This has resulted in textile designers exhibiting a huge diversity in their design portfolios. While most designs are invariably constrained by a design brief, the manner in which modern textile design can be executed is potentially limitless.

The textile design world is quite small but scattered over a large area: those involved in this world tend to assemble at such trade shows as 'Indigo' in France, 'Interstoff' in Germany, 'Comocrea' in Italy, 'Tex-Styles' in India, the 'International Fashion Fabric Exhibition' and 'Surtex' in the United States, 'Japan Creation' in Japan and 'Exhimoda Textil' in Mexico. This list is by no means comprehensive; suffice it to say that almost every major textile-producing nation hosts textile trade fairs which provide a platform for textile design. The leading and established textile-design agents and studios, such as Tom Cody and The Colorfield in the United States and Timney Fowler and Rowena Bristow in Britain, regularly exhibit at 'Indigo', which is one of the premier textile-design fairs in Europe. These occasions are viewed not only as major sales trips, but they also provide opportunities to source information about predicted trends for the coming season.

Design Practice

For the majority of designers in the middle market, where emphasis is on the mass production of averagely priced goods, personal creative freedom becomes rather transitory as designs are produced impersonally and in abundance, to be sold to unknown clients through agencies. Nonetheless, the role of the designer remains one of the most creative among options available to the textile graduate. A designer receives a brief and guidelines from his or her agent, client or studio; these, along with a recommended colour palette, are the constraints within which the textile designer will work. Guidelines provide specific visual or printed information outlining fashion or interior directions to be considered when designing. In addition, the designer is equipped with a general impression of the 'mood' a collection of designs should be based on, or even appropriate methods of presentation that the final design idea should take. This would include issues such as scale, motifs or decorative effects which are sourced by whatever means the designer deems suitable – be that a historical reference of sorts, such as those used by Sanderson, or computer-generated imagery like that used by Bullen Pijja. Equally, there may be communicated to the designer technical requirements such as which yarn to use, fabric construction specifications, texture and handle. At this stage it is down to the individual designer to interpret the information he or she has been given and to undertake the task of designing – hence, versatility is a great virtue for a designer. The capacity to tackle confidently any design brief and to adapt creative styles and processes to whatever design 'story' is presented is an excellent ability to have.

Agents or studios play a critical role in taking a textile designer's work to buyers. The designer's relationship with agents and studios is tremendously valuable, since they play a key role as mediator between the designer and industry. Often this is the only method of representation that designers have – unless of course they choose to represent themselves, which some do. Normally freelance designers regularly send work to their agents, who in turn organize: contacting and meeting with clients, many of whom are overseas; managing any financial transaction such as debt-collection or invoicing on behalf of the designer; dealing with any copyright and legal issues; and perhaps generating design work themselves.

From the moment a sale is made there is an absence of any further communication in the form of market feedback; the original creators of the work are rarely aware of where or in what format their designs finish up. Thus textile designers are rarely given recognition through the sale of what was originally their work unless, of course, they previously had celebrity status. Fashion designers such as Ralph Lauren, Versace and Jeff Banks have successfully managed to use their 'star' status to infiltrate the world of textile design for the interior by launching collections for the home. In addition to this some fashion designers such as Armani also produce designer fabric for sale off the roll, through exclusive outlets such as Liberty. Considering the global magnitude and presence of the textile industry, it seems that textile designers have a somewhat low visibility if compared say with fashion designers, where a 'star' system is in place. It seems that textile design is not recognized for its own merits, yet is seen as a feeder to fashion, interiors and any other sector that requires it.

Studies such as the 'Ph2 Textile Research Project' (www.csm.u-net.com/index.htm) have investigated the state of the textile design industry. It has been suggested that although freelance textile designers are fundamentally self-employed, often working in solitude and managing the responsibilities that accompany this role, their work flourishes and they are happy to operate in this way as it allows a valuable degree of creative freedom and offers flexibility in lifestyle. Normally, freelancing would involve working alone and from home with a personal client base, and might include entering into contracts with agents and studios. Often designers will register with organizations such as the Register of Apparel and Textile Designers (RATD) and the Chartered Society of Designers (CSD) in Britain or the Surface Design Association (SDA) in the United States.

Organizations such as these could possibly lead designers to potential sources of income or opportunity. It is evident that designers, agents, studios and manufacturers have a common interest in textile design despite having variable aims.

It is still difficult to define the term 'textile designer' with some clarity as it cannot be assumed that this group of professionals perform a specific and set combination of tasks. It is the complicated nature of their responsibilities that makes categorization difficult; bearing this in mind, it has been hypothesized that

> freelance textile designers are not a distinct profession but a group with diverse and flexible skills who enter a complex international business environment with varied abilities to weather that turbulence . . . Some freelancers also acted as agents. Some fabric designers also produced (manufactured) fabrics or products and yet did not see themselves as 'industry' and were unsure into which category they most closely fit. (Jones, S., 1997)

This only reinforces the idea that many textile professionals possess skills which are easily transferable from one field to another. Crossovers between specialisms often occur which raises the issue again as to what distinguishes a textile designer from a textile craftsperson or from a textile artist. In order to illustrate this point, we only have to look at how textile professionals categorize themselves for specific situations. For example, individuals such as Victoria Richards (Coatts, 2000: 20–3) and Sharon Ting both describe themselves as textile designers, makers and artists; in so doing, they manage successfully to combine a variety of practices with ease. Not only do they market themselves appropriately for specific activities but they are also able to maximize their employment opportunities. For many the variety of work, of itself, becomes a stimulus: as Sharon Ting says, 'At "the beginning" it was more out of necessity at present it is out of choice'.

Independent designers who choose to represent themselves will more often than not have begun their career as either freelancers or in-house designers. During this time they will have gathered a wealth of experience and an essential understanding of the intricacies of various market levels within industry. Inevitably, rather than just representing themselves, they are more likely to establish themselves as agents or studios. In this situation they not only collect the commission which otherwise would have gone to their agent but they also reap the commission from other designers' sales. There are pros and cons within this scenario. On the plus side it is true that the middle man is cut out, and those designers who choose to run their own practice and represent others receive the full design fee for the work they do. However, independent designers who assume this role also have to undertake extra administrative responsibilities in order to manage their practice. These designers-cum-studio-managers really don't have any alternative but to represent others too. They also have to increase their chances of potential sales to cover business expenses such as those for sales trips. The rewards can be lucrative, but there is no cast-iron guarantee that a design will sell: formulas for success come with experience and knowledge.

Global Comparisons of Textile Design

While the global textile-design industry is not vast, it remains too large to be succinctly described here. The focus of this section will therefore be to highlight some of the organizations and individuals that are globally recognized within the sphere of textile design. One of the most obvious comparisons that can be raised is the difference between the Eastern and the European approaches to textile design. The Far East's strength lies within traditional skill and technological innovation, whereas European textile design reflects a solid heritage as well as a contemporary avant-garde approach. Technological advance in design is now being stressed as a major factor in maintaining success in today's global market. As well as the appeal of scientific and industrial innovation within textile design, historical references in the form of patterns or craft techniques are often used. History and tradition are often applied to textile design in different ways. For example, it is commonly believed that some countries and regions of the world have quite particular received philosophies about textile design. These philosophies are often an extension of local historical craft attitudes, aesthetics and methods. When they are applied in the sphere of contemporary design, it can result in distinctive approaches to the use of technology, materials or imagery. In this context, Japan is often cited as demonstrating innovative combinations of old and new, applying sophisticated design traditions to new materials and processes. Japan is held in high esteem for cutting-edge and scientifically advanced fabrics, although it would be wrong to measure the commercial success or popularity of any textile design purely on technological expertise or process. The result and the approach is very different to the way 'history' is used elsewhere. In Britain, for example, modern 'historical' design is deeply embedded in a legacy of traditional patterning rather than in a craft philosophy. In considering a global representation of contemporary textile design, we tend to focus on specific continents, linking the expertise of various textile personalities or organizations with particular countries. We also perceive that design and taste preferences can vary greatly from country to country. What follows is a small sample of the approaches to contemporary textile design from various parts of the world.

Historical reference in textile design is a strong tradition in Europe and is still evident today. We are able to detect signs of this from current prominent textile design and manufacturing companies such as Sanderson (www.sanderson-online.co.uk) and Liberty (www.liberty.co.uk) in Britain and Dolfus, Mieg et Cie (DMC) in France. Archives for Liberty and Sanderson date back to the 1880s and

Figure 7. 'Bird and Anemone fabric and Acanthus weave'. New Morris & Co. Collection, Autumn 2000. Courtesy Sanderson.

1860s, respectively. DMC's stretch back even further, reflecting 250 years of printed fabric experience (Durie, 1998: XXXVI–XL). The worth of textile designers in large organizations can be pivotal to a company's success. Because of this, it is DMC's philosophy that their designers (who number almost one hundred) are valued and have frequent contact with clients in order to be aware of market needs. This reflects a general trend and mirrors views about textile designers held in industry.

The idea to borrow from the past is not unusual for many European textile design houses, who delve into archives in search of inspiration for new collections. Josef Otten, an Austrian mill, not only looks to past examples of textile design but also interprets the work of artists in the form of jacquards and prints. For Josef Otten, textile designs evolve as re-interpretations of works of art and design from artists such as Sonia Delaunay, Lubov Popova and Tone Fink. These commercial translations are still sensitive to the artist's original work and because of this, permission is sought to use them (Higginson, 1997).

The two UK companies Sanderson and Liberty have much in common when it comes to their distinctive approach to design. Sanderson, like Liberty, export their fabrics worldwide and are distinctive in terms of textile design as they coach their designers in perfecting the skills of botanical drawing and floral design. Because of this, the Sanderson style and heritage is handed down from one generation to the next. The in-house studio designers at Sanderson, like their counterparts at Liberty, dip into an archive which amounts to more than 25,000 designs, providing continual inspiration for new collections. This resource also contains original hand-blocks and samples by William Morris, one of the founders of what we now regard as modern textile design. His original designs are still re-coloured and re-worked, and marketed under his name.

Liberty textile designers, like Sanderson's, constantly return to historical reference when formulating contemporary designs. Liberty has one of the most recognizable printed textile-design styles in the world. Their archives also contain woven designs that are still produced. Today, well over a hundred years since they began, they still have a stronghold in contemporary textile design, wholesaling their collections throughout the world. Liberty fabric was originally inspired by the Art Nouveau movement in the late nineteenth century, and traces of this are apparent in some of their fabrics produced today; this is probably down to the in-house design team using the archival material as a constant source of inspiration for new collections. Although they are reworked and recycled, Liberty designs retain the essential Liberty handwriting that consists of colourful patterned textiles characterized by their 1930s small-scale dainty floral, which is now known as the signature 'Liberty Print'. Over the years, top couturiers have adapted Liberty prints for their own tastes. Past examples of these include Jean Muir, Mary Quant, Bill Blass and Yves Saint Laurent, and more recently Paul Smith.

The 'patronage' that prestigious haute couture designers can bestow on printed fabric companies like Liberty also extends to the producers of luxurious embroidered fabric – for example, Switzerland's most famous embroidery house: Jakob Schlaepfer and Co AG. Swiss textile design relies on intricate motifs and metal thread effects; its prints may incorporate over twenty colours, and lavish silk jacquards often include complex combinations of pattern and yarn. Like Liberty, Schlaepfer has a history of supplying high fashion since the 1960s. Because of high wage levels, Swiss companies are more likely to compete on grounds of quality rather than price. As a result, emphasis is on the creativity of the textile designer and it appears that this alone assures the potential success of a fabric. As we analyse the reasoning behind the success of textile designs with historic or traditional reference, it emerges that specialization within a specific field, utilizing the talents of trained textile designers and aiming for the finest quality, results in a well defined, globally recognized textile design profile. Associations with high fashion also assist in elevating the status of textile design companies.

In contrast to the industry in Europe, Japanese textile design is symbolic of the most radical fabric innovation. On the surface this seems at odds with their traditional textile crafts but the underlying creative philosophy is the same. Japan is a dynamic leading force in the world of textile design and enjoys an international reputation for producing some of the most pioneering textile designs (Guth, 1999: 54–9). Time-honoured materials and techniques are used in unexpected ways, and there is a quest for alternative materials and high-tech processes. Therefrom, Japan is home to some of the world's leading textile designers, not only in terms of aesthetic qualities but also with regard to the development of innovative materials and techniques for weaving and printing.

The Japanese are often seen to be the engineers of the textile design world. This is perhaps due to the intimate working relationship that can develop between manufacturer and designer. This affiliation with industry makes designers alert to the various limitations or functions of industrial machinery. This knowledge forms an integral part of the Japanese textile designers' psyche, enabling them to simultaneously refer to and challenge traditional Japanese and Western conventions in terms of industry and craft tradition. The central theme of Japanese textiles, ingrained in the consciousness of modern Japanese textile designers, lies in fibre and fabric finishing technologies. Traditionally these are the two most important aspects of Japanese textiles. Exploration of material structure and coatings are investigated, synthetic fibres are embraced and technology is harnessed as 'par for the course'. The basic design concepts in Japan have changed little – it is the technologies utilized in the execution of these designs that has changed.

This brings us very neatly to the stars of Japanese textile design. Jun'ichi Arai, has for many years been widely known in the textile design world for the interesting new materials that he has developed. He designs the structure and texture of a fabric rather than its pattern. By means of his design process, he is seen to combine the 'best of past and present' in that there remains a strong link between the industrial and craft elements within his designs. Arai investigates and researches traditional processes in order to gain an understanding of the origin of modern technique. Traditional methods of production have largely stimulated contemporary methods in Japan. Incidentally, Japan has a long tradition of 'wrinkled' or creased textiles, created in a variety of ways; it is interesting to note that the Japanese do not have a tradition of ironing, as is the case in the West. Wrinkled or textured fabrics are very prevalent in the Japanese textile industry today (Baurley, 1997: 35–6), though they are produced by means of contemporary, mechanized methods (Mahoney, 2000a).

Jun'ichi Arai originally co-founded the Nuno Corporation (www.nuno.com) in Tokyo, and is widely regarded as a pioneer in the field of techno-fabrics. Reiko Sudo is now the Director of Nuno Corporation and also happens to be the company's head designer. The Nuno Corporation is considered paradise for any constructed textile designer. They make beautiful fabrics and incredibly interesting materials and weaves. Metallic yarns are also a traditional part of Japanese textiles.

For example, Washi (paper) slit gold leaf yarns were used in nishi-jin weaving to produce the obi sash. The modern day version of this exists in the form of stainless steel spattering the surface of a polyester fabric, creating a metallic coating. For the textile designers at Nuno, traditional processes are only one source of inspiration and though they play a major role, their importance should not be overrated:

> Many of the fabrics produced by Nuno reflect the blend of the anonymous (urban) and the personal (human) found in the district. Some take discarded objects as inspiration. 'Scrap yard – Nails' involves the selection of particularly rusty nails . . . Another design was inspired by rubber bands lying on a sunny windowsill . . . The designer initially considered adhering actual rubber bands to a fabric . . . Printing layers of silicone resin onto linen fabric . . . the designers' surroundings or travel form the basis for some of the pattern and fabric structures. Shutters' is a nylon fabric inspired by a trip undertaken by one of the Nuno designers to Mexico. (Mahoney, 2000a)

It is worth noting that in the same way as Liberty has associations with various fashion designers, Nuno Corporation create new fabrics specifically for Japanese fashion designers Rei Kawakubo and Yoshiki Hishinuma. Makiko Minagawa on the other hand is a name virtually unknown in comparison to Jun'ichi Arai or Issey Miyake, and yet her innovative creations have gained her accolades on fashion runways around the world. Her collaborations with the fashion designer Issey Miyake (www.isseymiyake.com) have culminated in a remarkable body of work, utilizing a range of fibres, weaving processes and finishing techniques. Now the textile director of Miyake Design Studio, Makiko Minagawa oversees eight textile designers. Although a degree of design direction came from Issey Miyake, Makiko Minagawa has a personal approach:

> her beautiful, rough textured fabric that combined different yarns, often inspired by images of nature such as landscapes, tree bark, water ripples or parched earth . . . Many of Minagawa's innovations arise from the absence of preconceptions in her approach to technology and design . . . Minagawa researches the manufacturers that may potentially be used to produce the textiles she designs, learning about the functions and limitations of their machinery.
>
> (Takeda, 1999)

The work of the Japanese textile designers is exhibited at 'Japan Creation' in Tokyo, which provides a platform for the country's many creative textile talents. Textile designs, indicative of the blend of traditional technique and futuristic manufacture, are shown as impeccable examples of high-tech, modern textile designs. These fabrics perfectly reflect the Japanese ethos of textile design. Japanese textile culture presents some ideal situations for the conduct of discourse. Textile designers, textile artists and textile craftspeople within the country share a common ground within their disciplines, exploring similar visual and tactile effects. When we consider contemporary Japanese textiles it is obvious to us that, as a specialism borne out of traditional Japanese craft, it enjoys the same status and respect as the fine arts. This is unlike its counterparts elsewhere. Highlighting this issue emphasizes the notions different countries have toward textile design.

Futures

As the practices of the textile design world evolve, it is anticipated that so too will the appearance of the textile design 'portfolio'. The portfolio is already in a constant state of flux as the normally expected formats and contents change over time. We have to consider what possible consequences a 'digital portfolio' will have on fabric presentation and perception. This idea sends those of us who regularly interact with cloth into a state of panic. It is very difficult to imagine a world without touch, or a life devoid of those essential sensory pleasures. Even the use of colour-matching systems does little to match a screen representation or computer printout with what ends up on cloth. While the internet may impact on the sale of known designs or even perhaps the sale of the new, it is hard to foresee that the design community would give up the opportunities that a more direct intervention and experimentation with cloth permits. On the whole, one imagines that the majority would find the prospect of an entirely digital portfolio totally alien to the innate nature of the subject and therefore unacceptable. However, textile design never stands still, and if the only way to stay competitive is to be electronic, that is what will happen. In the age of the DVD, the laptop and the camcorder it is reasonable to expect that things might eventually prove to be very different to what went before.

The Designer-Maker

Designer-maker is a title or term recently used in some countries to describe someone who designs and produces items in small or batch quantities, usually operating as an independent or in a small-business context. The term itself seems to be gaining a growing international acceptance and is applicable to a range of design disciplines including textiles, furniture, ceramic and product design. Designer-maker practices have recently been the subject of an exhibition, *Industry of One: Designer-Makers in Britain 1981–2001*, at the UK Crafts Council Gallery, although the use of the term is somewhat retrospective. The term is also currently in use in Australia, as evidenced by the Designer Makers Tasmania Co-operative Society (www.designer makers.com.au). For textile designers and craftspeople the designer-maker model of practice represents a new and emergent career opportunity. Textile designer-makers produce items across the range of home, lifestyle and fashion goods – for example cushions, scarves and bags. They may also incorporate other materials and technologies creating such products as lighting, room dividers, screens and blinds. Some designer-makers are truly interdisciplinary, covering more than one design discipline or marketing a co-ordinated collection of products. The term is a useful one allowing some distinctions between different types of business, and also helps to highlight the often complex relationship between designing, making and manufacturing in very small or 'micro' businesses based around one or two creative makers.

The term designer-maker is often applied on the simple basis that work produced is contemporary and stylish, but it is worth making a distinction between a *craft* approach and a *design* approach to making. In fact there is often a continuum between the two approaches. Traditionally craftspeople, while sometimes producing batches of product that are the same, will retain personal control over the individual making of the product from beginning to end. It may also be the case that their design vision is only reachable through a craft process, and that industrial manufacture or contracting out will not achieve the effects they desire:

> Gillian Little produces a limited edition of hand-woven scarves in natural fibres and vegetable colours to create intriguing woven structures. Wool, cotton, silk and linen are skilfully worked together on the loom and later a burn-out technique creates a skeletal framework of fibres. (Jones, B., 1997)

Figure 8. Handwoven bag. Liz Marchetti.

A pure craft maker essentially deals with handmade and hand-finished goods. Some craft makers probably prefer or naturally accept being described as designer-makers because of the image the term projects and because of how they want their work to be seen. In many respects, issues of starting and running a business are similar for both craftspeople and designer-makers. Many craft makers move in the same business world as do designer-makers, located in common studio facilities and complexes and selling through the same trade fairs or retail outlets.

Designer-makers in a sense could be defined by the way in which a design approach permits the possibility of using pre-fabricated components or subcontracting aspects of manufacture and assembly. Emphasis is more on designing than on the making of individual pieces, mimicking the industrial system and sequence of manufacture. A further difficulty in distinguishing between the craftsperson and the designer-maker is the way in which design itself is undertaken. For many designer-makers the development of an original or prototype design is through the craft process, and designer-maker products often demonstrate the craft origins of their design. Indeed this is often what makes designer-maker products attractive and successful. If there is a distinguishing characteristic it is that point at which the integrity or ambition of craft gives way to such typical issues of design and manufacture as economy, efficiency or ergonomics. Occasionally the result of this process is a reversal of conventional practice, whereby designers come to use industrial processes to achieve the conventional outcome of craft, unique one-off pieces. In this situation designers are often defined by the arena of their work: they are not artists in the generally accepted meaning of the term, neither are they the old model of designers, and certainly they are not craftspeople.

While the cachet of auteur or artist is key in the marketing and promotion of designer-maker goods, the true designer-maker practice is ultimately a reflection, a miniature, of the entire industrial cycle of origin and supply of designed goods to the market place. The dilemma of independent practice is always this: if you can't do everything and play every role, which or what do you give up or pay for someone else to do? A craftsperson would be reluctant to give up the activity of making or for making to have anything less than a central and main role. A designer-maker on the other hand would be conscious of making as only one element in a broader process and something of variable importance.

The Origins of Designer-Makers

The growth of interest in design and designer goods represented by lifestyle journalism has to some extent accelerated the visibility and success of designer-makers in an increasingly 'label'-conscious marketplace. There is a certain mutuality of interest between the journalist's need for design 'stars' and stories and the designer's need for exposure and publicity. While this symbiosis is transparent, the underlying factors which gave rise to the designer-maker in the latter part of the twentieth century are more complex. Contributing factors include employment opportunities; changes in the marketplace; various state, private and regional interventions in the economy; the role of buyers and professional trade shows; and finally the increasing community of designer-makers themselves. As these factors vary around the world, designer-makers are less likely to be found where employment and pay for designers is good or where support and opportunity for new business start-up is poor.

In a sense the designer-maker is a post-industrial phenomenon, dependent on a sophisticated social and market context, utilizing modern communications and flexible business strategies but perhaps, above all else, having high expectations about his or her working environment and the experience of work itself. It could be said that the designer-maker's enterprise is little different from any typical new business venture, but this would overlook the fact that designer-maker businesses usually revolve tightly around one individual. Ultimately the designer-maker combines the freedom of the artist with modern industrial design and spins a living out of it.

Employment

For many who graduate from a design course, much of their educational experience has been about discovering their own creative powers, personal philosophy and career ambitions, and this is true around the world. The subsequent reality of the employment market can sometimes be depressing – repetitive or uncreative design work; poor pay and job security; little opportunity to do 'your own thing' and so on. Situations will vary locally, nationally and internationally but obviously it is not all bad: some will find good design jobs and others will find employment in related areas that don't directly involve designing. However, for determined, ambitious and creative individuals the prospect of being independent and in full control of their work and career is too attractive a prospect to pass over, even if they don't initially know much about business. It is reasonable to assume that many graduates who go on to be designer-makers retain a stronger interest in designing and the associated lifestyle than they do in establishing a business or making a lot of money.

Given that the designer-maker is a relatively recent phenomenon, the realities of long-term survival as a one-woman or one-man design-based business are yet to be understood or, indeed, proven as a reliable alternative to being a regular employee in a larger business. What is true is that an increasing number of individuals are prepared to try to survive on an independent basis either in the short term or as part of a mixed and changeable pattern of employment.

Market

There has been an increasing demand for distinctive goods in both home and public environments. This increased demand is not simply based on 'fashion-conscious-ness' in the old sense of simply wanting to be seen to be up-to-date or youthful. For the consumer, fashionability is now just one criterion among a range of motivations; it is also only one part of modern lifestyle psychology. While stylistic and seasonal change is symptomatic of traditional 'the fashion' or what is 'in' at the moment, the market place for designer goods differs to some extent being increasingly marked by a growing diversity of products. This diversity can create opportunities for niche products as well as market stability – for example, a product that errs on the side of eclectic design rather than fashion will not 'go out of fashion'.

The supply and demand for designer goods are stimulated by journalism, television programmes and what we show we like through buying. While journalism and entertainment related to consumerism are the most visible aspects of the designer-maker's market, there are other influences at work. There are various permutations of the relationship between product change, product innovation and the consumer. This not only incorporates issues of fashion (same product, different style) but also the issue of niche markets (same product, same type of people) and creating new markets (new product, new customers). Niche markets and new markets can both prove key to the success of designer-makers. Producing small or limited runs of products means that specialist or niche markets, limited in nature and with a relatively low level of demand for goods, are an ideal outlet or starting point. There are also often very clear marketing needs and retail issues. However, if a designer-maker produces a very successful product, suitable for a mass market and requiring volume production, unlike most craftspeople they have the option of subcontracting manufacture or selling the copyright or patent for their work. This illustrates the essentially industrial model to which they work:

> As well as creating limited edition or one-off pieces, designers such as Diane Jameson are working on projects for high street fashion retailers. Jameson's knitted bags are refreshingly simple. Bands of colour blend together in the felting process and hand-stitched flower details are picked out in lambswool. Jameson has been commissioned to create a range for Jigsaw later in the year.
>
> (Jones, B., 1999c)

New products and new markets are a little harder to understand than niche markets. For people whose origin is in textile design and who wish to create a marketable product, there is always an initial problem of finding a product archetype that can carry what is, essentially, a component product – i.e., fabric. Some archetypes come readily to mind, such as scarves or cushions. These types of product are often very dominated by fashionability, and market competition is fierce. There is an obviousness about these types of product as vehicles for fabric and in many ways a preference for them. The transformation from fabric to saleable item seems short and not too difficult. For example cushions, beyond fabric production or purchase, only require seams, a filling and a label and so on, all of which can be readily sourced and/or bought in. It is this very straightforwardness of manufacture that can later cause problems on the business front: because there is essentially no market advantage or control in the manufacturing process, competition is based primarily on business acumen or design value. Occasionally designer-makers become involved in product innovation, either creating new archetypes or radically altering old ones. Such outcomes are often due to a mixture of artistry, happy accident, design process and changes in such other areas as new materials or new technology. The freshness of a previously unseen product, something that really feels 'new', can cut a swathe through lifestyle journalism and is usually immediately noticeable at trade fairs. It is often quickly copied. Consumers can also quickly tire of the product if there is little more than stylization or gimmickry involved.

The relatively small levels of production a designer-maker is involved with – whether it be a single commissioned piece, multiples or a small range – usually means that to earn a tolerable income, design must significantly add value to the products. As a result most designer-makers must work at the upper-middle to top end of the market, the only exception being when they work as 'designers' rather than as designer-makers. Often designer-makers' work will draw synergies from other activities they may be involved in: gallery exhibiting, 'artier' or one-off projects, collaborations and so on. These can add to the public perception of designers or add cultural connotations to their products, enhancing publicity and value. Via this route they can approach the status of the design star who, seeming to be neither one thing nor another, still has a very definable practice and product – for example Petra Blaisse, designer of textiles, landscapes and interiors (Bullivant, 2001: 30).

The amount of time designer-makers spend designing varies according to their business and market. The life expectancy of a product (how long the public will like it or want it) varies from sector to sector and product to product. With classic or highly idiosyncratic styles of design, the expectation might be that assuring distinctive quality is more significant than the perpetual generation of new products. For more edgy or contemporary styles, often adapting to fashion is easier than instigating fashion. Finally, responsiveness to market and business forces may dictate the creative direction of products. What comes designer-makers' way, the nature and quantity of work, business successes and failures, ultimately prove and test their entire operation from design to manufacture to retail.

Business

The business climate for designer-makers is dependent on having access to an affluent consumer group and client base, private and public support, and finally promotional opportunities. If any of these is missing it is unlikely that designer-makers can survive. If all these features are present then the designer-maker business can benefit from being lean, adaptable and sought-after. Economists and politicians often see the creative industries as critical in industrial and economic regeneration. They can have a key role to play in urban redevelopment and urban rezoning. A problem facing many countries is that mass-manufacturing industry becomes an increasingly volatile sector; large employers seek cheaper costs, inadequate supply industries cause hi-tech companies to move on, and so on. Consequently strategic economic policy demands the formation of new businesses and companies. This is for two reasons: first, by the law of averages, some of these companies will become longer-term players in the industrial and economic landscape; and second, some of these companies will scrabble toward new and unforeseen market sectors and share. None of this means the life of a designer-maker is easy but it can mean that support is available at need. Charitable organizations can also have a significant role to play, in Britain for example, The Prince's Trust has often played a main role in supporting new designer-maker businesses (www.princes-trust.org.uk).

The market for designer-makers varies depending on the product they offer. The makers of scarves, handbags, cushions, rugs and throws will often sell to or through specialist retail outlets and the designer sections of prestigious stores. Larger retail chains and stores seeking to reinvent themselves or to hold on to market share, increasingly need highly visible and exciting products on their premises. The role of the buyer has become increasingly important in sustaining High Street identities and reputations. Buyers are thus a very important point of contact for the new designer-maker. Some makers will also sell through annual craft fairs or even craft 'villages'. The general growth in the consumption of goods with 'design content' and the competitive nature of the market has given rise to a well established and growing calendar of events around the world. These provide some security and opportunity for new business ventures. Increasingly, small independents start to take stands at the larger trade fairs such as *Top Draw* or *100% Design* in Britain, hoping to attract the attention of buyers or commissions for their work. Each trade fair has its own 'accent' and deals with a particular range of products. Canada's *The Interior Design Show*, a typically large event, anticipated 300 exhibitors and 48,000 visitors in 2001 (www.interiordesignshow. com). Some are more conducive to the small independent than others: there can often be advantages in being new on the scene, and new young designers can add interest to the proceedings and provide good copy for design journalists. Without the stable presence of lifestyle magazines, product fairs and regular consumer demand, it would be difficult for small independents to establish themselves.

In general designer-makers have a variety of markets open to them in order to survive in business, most of which involve straightforward selling in the following ways:

- finished products direct to the public either at craft or trade fairs
- through niche outlets such as gallery shops or fashion boutiques
- through the internet or magazines
- to retail or other trade professionals at trade fairs
- direct to company buyers

Also, sometimes, opportunities arise to work to commission.

To pursue these opportunities the designer-maker needs to develop a complete range of business skills. Together the public and private sectors can create a climate of financial and professional support for the designer-maker, providing everything from advice on business plans to financial support. This can include establishing studios, purchasing equipment and undertaking marketing. In many countries there exist various foundations and fellowships with the explicit purpose of promoting one or more of creative arts, personal development or business initiative. There may also be regional or national initiatives to stimulate the creative sector. Quite often the designer-maker must adopt a patchwork approach, seeking separate sponsorship for studio space, for equipment, start-up loans, free marketing advice, financial support to attend trade shows, assistance in product promotion and so on. Cumulatively, individuals can build and establish their business using a complex network of charities, foundations and local government offices. More often than not there will still remain the burden of finding other sources of income, particularly during an establishing phase.

As the number of people who elect to follow an independent path in business grows, the increased community of designer-makers has various effects, regularizing and consolidating practices and opportunities. One consequence is the way buyers and retailers develop a growing confidence in small independents as a reliable source and supply of product. Another is the learning and sharing of strategies, techniques and information among the design community, whether through the educational system, by meeting at professional events or through sharing workspaces. Ultimately the size of designer-maker communities depends on how ready the public are to buy their goods. Local circumstances such as the size of population and the amount of disposable income will affect the size of the market for what are usually above-average-price or niche goods. The ability to produce independently may also be affected by local manufacturing capacity both in terms of its type and access to it. Finally the very possibility of there being any designer-makers can be dictated by local cultural perceptions, social structures and markets. In many cultures the purchase, import or copying of foreign brand names or designer goods will suppress the development of local design entrepreneurs. Similarly, a strong traditional design and manufacturing base can obviate the desire to start up independently.

Case Study: Lindsay Bloxam

Lindsay Bloxam's first studies were in embroidered textiles. By the end of her postgraduate studies she had already established a form and style of decorative lighting that was to become the key to her success as a designer-maker. Her professional career highlights many of the issues and dilemmas of the designer-maker's practice: establishing a business; mixed employment; mixed commercial and cultural practices; product development and diversification; complex management of commissioned design work; the personal burden of the independent. Her case is of particular interest in that it shows how, from a firm origin in textile design or textile art, it is possible to evolve toward a more generic or interdisciplinary form of design practice. Operating primarily in the area of commissioned and architectural work, she is less well known to the general public than many other designer-makers but she has an outstanding reputation in her own field and has had a major influence on the direction of contemporary lighting design.

Lindsay operates her business from a design retail studio based in the prestigious Oxo Tower Wharf development on London's South Bank. Her work has been developed to enhance and energize interior social spaces through the use of light and decorative sculptural form. As her business has developed she has increasingly concentrated on large commissioned pieces but she still sells limited-edition domestic lights and chandeliers through her studio shop. Her work has been placed in many public and commercial environments such as bars, shops, foyers and atrium spaces. Her clients have included Harrods and Mercedes. She often undertakes work destined for highly visible public locations, such as a recent project at Trinity College Dublin Dental Hospital or the Christmas lights at the Oxo Tower. Her reputation as an innovator in the area of lighting is amply demonstrated by a recent collaboration with Dr Christina De Matteis, a molecular modeller. Undertaking a project combining science and art, with the financial support of the National Endowment for Science, Technology and the Arts (NESTA), they developed a range of domestic and interior lighting based on the sophisticated architecture of the molecular world.

Figure 9. 'Chandelier'. Lindsay Bloxam.

Personal Issues

Entrepreuneurialism

Did you imagine that you would be an entrepreneur? Was it an ambition?
I knew I wanted to work in my own studio but I didn't really know what that would involve. I suppose I had a creative ambition.

Lifestyle

What would you say about the quality of life you have as a designer-maker?
No one tells you what to do, you make your own decisions, you choose the projects you want to work on and when you do them. The nature of the work is stressful though, every job I do is a completely new, individual project. The majority of my work is project management, which can be very demanding, there is no boss carrying the burden, I am always responsible . . . and I have no support system like you might get with an employer.

Creative Path

Is there a personal creative path in what you do? Do you consider the business activity an extension of your creative identity and evolution or does it have a more direct influence on what you do?
It's not the same as a fine artist, not art for art's sake but I take on board and go for jobs I find more interesting (enough jobs come along). I enjoy problem solving . . . that's what keeps my brain going, something comes along and I think . . . ah! That's what attracts me to particular projects.

Textiles

Do you think a background in textiles has given you any advantages or special qualities as a designer?
I couldn't have done what I've done without having that background. I approach design in a different way to somebody like a product designer (at least I think so), I start with the overall look. You start with the image, you work the problem round the 'wrong way'! I respond to the way I draw, the aesthetics come first. It's not what I do, it's the way I do things, I don't start to tackle the problem by looking at the electrics or the materials, and I don't do technical drawings. I begin with the overall image of what the work will look like and if that's to do with textiles, then that's proved really important, invaluable really. I start with the image and then I think 'how do I stick a light bulb in this then?', I also think work can be more interesting if you mix disciplines, you get more unusual results . . . there are lots of extra possibilities with textiles.

Establishing a Business

What Designer-Makers do

What does a designer-maker do?
I think you've answered that quite well in your writing; of course others may disagree.

Starting Points

What do you think you have to have to begin?

Some sort of service or product. In an ideal world people should pretty much have a fully developed and worked out product, so they know exactly what they're doing, exactly what they're selling. I started with a lampshade, I thought it would be my 'bread and butter market', I took it round to buyers and asked them what they thought, whether they would buy it or not and if not why. Things like colour proved very important, if people were going to have it in their home, it would have to fit in. I learnt a lot from the buyers about what was needed.

Support

What kind of support do you think has helped you along?

Financial support was very necessary, if you haven't got the finances then there is no point in starting really, it's very difficult when you're a student. For example if you've got no sewing machine you've got to buy it, some people can start with very little money, it depends on your business. You probably won't make a lot of money in the first three years, therefore you need to be prepared for that, you'll know if you are succeeding in five. Business advice has been really essential. I have three different companies that offer me legal, financial and business advice. So if I have a problem I can phone them up, they check letters and things for me too. *The Federation of Small Business*es has proved very useful as well. When you work on your own, at the end of the day you need somebody at the end of a phone; it's really reassuring to know that, because a lot of situations you won't have come across before.

Key Issues

What have you been most concerned about as you developed your business and practice?

Perhaps it's a personal thing but more and more of what I do is now made by other people, manufacturers, which means the making, the part I enjoy most, is done by other people. I'm on the phone all day. I'd like to turn that around but I'm not quite sure how to do that at the moment. I'm probably turning into more of a manager. I have a huge network of people who will do particular jobs for me depending on the type of project. I may only use them once or twice a year. Normally about seven small companies would be involved in one of my projects. As each of my projects is unique, each one takes a lot of time, identifying new problems, finding new solutions, finding out who can do them. Setting up machinery for what are often short runs is not particularly economic either. It's a disadvantage of the kind of work I do.

Location

Do you think you have to be in a major or capital city to do this?
No but maybe it helps.

Selling Stuff

Trade Shows

What is your experience of trade shows?
They are very important, it tends to be where you get a lot of exposure to the people you need to be exposed to, to get your product sold. There are always a lot of the press there, all the trade magazines and so on. I have had to do very little press of my own; I must admit I don't put much into it, unlike *Salt* who are very good at press and put a lot of work into it, although I guess their market is very different to mine. (*The company Salt comprises two textile designers also located in the Oxo Tower who are well known for their sophisticated range of screens and blinds and are regularly featured in the British design press*).
Yes, you don't seem to be very well known to the general public, why is that?
I am probably in trade magazines more than consumer magazines because those are the people I deal with. Consumer products are not my main market.

Retailing

You run a small shop and you've sold to shops, what's that like?
I don't see it as a shop, I see it as an extension of my studio. I don't know how to run a shop, I see it as an interaction with a client. I haven't got an ambition to develop a retail chain, the commissioned work is much more interesting to me. Though I have to admit the shop does pay for my studio, sometimes I have to lock it so I can get on with my work!

Commission Work

How have you come by commission work and what has been your experience with it?
I come by work through trade shows, the press, possibly word of mouth. I don't ask how people have heard of me, I just make assumptions.
Don't you think you should know?
I have been to business class, business advisors often get exasperated, I'm not in it for the cash. With teaching I do have money to fall back on, it means I can afford to take the risks (*Lindsay teaches part-time at Hertfordshire University*).
My experience of commission work is that it is stressful, exciting and experimental.

Clients

What do you think are the main rules for dealing with clients?
Communication. I am often involved with quite large building projects, I'm usually the afterthought, the 'decorative bit', and usually a lot of the people involved, (particularly those on site) are unaware of my role or the requirements for my work to be installed. I make a point of 'cc'ing everybody I can. Sometimes you have to be quite assertive, make your presence known, explain who you are and start sorting things out. (*Lindsay recounts the tale of how, when turning up on one building site, she discovered that the building was complete but the power supply for her light piece had been 'overlooked'. It cost £2000 to rectify the oversight.*)

Sub-contracting manufacture

What is it like trying to manage other people and companies in the production process?
You have to develop a trust and a good dialogue. Ask people their views, they will be more willing if they feel involved. The stuff I ask people to do puts them under pressure as well, no project is straightforward. I have to respect the people I ask to do work for me, I'm usually presenting them with a problem they may never have to solve again, so any solutions they come up with, only get to be used that once. That must be annoying if you are in business, they don't get much benefit from their 'research' effort. Of course sometimes you have difficulties, particularly if you are a woman, you often have to win respect dealing with electricians, builders and engineers. Sometimes though, people really respond to the challenges in the work and then it can be as exciting for them as it is for me. On the NESTA project for example I employed a precision engineer, a CNC machinist called Jim Day; he was really thinking about what I wanted to do and came up with lots of suggestions – it was a beautiful piece in the end.

The Broader View

Interdisciplinarity

Your work and business has required you to combine many different types of skill and deal with lots of other specialists. Do you think that is a necessary part of being a designer-maker?
I suppose it depends on your personality; I really enjoyed working on the NESTA project but then I'm seriously fascinated by science. In general I respond to problem-solving and my work and my business both involve a lot of skills, techniques and knowledge. I can't do what I do without working with others.

Progression

From a very clear origin in textiles you seemed to have moved increasingly toward becoming a straightforward lighting designer, retaining the option of using textiles. You also work closely with people from other fields like electronics. What would you say about that drift and do you see yourself returning more fully to the use of textiles at some point?

I don't know, I think I'm probably more of a general designer now. I'd like to go back to doing more textiles but my answer to that probably changes from year to year. I think my work has been characterized by an approach which seeks new forms and different materials and I see that as direct continuation of my textile experience. It has been an interesting progression, but for me where I am now, textiles as a material is just part of my repertoire; it will to some extent depend on the projects which come my way.

Exhibiting

You have a very varied career mixing lecturing, running a business and exhibiting, how has the gallery exhibiting fitted in?

If it seems like a good idea, for whatever reason, I'll do it. I enjoy the idea of exhibitions – it gives you a bit more freedom. I don't really approach galleries, things arise; the Sparks festival was a case in point. *(The 'creating Sparks' festival took place in Kensington, London in 2000 and celebrated collaborations between artists and scientists).*

Personality

What virtues do you think a designer-maker should have?

Hard worker, self-motivation, flexibility, perseverance is very important. You have to do every job that you would find in a normal company, you are the director and the cleaner, the project manager, the press officer and the secretary. I am not bossy but I have to drive people, you have to be firm with clients and the people you employ to do jobs. Last of all there is negotiation, a lot of my time is taken up in telephone conversations, trying to match *a* with *b*, trying to move projects on. You have to be good with people, keep the dialogue going, while all the time at the back of your mind are deadlines and difficulties. The satisfaction for me in the end, is the feeling I've succeeded in adding something special to the world, often against the odds.

Thankyou for your time.

It's been a pleasure.

–6–

The Craftsperson

Essentially and absolutely a craftsperson is a maker. Craft textiles, as a distinct category, are commonly perceived as multi-media, exploring the inherent qualities of different textile materials, sometimes in combination with other materials and objects. Modern craftspeople, in the process of establishing their practice, pursue and explore textiles in a wide variety of commercial and professional contexts. Often they draw on a range of cultural issues, or adapt to social trends, and form an individual, personal and expressive textile language. As stated previously, there are many similarities between the textile craftsperson and the textile designer-maker, which can give rise to confusion. There are major differences in the way they produce textiles but their modes of professional practice are alike; they may supply the same markets; operate within a comparable model of studio practice; finally, their work or products may be perceived in a similar context by the viewer. The craft approach to textiles is very much process-led; the actual pursuit of making by hand is of paramount importance for the craftsperson.

The personal interaction with making and the control this gives to the maker is indicative of craftspeople's attitude to their work. This is contrary to the attitude of designer-makers, who are not worried about using ready-assembled components or the services of a third party in the making process. However, we cannot escape the fact that there is a craft element underpinning the design process which the designer-maker is involved with, simply because to create a prototype calls for a 'hands-on' approach. Eventually, designer-makers choose to have their product completely or partly produced or manufactured by someone other than themselves. Having said this, today such craftspeople as Miglena Kazaski originate their product by means of craft, but in her case, in order to deal with the volume of orders placed with her, she is left with no alternative but to out-source the manpower required to carry out the work (Hoggard and Coatts, 2000: 38). Despite this, we can continue to term her trade as craft-based because her outworkers are still performing their tasks by hand and not by way of an industrially mechanized process.

When it comes to textile crafts, we cannot overemphasize the importance of the sense of touch which can carry a status at least equal to visual aesthetics. Also the dexterity of hands and fingers provide the craftsperson with creative opportunities not matched by machinery. Given this, the critical 'hands-on' philosophy

Figure 10. 'Pineforest Quilt – Applied, Used, Discarded'. Valerie Kirk. Courtesy The Powerhouse Museum, Sydney.

that the textile craftsperson adopts highlights the importance of the interaction between the hand and the material. This process creates sensitivities that are a central theme within the craftsperson's practice (Metcalf, 2000: 42–5). Tapestry weaver Valerie Kirk, in Australia, stresses the importance of the individual's role in the making process

> As a tapestry weaver it is all important that I create the work. It is not a simple matter of making by hand for the sake of this or as opposed to machine made or an adverse reaction to technology or wanting a handmade look. There is no technological process that can work in the way that I work as an artist creating in the process, making decisions each step of the way. (Kirk, 2001)

Given that the approach to textile craft is about instinctively responding to materials and handling them, we can assume that the textile craftsperson must have a natural or developed affinity with fabric and yarn. Most craftspeople embark on a period of training when the skills and dexterity for their practice are acquired and perfected. They usually find their chosen activity very fulfilling, absorbing, stimulating and complete. Working in such a self-absorbed manner takes an elevated level of commitment, discipline and perseverance. Sometimes striving for perfection within a discipline can take years, and it can entail a considerable degree of emotional commitment. It can also involve the sort of passion that arises as a result of applying one's efforts in an intense fashion, making both the work and the process significant. This strong vocational (almost spiritual) emphasis is part of the popular 'image' of craft and is often coupled with a romantic idea of where craft takes place. Textile craft disciplines are often perceived to have a history of association with cottage industries which embody notions of work of a skilful nature performed in familiar surroundings. Rather than erring on the 'design' side of the fence, craft sits firmly on the 'art' side. It is nigh on impossible to take the art out of craft; after all, to attempt to do so would strip the craft of its artistic expression. However, textile craft cannot be decanted into purely conceptual thoughts – as textile art can. The 'craft' stamp exemplifies a skill that is historically weighted and demands a physical interaction. In order to earn the label 'textile craft' the object needs to indicate its handmade value: if not, it is no longer craft.

Craftspeople's personal identities are often linked to their practice. Craftspeople express a commitment to their work and strongly identify with what they do and the way they feel about it. When people refer to themselves as weavers, ceramicists or jewellers, they are not simply speaking about the field they are involved with but are also making a statement about their individuality. Peter Collingwood is regarded by his peers not just as a craftsman, but as a Master Weaver. Collingwood has devoted his life to researching his craft: for him the craft of weaving involves mathematics, engineering and architecture (Seeling, 2000). There is often a

common bond between craftspeople. Collingwood's approach is very comparable
to the spirit of the Japanese attitude to textile crafts, so it is probably no surprise
that Collingwood and Jun'ichi Arai, the Master Weaver of Japan, share and express
a similar empathy for their craft.

Of the textile disciplines, weave, knit, embroidery and feltmaking are textile
practices which lend themselves readily to the craft environment. However, the
same tends not to be said about the medium of print – perhaps this is due to the
intrinsic nature of the subject. In contrast to other textile specialisms and methods,
modern print can fit neatly into the contemporary commercial framework. This is
possibly because the print methods used by independent designers are very similar
to their industrially mechanized equivalents. It can be very difficult to spot the
difference between a material which is precisely screen-printed by hand and its
commercially produced counterpart. That said, though, print is historically also
steeped in craft traditions, its origins stretching back to an age of block-printing.
Modern day printers who fall into the craft category tend to gravitate toward the
world of luxurious fashion accessories, or designer goods. To some extent the
different categories are increasingly blurred anyway, modern craftspeople being
free to mix and match processes as they feel appropriate to their artistic vision.

Comparing Makers

With some fundamental differences in practice between the designer and the
craftsperson having been determined, there is still the matter of the difference
between art and craft. Textile artists (or fibre artists) have often striven to reach
the status of 'high art' they believe they deserve. In comparison, the word 'craft'
still carries a stigma in some creative circles. Rather than celebrating its rich heritage
of process and technique, craft is often seen as a poor cousin. In an attempt to
break away from and create space between itself and other textile practices, textile
art has gradually become a more theoretical activity. This seems a little odd in
contemporary society, where the tangible margins of subjects are evidently eroded.
Our desire to categorize the intricacies of contemporary textile practice is
questionable. Gopika Nath summarized these issues at the close of the twentieth
century:

> Having worked within the realm of textiles for more than 20 years, I find the idea of
> having to define myself as designer, craftsperson or artist as rather perplexing, for I
> find that I work as all three and at given times, in certain contexts, this medium has
> allowed me to indulge and also emphasise the many facets of my creative being. But
> society today decrees that we make demarcations and categorise artists by the medium
> of their expression. At a certain level, it is to the advantage of practitioners working in a
> specialised medium to do so in a relatively insular way, to develop techniques and levels

of skill, and therefore expression, to standards of excellence that may well be thwarted when competing for space in the larger context of 'art'. (Nath, 1999)

If we must rank creative occupations within textiles, we have to consider the particular environments the work is destined for. For instance, we may find the work of a textile craftsperson and a textile designer-maker at the same trade fair or retail establishment, but would be hard pressed to find a textile artist on the same ground. The textile craftsperson easily crosses over and shares camp with both the textile designer-maker and the textile artist, yet the designer-maker and the artist hardly ever cross paths; they are quite different from each other. Occasionally, we find the craftsperson and the artist sharing the same territory, usually in the form of exhibiting space or competing for work, such as commissions. When required to categorize the craftsperson and the artist, we see that they have specific identifying characteristics. The textile craftsperson's work often arises out of an affinity with material in the pursuit of a process-based practice. The inspiration for this type of work varies: it can be either very prosaic and literal or alternatively quite thought-provoking. Conversely, the work of a textile artist is more likely to be conceptual in nature, drawing comfortable comparisons with fine art. It would be wrong to demean craft in comparison to art because of its lack of intellectual debate, since it compensates with its own particular virtues. Craftspeople carry a high level of unspoken, implicit knowledge and, in their defence, they have rather more flexible options regarding destinations for their 'craft' type of work. At times, as practice changes, the whole debate itself seems anachronistic:

> students have been experimenting for some time with new and unconventional materials which have been pressed into service to take knitting into new areas, breaking down barriers between craft, art and fashion. Experimental 'yarns' include wire, paper and plastics and knitted fabrics have been treated to a wide range of processes – perhaps printed, laminated, rubberized, felted, sprayed, or dipped in resin. (Black, S., 2000: 30)

When comparing the textile craft product to that of a textile designer-maker product, there really isn't any dispute about status. The basis for an equal footing is that there is no conflict on the grounds of intellect or cultural worth. However, issues of status and identity may occur in the area of selling products commercially. The onlooker's perception of a product can be swayed enormously according to the 'label' attached to it. The craft label sometimes carries a stigma and so too can the design label. There can be cultural and generational differences in reactions to labels, and craft may demand more respect than design in some parts of the world while design may be seen to be rather more hip and groovy than craft. The way in which textile designers and textile craftspeople label themselves is quite interesting too.

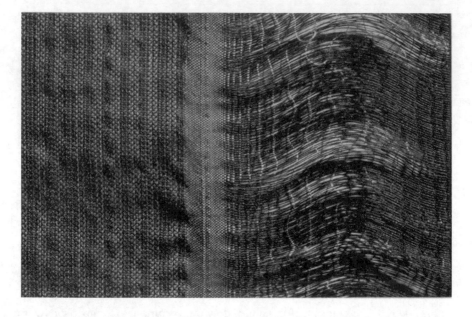

Figure 11. Sample of handwoven fabric. Liz Marchetti.

Elizabeth Marchetti makes hand-woven bags for the luxury end of the market, supplying stores such as Harvey Nichols in Britain and other boutiques internationally. Of her practice, she says:

> Although my practice is craft based, I don't like to be labelled as a craftsperson because of the stigma attached to that. The only element of my work that describes me as a craftsperson is the fact that I am a hand-weaver. I would like people to think of my products as contemporary and modern rather than be perceived as traditional because of the method I use . . . Obviously, the making is the most important thing for me. Process is key, I have to weave the fabric, if it was woven commercially my products would not be the one-off luxurious items that they are. The label 'weaver' is critical because I want to be recognised for my skill and be associated with the quality of my hand-woven bags, so it is important that my name is attached to my products. (Marchetti, 2001)

With the more obvious differences between the craftsperson, artist and designer now marked out, subtleties still remain. We can, even now, raise similarities between the spirit of textile crafts and textile art, in that it is common for almost all textile practitioners to have a certain affinity with material and process. For example, from this extract, it is difficult to categorize Alice Kettle, whose approach to making appears to have shifted from a more consciously 'art' basis to a craft one:

My work isn't any longer a frantic search for discovery, a race against time to express everything inside my head before it evaporates . . . And that has always been the paradox of stitching, balancing together its slowness in the making with the constant emergence of new ideas. Sometimes you grapple with both and you dart between one piece and the next with impatience, while at other moments the rhythmic flow of the work lets the ideas form themselves. (Kettle, 1999)

The Importance of Process-Led Practice

The intrinsic nature of process is satisfying in itself, almost sustaining the craftsperson. The research results of Mihaly Csikszentmihalyi, a psychologist investigating the nature of satisfying action, seem appropriate to the realms of textile crafts, the connection being handwork. He identifies a pleasurable action which he refers to as 'flow'. Those activities that stimulate 'flow' have obvious challenging aims and are importantly characterized by intense focus and concentration: 'The combination of all these elements causes a deep sense of enjoyment that is so rewarding people think that expending a great deal of energy is worthwhile simply to be able to feel it' (Csikszentmihalyi, 1991). Given this, at the very heart of absorbing craft practice lies a satisfaction and pleasure that is almost therapeutic. Although craft is a slow, contemplative process, it is rhythmic and the craftsperson finds enjoyment in the measured and calm pace of the work.

Far from being easy, craft can at times demand raw energy as well as exhausting mental activity. Process is the dominating characteristic of the textile craftsperson's world, the aim, the making of an object. Sometimes the process can become so commanding, it virtually takes over. Linda Behar, maker of embroidered miniatures says:

Embroidery appeals to her precisely because it demands such direct engagement . . . 'the stitching just took over . . . I have a very tactile approach to art making . . . When embroidering, I respond to the feel of the fabric in my hands and the quality of the threads I use'.

(Harris and Lyon, 1998)

To the textile craftsperson, the physical act of stitching can create a mood of reflection and be emotionally comforting. These are the same emotions we might anticipate a viewer of the work to experience. Carol Eckert has a working practice identifiable with Behar's. She too works on a miniature scale, which is perhaps part of the charm of a crafted textile object. In producing coiled vessels, she skillfully envelops thin copper wire in cotton embroidery thread, using her 'figure eight' stitch. Her meditative craft encompasses her work ethos of discipline, persistence and a piecemeal, solitary practice, characterizing the typical craft approach to textiles. Intriguingly, Eckert busied herself as a child with scraps of fabric, needle and thread: perhaps this is a common formative personal experience and explains how some textile craftspeople become attached to materials (Brandt, 1999). As a child Peter Collingwood was also conscious of the process of making, exercising intellect and skill as well as relating to the physical world of materials.

A Role in the Modern World

With consumers becoming more sophisticated and the world more technological, it is interesting to reflect on the value of textile craft practice in the twenty-first century, to consider whether the need for handwork exists. Certainly many like to believe that there is a place for wistful, romantic nostalgia in our lives, which older craft practices quite happily fill. Today, however, textile craft is also seen as an alternative to mass production, expressive of the 'human touch'. It offers an element of exclusivity that the consumer is able to buy into. In contemporary life, the creative qualities found within textile crafts are seen as virtues and add to the value of these crafts as commodities. As consumer tastes grow ever more sophisticated, there is a preference for individuality. Craft objects become favoured over the conventional 'run-of-the-mill' item.

While the demand for craft objects persists and perhaps may even grow, the opportunity to become a craftsperson in advanced societies seems to be diminishing. In modern society a life dedicated to craft often doesn't equate to a worthwhile vocation or a financially rewarding one. It conflicts with what people ordinarily believe is normal work, as well as with their expectations about standards of living. Above all, it is not a financially driven career path; on the contrary, anyone who is involved in the making process doesn't do it for the lucrative economic prospects – the fame maybe, but not the cash! It is doubtful as to whether, for the vast majority of contemporary craftworkers, craft is an economically viable practice at all. In order to survive, many textile craftspeople will produce a diffusion range of products for the commercial market alongside making one-off signature pieces. Alternatively they may find other means of income to support their practice. In terms of quality there is still a place in the contemporary world for the benchmarks that the craftsperson sets. While craft to the consumer and general public may often be perceived as having low intellectual status, it more than compensates in terms of the production standards and aesthetic values it sets.

Although that may be so, there are numerous textile crafts sustained around the world, particularly to support the tourism industries and as a feeder to fashion. It is almost inevitable that over time all ancient and original craft traditions will disappear. Given this, contemporary craftspeople such as Miglena Kazaski and Anne Belgrave are reinterpreting and keeping alive an ancient medium of textile crafts – felt. Their respective approaches to communicating the same craft in a modern world are very distinct from one another, one operating in a commercial sphere and the other on a very creative and expressive level. Kazaski sculpts what is historically perhaps the most primeval of fabrics to make bags, clothes and other fashion accessories which sell at venues such as London Fashion Week. Though Kazaski's work is sold by commercial means and sits comfortably in the retail environment, it is very apparent that its roots are in the craft world. Her work and practice show how closely intertwined the worlds of the craftsperson and the designer-maker are. In contrast, Anne Belgrave simultaneously works on making a range of accessories alongside her dramatic sculptural forms. She describes her relationship with the material she uses to 'make':

Figure 12. 'Buffalo Bucket'. Anne Belgrave.

The essential idea of felt appeals to me . . . I feel I'm finally going back to my roots. I started out as a sculptor and, this year, the last thing I've wanted to make is functional pieces . . . In some ways felt-making is like hand-building with clay. There's an intrinsic randomness I really like. There's no foregone conclusion – and at some point the 'thing' almost makes itself.

(Hoggard, 1998: 44)

The modern designer is often seeking the craft qualities within textiles, and the fashion glossies are keen to highlight work such as that of Kazaski in the claim that traditional textile craft is making a comeback in fashion. We have to consider whether fashion designers have ever actually abandoned traditional textile crafts in the first place. They have always used traditional hand skills like beading and embroidery for example, in a modern context and as a source of inspiration for their collections. Fashion can be a vehicle to take traditional crafts into the contemporary world. In Western fashion-design culture, it is often assumed that Western style is modern and all other styles, by default, including those of different cultures, are at once ethnic and historical. Consequently traditional crafts from around the world fuel the fantasies of Western designers' mood boards and 'exotic' collections. Elsewhere, the desire to market or develop the local fashion industry by retrieving local tradition can become a matter of genuine economic strategy.

Today, through necessity as much as through choice, the modern textile craftsperson will engage in entrepreneurial activity. This immediately narrows the gap between the world of the craftsperson and that of the designer-maker. In addition to producing unique pieces, craftspeople such as Anne Belgrave and Elizabeth Marchetti employ their distinctive skills to develop commercial diffusions of their craft. They are under pressure to do so, particularly for financial reasons, which are paramount. There is a defined niche in the commercial world for craftspeople. The items they make, often in small or limited-edition batches, will normally go on to be sold through craft and trade fairs, semi-commercial galleries or retail establishments. In the United States, craft fairs are held annually and are considerable in number – the most popular being in Ann Arbor, Michigan or State College, Pennsylvania. It is at such venues that the buyer can interact with the maker of the goods – enabling them to associate the product with a tangible identity.

The Appeal of the Handmade

Sometimes, although the craftsperson may produce small batches of the same item, it would be rare to find two that are absolutely identical. This is simply because they are made by hand and as such, more often than not, will contain the odd flaw. It seems that this only acts to enhance the handmade quality of the object further, making an object more charming as it becomes a symbol of the 'humanness' of craft. Thus the unique identity of individual makers and their products ultimately fuse, to create something quite special for the market.

The craft consumer, the buyer and user of handcrafted textile products, will generally not be aware of the context and circumstances of production. Neither are they likely to be aware of the contentment and fulfillment its creation brought to its maker. Considering this, it is difficult to assess how craftspeople measure or determine the worth or significance a buyer attaches to the object they have made. It's necessary to make an educated guess and assume that the consumer places a degree of significant value on the craft process, so as to justify investment in the crafted object. Alternatively, if consumers are not aware of the worth of craft or have no interest in the technique used, their motivation is harder to understand. It might be that the crafted object projects a status through its handmade quality; the appeal of a piece can lie in its total originality and unique nature. A very attractive characteristic of the handmade is that, in the entire world, no replica of it exists.

The way in which antique or ancient textile practice is perceived could be seen as either an asset or a hindrance. For example, the idea of buying a traditional handmade crafted object could be perceived as a sign of education, status or sophistication, an expression of knowing the cultural, historic and artistic worth of an object. The value of many craft products is in the way in which high quality and fine workmanship reflect or add to long-standing traditions and techniques. These virtues are perhaps not always as appealing to the modern generation, for whom craft in its widest sense is perhaps seen as an antiquated practice, and the crafted piece has no perpetual place or special significance in their modern world. It may prove that in a digital age the value of such fine craft will return. Of course not all craft needs 'fine' materials and meticulous processes; there is equally a place for humbler, expressive products that defy the anonymity and uniformity of mass-manufactured consumer goods. In essence handmade objects represent their originators and their creative endeavours and skills – fundamentally this genuine and marvellous quality is what stimulates a desire to touch, feel or own a craft object.

Supporting Organizations

Rich histories of textile traditions are present in almost every nation on the globe. Both nationally and regionally, various bodies are organized to represent and support textile traditions and communities. Most countries have an organized agency responsible for representing and promoting their nation's crafts internationally. Such agencies also play a role in increasing public awareness of contemporary crafts. Bodies like The Crafts Council in Britain (www.craftscouncil.org.uk), The American Craft Council in the United States (www.craftcouncil.org) and Craft Australia (www.craftaus.com.au), typify established national craft organizations.

Complementary to these national craft associations is The World Craft Council (www.wccwis.gr). The World Craft Council is not affiliated to any one government or country; instead, it is representative of five regions in the world: Africa, Asia, Europe, Latin America and North America. Its mission statement is one of encouraging, strengthening and unifying craft communities as a cultural and economic force around the world.

Agencies also exist to monitor the state of traditional and contemporary ethnic textile craft throughout the world. Some operate at a high political level, one such example being UNESCO (The United Nations Educational, Scientific and Cultural Organization) (www.unescobkk.org/culture/devclt.htm). Its strategy is to protect and promote creativity, encouraging the growth of the cultural industries. These cultural industries have over time defined national identities and shaped the societies of the world today. Much craft that takes place in the poorer parts of the world is undertaken out of economic necessity and for basic survival rather than with a romantic notion of sustaining a handmade or traditional practice. Similar to the World Craft Council, UNESCO's role is one of encouraging global economic development through creativity.

India is one of the few countries that demonstrates a commercial approach to their traditional crafts. The continuance, survival and preservation of traditional Indian textile crafts exists not in a museum but in the form of 16 million crafts-

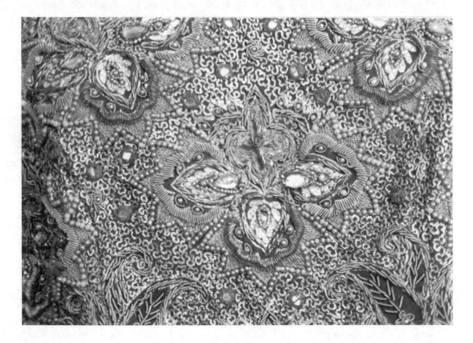

Figure 13. Example of Indian embroidery incorporating beads and crystals. Courtesy Kandola.

people, weaving, dying, printing and embroidering. Fashion designers, both within India and elsewhere, help create the demand that sustains this huge craft industry. These designers have become the modern-day patrons of traditional Indian textile crafts, sourcing materials from the handloom and craft centres, in a quest to revive and benefit from the craft techniques of the past. The Indian craft industry is one of the last of its kind; whether it can survive the modernization and economic growth of India is a moot point. Generally the future of textile craft in the new millennium and the role of different agencies presents a mixed picture. For some countries, such as India, it may be a fact of economic survival or a way of sustaining communities while industry develops. It might alternatively be that new markets sustain and develop a demand for crafts. For other countries there may be broader issues of cultural identity or the role of culture and the arts in their communities. All the agencies, institutions, communities and individuals involved in sustaining and developing textile craft face similar and growing problems about issues of stability and sustainability. We can only be certain of two things, history has taught us that crafts and craft knowledge naturally disappear, but it has also taught us that new crafts have always emerged and developed because people want and enjoy beautiful things.

The Textile Artist

It is possible to develop a very personal relationship with textile work. For many practitioners this will dictate a career route or a set of experiences that lead them to undertake what is commonly called textile art. In so doing they may well experience difficulties of creative identity and status, because textile art is as yet an uncertain definition of practice. This chapter provides an overview of what textile art currently entails and offers observations on the philosophical and institutional problems it can provoke when compared to dealings with fine art or textile craft. Much of the chapter pursues and tests the comparison with fine art, as this is often a prime source of confusion, but it might equally have pursued and tested the difference with textile craft and design. Nonetheless there is sufficient material to indicate the professional dilemmas and questions facing the contemporary textile artist, not least being to determine what textile art actually is.

Textile art (or alternatively fibre art) is a term that has gained increasing currency in recent decades and is used to describe textile works that, like sculpture, paintings or installation, can exist in galleries or public spaces. While some modern textile art can be seen to bear similarities to activities and material approaches within modern fine art, for example the work of Eva Hesse (Lippard, 1976), it provides a broader practice that can include decorative values or the intrinsic pleasurable qualities of fabric. The vast majority of contemporary textile art can be seen to have grown directly out of the more generic textile art and crafts traditions, particularly weaving, embroidery and tapestry, as these have mirrored the evolution of modernism in other creative disciplines. On occasion when textiles has found itself adjacent to some art historical period or group, it has undergone a degree of inclusion within the art historical perspective of cultural history, as for example the weavers of the Bauhaus (Weltge, 1998) or the textile designs of Russian Constructivism – particularly those created during the 1920s by artists such as Stepanova and Popova. The term is now widely understood but not in all countries, and in various parts of the world textile art does not exist as a defined form separate from fine art or textile craft. Many people find that both the use of the term and the characteristics of the work create problems of categorization. For these reasons textile art is an unclear concept, but remains nonetheless an increasingly visible and popular group of practices, with many willing to take on the mantle of 'textile artist'.

In the second half of the twentieth century, various parts of the textile art community became increasingly organized, establishing for themselves identifiable forums, groupings and exhibiting opportunities. These developments lent credibility to the types of work textile artists undertook, created support networks and added substance to the concept 'textile art'. With much of the groundwork having by now been established, if textile art is henceforth to be confirmed as a single, separate and coherent discipline, it is probably at a crucial stage in its development. There would be benefits to the wider textile community if this confirmation took place. The potential role of textile art in stimulating the broad cultural status of textiles is not to be underestimated. The great social status that textiles once had, particularly in ancient cultures, by and large has slipped away. Textile art has the power to recreate such status. Where previously textiles expressed power, mystery or wealth – primarily through opulent and dazzling clothing – now textile art can make complex statements or seductive overtures through the media, in public spaces and in the home. In doing so it could reassert the cultural status of textiles.

Textile Art, Craft or Design?

Any attempt to explain textile art begins with some fairly fundamental problems of definition. Many textile practitioners define themselves as textile artists but the title belies a friction between the world of fine art and the world of craftspeople. Increasingly there is an intellectual tension within textiles itself between types of practice premised on traditional techniques and material sensibilities and more conceptually led forms of practice:

> One of the central problems of the issue is a general lack of honesty as to what is actually being discussed. Decorative artists and craftspeople are now employing writers to 'talk up' their work into something more allusive and philosophical than it actually is. Look at it hard and it begins to seem that the debate about art, craft and design is about pretensions motivated by ambition, perhaps even greed, and the desire for personal glory. (Colchester, 1991: 11)

This tension is matched by an ambivalent, sometimes frosty, relationship with galleries, funding organizations, arts policy-makers and the fine art establishment. Whatever the problems of pursuing a definition, the term textile art reveals a broad and lively set of issues about textiles for love and textiles for its own sake on the one hand, while on the other textiles as high culture, vying with other art forms for status, funding and opportunity.

Within textiles practice itself, the term textile art is applied to many different levels and varieties of work. Hobbyists will often call their work textile art when it is little more than traditional samplers or tapestries. Craftspeople of varying degrees of sophistication will call their work textile art as if to appropriate some higher status for what they do. Sometimes textile designers enter the arena of textile art. Community artists will use the term as a catch-all making it easier to explain the materials and processes they work with. Some textile artists explain it as a practice separate to fine art but of equal parity; others state that textile art is simply a genre within fine art. Some fine artists work with textiles but simply see it as part of their material and conceptual repertoire and consider themselves as fundamentally fine artists. Finally some practitioners are happy to have identities to suit work or context, moving between art, craft and design.

The problem of definition, in general, is attributable to a centuries-old philosophical intervention which drew a distinction between high and low culture and put fine art in the high culture category:

> In the Critique of Judgement Kant divides the arts in general into mechanical and aesthetical ones . . . in Kant they (*the mechanical ones*) are firmly subordinated to the aesthetical ones, on the ground that they are disagreeable in themselves and draw what positive value they have from their results. (Sorell, 1991: 72)

Kant also compounded the signifier of a 'work of art', the contingency of an expression or idea with a form, by differentiating between pleasure consisting only in sensations and pleasure consisting in modes of cognition (the latter of which he, along with successive generations of fine artists and art historians, took to be superior). Obviously for textiles, an expressive medium with 'sensations' at its very heart, Kant's opinions damned it irrevocably. Caught between being a 'mechanical' craft of little cultural value and an 'aesthetical' art of high cultural value, who would not prefer to be a fine artist? Interestingly, in textiles some people prefer the label of craft because they presume, and are annoyed by, art's avowed conceptual nature.

The culture of fine art has managed over the years to accumulate some silly and problematic bits of philosophy, such as the idea of the avant-garde:

> The artist rarely uses it as a term of self description; there exists a certain etiquette, involving modesty, that makes it a slightly embarrassing label. For the critic to describe something as avant-garde usually indicates a certain mystification in the face of the object, and as such the term legitimates incomprehension. For the gallery owner, the avant-garde indicates a relatively under-colonised domain that is ripe for commercial exploitation at the same time as improving the gallery's reputation for supporting daring and innovative work. For the curator, the avant-garde represents an opportunity to construct new trends and to codify what might otherwise appear as disordered and polymorphous. Definitions are thus strategic (Ford, 1994)

In essence textile art finds itself entering a marketplace already occupied and strategically managed, one in which a particularly elaborate auctioneering process is always in progress. Nonetheless, being able to participate in the auction is essential to seeking exhibiting opportunities, funding opportunities, commissions and sales. The issue of textile art is not fundamentally about whether it is fine art, design or craft; it is about accessing fine art's industrial infrastructure, which is increasingly just a part of the media, leisure, tourism and interior decoration industries.

It is worth noting that while there may be no clear definition of what textile art is, the definition of fine art is no better. Within the fine-art education system and in many fine-art publications and journals the impression is given that there is no middle or lower market associated with fine art. Equally the impression is often given that practice is always 'contemporary' or 'modern', that craft is not a significant aspect of much fine art and, finally, that content is 'high' or 'clever'. It is a patent reality that the majority of fine art in the world is pedestrian, craft-based and historical. This much it has in common with textile art. Both disciplines can be seen to have a high, middle and low culture. Also, they both diffuse into craft, tradition, design and commerce. The most interesting questions therefore remain at the higher end of the debate, whether there is some pure centre, some integral formula or proposition that makes textile art and fine art fundamentally different.

The Reason of Textile Art

The simplest characteristics that qualify something as 'textile art' are that it predominantly incorporates textiles, that it is appropriate to be displayed in a manner or context we associate with fine art (such as a gallery), and that the artist describes him- or herself as a textile artist. A contentious thesis would be that textile art can in some way be understood as an extension or elevation of textile craft or design into a 'higher' realm. This would imply textile art is the conceptually superior cousin of textile craft and design. This takes us down the road that 'art' is *better* than 'craft' or 'design' (rather than just *different* from them). Typically this debate would be informed by an interrogation of philosophy, starting perhaps with the work of Kant; typically also, this would result in a great waste of time and breath.

We cannot ignore the relatively recent appearance of textile art as a cultural form and as a practice. Nor can we ignore the realities of contemporary culture and the creative industries. An explanation of textile art that might clarify its position is to be found in motivations based on origin, sentiment and sensibility. The prior experience of textile artists, for example the nature of their background in textiles, and what the artists feel as significant in a work, will all affect the content, perception and explanation of the work:

I wanted to make work that recognised the strength and integrity of early patterned textiles, acknowledging their use of loose geometry and sequential elements. I also wanted to question the derisory manner in which textiles continue to be discussed within the wider spectrum of the visual arts. Patterning and decoration in particular were used as critical terms to indicate either a lack of ideas or superfluous overworking (Brennand-Wood, 2000: 51)

It is the artists' perceptions and explanations that provide a key as to what, if anything, textile art could be said to be and how it differs from adjacent categories. In a sense what textile art most suffers from is a lack of history; it needs more curations, landmarks and artistic groups. Textile 'art' after all, has a shorter history than 'art' photography even though its roots and its aesthetic sensibilities stretch far into the past.

In Britain the same figures have dominated the 'high culture' textile art scene for some time. Artists such as Sally Greaves-Lord, Sally Freshwater, Polly Binns, Caroline Broadhead and Michael Brennand-Wood, begin to seem like permanent central fixtures on the scene. While new talent may appear from time to time (Dawney, 2000), more often than not they swiftly disappear, lacking support, opportunity or influence. As in many other countries, it seems as if the size of the textile art community is, as yet, too small. Undoubtedly a close relationship between textile art and critical discourse can prove essential in creating a larger, more dynamic community; it is also a necessary part of establishing a cultural market. There is no need to presume that this might simply mimic the traditions of fine art. Increasingly there are appropriate opportunities, such as the recent *SHIFT* conference held at the Canberra School of Art (www.anu.edu.au/ITA/CSA/textiles/shift/shiftprogram1.html) and the *Textiles: What is Critical* conference (http://website.lineone.net/~nwtf) organized by the British North West Textiles Forum at the Whitworth Art Gallery in Manchester.

It is interesting to consider whether there are other disciplines with an origin in craft or design that now compare or compete with fine art. Certainly fashion has made claims to the gallery space, as have photography and video. The adjunct 'art', as in art house movie or wearable art or even perhaps performance art, connotes only the entry of these disciplines into a different institutional framework, where valuation and purpose are of a particular kind. Entry to, or the adoption of the fine-art industrial framework by these disciplines, does not simply either amount to their assimilation by fine art or constitute an extension of it. As much as we might say that any of the 'new arts' are brought about by the behaviour of the artists themselves, it seems an aspect of the postmodern idiom that there is a general pressure for creative disciplines to increase the conceptual dimension of their work. This is true across all spheres of craft and design. This results in a high-culture version of many craft and design subjects (subjects that previously were the

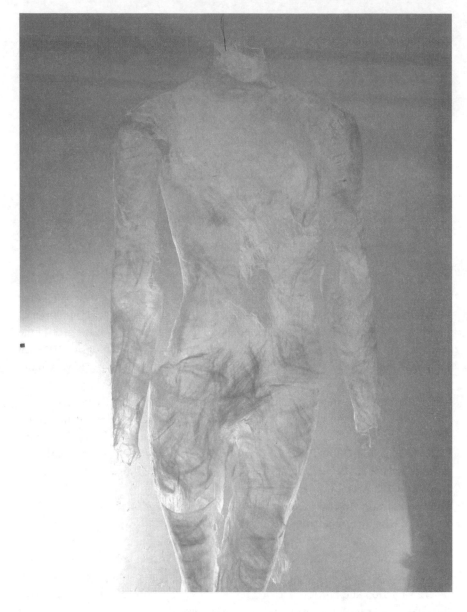

Figure 14. 'Body Cast'. Kei Ito.

Kantian lowly 'mechanical arts') stimulating new and different forms of appreci-
ation of new and different forms of expression, detached from simple utility. The
evolution of textile art is a symptom of the evolution of postmodern, post-industrial
culture.

Issues of Content

Textile art differs from fine art primarily on grounds of the importance of aesthetic content and the importance of technique in construction. In many other ways textile art shares the forms and modes of presentation of fine art but the central priorities of textiles (touch, handle, texture, colour, surface, pattern), its inheritance, are never abandoned. Of the two defining features that mark out textile art, technical process is what most closely links the art with the craft. Within textiles, particularly perhaps within the traditions of constructed or embellished textiles, such as weave or embroidery, process and technical knowledge are often seen as part of the rite of passage. Close knowledge of technique, yarn and so on, or the observation of it, can be part of the fascination with textiles. It is also something that, in the absence of philosophical discourses, preoccupies the conversation and establishes the professional bond among those who work in textiles. This is an important point: there is undoubtedly a sense of collectivism, a shared almost masonic culture, that runs through the textiles community, which is based on an esteem for both the material qualities of textiles and the way they are made.

While textiles shares the common aesthetic language of form, composition and so on, as with many disciplines concerned very directly with materials there arises a special sensitization to complex phenomena particular to the medium – for example, phenomena occurring in or on the surface of fabric through differing densities or depths of yarn; modulation of matt and shiny surface; unusual or unexpected combinations of yarn; aspects of performance such as stretch or shrinkage; illusion related to handle (e.g. a fabric that looks heavy but is light). The list is not endless but it is elusive and only available to the cognoscenti. As with fine art, in this way textile art and textile craft assert and establish their own version of elitism through a private and sophisticated language that the public is invited to discover, reflect upon and enjoy.

Something which can be said about the aesthetics within contemporary textile art is that beauty, on its own, often seems a legitimate goal and is seen to be a sufficient mark of content. This is in sharp comparison to much contemporary fine art where beauty is often eschewed as vulgar or naive and is seen to be without intellectual substance; this often results in a lament or inappropriate comparison from those who comment on textile arts:

> How sad that it has become fashionable to malign beauty in art. Helena Hernmarck's work is for those who can still be uplifted by masterful handling of material, virtuosity of design and visual pleasure. Like the tapestries of old, her thoroughly contemporary hangings will stand the test of time. (Weltge, 1999: 42)

What is a cultural strength of fine art, its conceptual content, can occasionally amount to a narrowness or a strategic weakness. Textile art, sometimes portrayed as lacking critical intellectual content, in fact only appears so in relation to terms set down by a part of the fine-art community. On its own, or most people's terms, textile art is a tolerant, broad-based art form, equally at ease dealing with pleasure and nice things as it is dealing with the adult or the intellectual. This plurality and diversity of outcomes is probably what makes textile art an art form for our times, a properly postmodern variety of art.

Various categories of textile art reveal its linkage to different practices and traditions. In particular the continuum between textile craft and textile art is uninterrupted, and it is difficult to say where one ends and the other begins. One type of work seems to have been generally influenced by modernist ideas in the visual arts and the pictorial traditions of subjects like tapestry. This type of work often bears much in common with the pictorial devices of abstract, semi-abstract or symbolic forms of painting and uses traditional textile skills of needlework, tapestry, patchwork and so on. Examples are to be found at the *Textilia Center for Contemporary Fiber Art* in Sweden (http://home.quiknet.com/textillia) and perhaps also at the *Bayeux Gallery* in Denver, Colorado (www.bayeuxgallery.com). Another kind of work seems a little less straightforward by virtue of being old and new in a different way. In *The World of Embroidery* (www.embroiderersguild.org.uk/worldofembroidery) we see examples of work by textile artists for whom, often, the physical form of the final piece or the technical processes of the work are not necessarily traditional to textile craft and yet, for example, the intensity of embellishment or the aesthetic result seems part of the conventional 'goals' of craft. Both these categories of work also seem to support the possibility of approaches to practice supposedly dismissed by fine art. For example 'light-hearted' work, with cute or fey imagery, 'pleasurable' work, with sensuous colour or nice shapes, and so on.

A further category of textile art seems to draw on 'high modernism' combining the traditional virtues of modernist sculpture, essentially a kind of physicality, with textile sensibilities and materials. The physicality referred to tends to defer a language-based reading of the work, instead drawing on an emotional, spiritual or dramatic repertoire likely to inspire such feelings as awe or peace. This type of work has few better exponents than some of the contemporary textile artists of Japan. The reputation of their work has spread throughout the world. A major touring exhibition of Japanese textile art *Textural Space* (www.texturalspace.com), curated by Lesley Millar and originated through the Surrey Institute of Art and Design University College, England, incorporates the work of artists such as Asako Ishizaki, Koji Takaki and Chiyoko Tanaka. The work is both different in ambition and in context to the kinds of textile art mentioned before and, as well, different to more craft-based Japanese textile art (Shepley, 1999: 49–53). Very much an art of

Figure 15. Textile art. Asako Ishizaki. From the Textual Space exhibition. Photographer Gerry Diebel.

architecture, public spaces and galleries, it shares some of the aesthetic resonances often implicit in the work of fine artists such as Cornelia Parker (Parker, 2000). The formal properties and presence of the artworks of many of these Japanese artists have much in common with contemporary fine-art installation (de Oliveira, Oxley and Petry, 1994). However, the motivations differ widely from fine-art practice and the more conceptually led categories of textile art:

> It can be seen that there are differences between the Japanese and UK textile artists' approaches to their respective work. Both base their work on a particular understanding of their chosen materials and the history of textiles. For both the Japanese and UK textile artists, the contextual framework is of primary importance, but for the Japanese the context is the harmony achieved, whereas for the UK textile artist the context refers to contemporary discourse.
>
> (Millar, 2001)

The *Textural Space* project shows an increasing level of international exchange within the textile community, exchange which will in the end establish and develop a discourse particular to textile art. Various spin-offs of this type of project (as a result of which the Surrey Institute are establishing an Anglo-Japanese Textile Research Centre) do much to establish a better infrastructure for textile art.

The issues of content in textile art fundamentally concern whether there is something particular, some shared set of principles and priorities, which make the term textile art a meaningful one to use. For the time being we can observe that as so many people are prepared to use the term in itself, this implies indeed something particular: textile art exists. If anything, textile art has been too apologetic about its distinctive qualities – its inherent multiculturalism, its sensuality, its humanity, its beauty and its prettiness.

Ownership

During the twentieth century, many new and emergent disciplines have had difficulties establishing themselves as high-culture gallery-based forms (for example photography). All have had to compete with fine art, and textile art has not been alone in struggling to define itself as a distinct *alternative form* to fine art. Part of the process of definition is the establishment of a discourse about practice, historicizing change and personalities, creating groups and movements, typologies and themes within the discipline. For example the *62 Group* in Britain (www.62group.freeuk.com) have not established an identity or fame comparable with that of *Magnum* photography, yet it represents many 'famous' textile artists. There is a problem of myth-building, of heroic reputations, a strategy that textile art has failed to develop. Another aspect is how textile artists themselves, as groups or as individuals, start to establish discourse and practice. There are difficulties in evading a fine-art model while having to share much of its rhetoric and strategies, not least the broader politics of 'ownership' of the subject: that is, any attempts to assert textile art as independent of fine art. The stronger textile art becomes the greater the competition over such resources as funding and gallery access. These are the politics of status, whether textile art is treated as a separately identifiable discipline or as a genre within fine art.

The issue of ownership is closely linked to the issue of subject definition, and both are further problematized by the fact that increasing numbers of practitioners and creatives find the old divisions, based on material, process and discipline, rather arbitrary anyway:

> Nowadays young Slovene textile and fashion designers or artists do not tie themselves to a certain production technique or specific materials. The concepts of their expressions are much more dedicated to an exploratory sensibility based on different forms of art. In their postgraduate studies in Slovenia or abroad, they attempt to combine the knowledge they gained about the behaviour of textiles with photography, video art,

lighting design, architecture, psychology, visual theory and electronic media. (Jenko, 2000)

Such 'Renaissance' aspirations are fine but they pose major problems of adaptation for the institutions in which these young designers and artists wish to ply their trade. The implied increasingly individualistic notions of content, genre, status and worth will also need to be balanced against more utilitarian definitions of subjects and practice. Interdisciplinary practice is rarely an easy route to follow and the need to claim a 'professional title' or sphere of work is inevitable. However, the question is raised as to whether there is a general trend of homogenization or convergence in the 'arts'.

Galleries, curation and a shared discourse collectively help to sustain and develop the status of textile art. There is an interdependence between galleries being sympathetic and predisposed toward textile art, the perception that there is a practice available for curation and, finally, that there is something interesting and edifying to say about it. There has been a steady growth in the number of textile galleries, galleries hosting textile exhibitions and textile competitions. For example, in the United States, Pittsburgh boasts the Society for Contemporary Crafts (www.contemporarycraft.org) and the biennial *Fiberart International* exhibition organized by the Fiberarts Guild of Pittsburgh, the interaction between these organizations and the local art community no doubt stimulating the development of new and interesting work. The San Francisco Bay Area has Fiberscene (www.fiberscene.com), its goals being education, promotion, exhibition and sales. In many cities, towns and rural districts, textile art seems able to successfully draw on its synergies with textile craft, textile design and local textile education. This synergy it can exploit to play a part in the tourism, entertainment and culture industries. In Britain the Bury St Edmunds Art Gallery has twice staged a major survey exhibition of British textile art (www.burysted-artgall.org) while the Crafts Council has stoically supported textile art for decades (www.craftscouncil.org.uk). There are now many websites relating to textile art activity including lists of exhibiting opportunities and professional associations. Increasingly textile journals such as *Fiberarts Magazine* are available on the web (www.fiberartsmagazine.com) adding to the popular literature that textile art stimulates such as the *Art Textiles of the World* series published by Telos Art Publishing (www.telos.net).

That there are established publishing and exhibiting activities associated with textile art is a positive indicator of its growing success, but in all practices that revolve around the single creative, it is usually the artists who pay the greatest price. The practice of any art is an uncertain occupation, and there is no reason to assume that the practice of textile art should prove any easier. It is possible to reflect that textile art has some difficulties with resolving the complex philosophical inheritance that often excludes it from a higher status. We can also see that many of its strengths rely on being able to access a middle and low culture in a way that fine art would be embarrassed about. However, it is also possible to reflect that culture in general is in a state of flux, that the philosophical debates are changing, and that textiles has some aces to play. Textile art perhaps needs some passionate advocacy, some exceptional visibility to bring it centre-stage. This might be a star, it may be a group, it might be an event: whatever it is, it will need to be newsworthy because that is the nature of contemporary high culture.

Part III
The Social and Industrial Context

−8−

Global Textile Traditions

The world is rich in textile traditions – in its entirety, the subject merits an encyclopedia and a sophisticated reading. The intention here is to give the reader a tentative overview and introduce some of the many complexities of the subject. The main emphasis provided here is on Asian textiles including those of Indonesia, Japan, China and India; there are also some references to African, European, Australian and American traditions. There is no substitute for seeing textiles and, particularly in respect of this chapter, the reader would be well advised to seek out examples of the work mentioned. Throughout the world there are many collections documenting textile traditions, some broad-based and others more focused on specific cultures or regions. Apart from specialist publications, a variety of textiles can now be viewed on the web (www.artlex.com/ArtLex/t/textile.html) along with scholarly research (Tanaka, 1995), thus increasing access to a quite remarkable diversity of styles, technique, history and forms. There are book publishers' sites such as the Indian www.vedamsbooks.com/textile.htm and useful web 'portals', such as Gwendolyn A. Magee's www.quiltethnic.com, which provides links to sites covering African, African-American, Asian, Haitian, South American and Native American textiles.

It is almost a contradiction in terms to speak of national textile traditions, given the complex origin of many of the world's textile styles. Textile traditions are never static nor geographically fixed, and they have constantly changed in response to interactions between different cultures. This is one of the great strengths of textiles and a major part of the way it has contributed to the world's cultural heritage. However, many national textile traditions arose from indigenous textile crafts, and these typically reflected local cultural traditions and had social meaning and worth. All people have a sense of their own culture and manifest it in their arts. For the majority of the world's cultures, textiles have provided a perfect vehicle for establishing, expressing and maintaining cultural identity. Within textiles various patterns and fabrics reveal expressions of spirituality, mythology, symbolism, wealth and tradition. These expressions are particular to each country and each people, and distinguish one region of the world from another. Textiles also mirror periods of national history, reflecting the way in which people see themselves, their culture and their lifestyles at a particular time.

Many nations are renowned for specific textile traits. India is a country of cotton and chintz, its mysticism enhanced with lavish and exotic textile crafts. China is a country of silk and intricate patterning, renowned for early technical genius. Indonesia's myriad textile techniques and styles maintain significant magical power and a sense of richness. Africa's textiles retain a strong heritage of storytelling and symbolism. Modern America has a relatively recent history of textiles but is identified throughout the world with styles associated with the pioneer and the settler. It is here for example that the domestic quilt has evolved from a functional textile craft into highly decorative textile art form.

Regional Exchanges

Historically, the textile trade has known no boundaries and fabric was one of the basic commodities of the earliest trade routes. Consequently there was a constant exchange of textile processes and patterning. Sometimes individual nations or regions have so dominated world textiles that the resulting cultural and stylistic influence has been profound. For example, from the sixteenth century to the nineteenth century India and China were responsible for making the bulk of the world's finest textiles. During this period Indian and Chinese textiles managed to cross the world and be distributed quicker than ever before. Many contemporary Western designs still have their roots in the fascination of earlier generations for the diverse and lavish decorations of the East. Along with such items as spices and ceramics, fabric was one of the main exchanges between the East and the West. The enormous range of Chinese and Indian patterns were to greatly inspire French, Italian and English textiles.

Various regions within Asian countries maintained their own indigenous textile traditions until the sixteenth century. At this time the introduction of new techniques and designs, via trade, encouraged an evolutionary mixture of the traditional and the new. This in turn led to numerous innovations in patterns and textile technologies which spread and developed. As a result of these advances, a system was established involving the exchange and distribution of textiles, and along with this there was also an exchange of cultural information. These events were to significantly shape textile cultures of the future. Chinese and Indian textiles were very distinct from one another in terms of pattern and process during this period, although previously Chinese textiles had been influenced by aspects of Indian and Persian design. Japanese textiles had always been influenced by Chinese textiles; however, through dealings with Southeast Asian countries, Japanese textiles also started to show traits of Indian textiles. Before Japan established its connections with South-east Asia, it had borrowed Chinese textile patterns, such as plum blossoms, circles of peonies and the linking swastika pattern, as well as other geometric formulations. The Japanese also adopted brocade and damask weaving

Figure 16. Ching Dynasty embroidery.

techniques, again from the Chinese. The diversity, richness and trading history of Asian textiles are well documented (Gillow, 1992; Gillow and Barnard, 1993; Harvey, 1996; Guy, 1998) and many fine examples of textile craft have been preserved to grace collections around the world.

Religion and religious groups have played a significant part in defining both the imagery of and the difference between textile traditions. Despite the fact that Asian textiles have been distributed across the world, have a history of influencing each other and share common traits, their individual characteristics have been well preserved. The perfect case in point would be Indonesia, in whose textiles the variety found corresponds with the variety of its people, who represent the religions of Islam, Hinduism, Buddhism and Christianity. Consisting of 13,667 islands and a staggering 300 cultural groups, speaking an astounding 200 languages, it is no surprise to learn that the textiles of this nation should be as diverse as its inhabitants. Indonesian textiles are representative of the great technical and stylistic variety found in South-east Asia and include techniques such as batik and ikat; there are also many types of pattern. As in Indonesia, the textile history of India has come into contact with and been enhanced by traces of many religions, all adding to its Hindu origins. Islam, Jainism and Buddhism have all been incorporated into the language of Indian textile-design. There is also the more recent Western inspiration. Influenced by the variety of its religions, India has a rich heritage of textile crafts such as weaving, printing and the embroidering of fabric, with styles as varied as its topography and the cultural diversity of its population. Each district or village in India makes a distinct local interpretation of its textile traditions.

Although the adoption of textiles from other nations was strongly evident on the Asian continent, it was not exclusive to just that part of the world. African societies combined imported materials with their own traditional textiles – for example, the original 'ashanti' cloth was woven in blue and white symbolizing innocence and joy (www.du.edu/duma/africloth/strip.ashanti.html) – but as trade increased, weavers were able to purchase colourful silk cloth from Southern Europe and unravel it and use the silk thread for weaving. Cloth was transported between the cities of West and North Africa via the trans-Saharan trade caravan routes which passed through Afghanistan, Persia (now Iran) and Turkey. Foreign textiles also found their way to East African ports on ships working the monsoon trade routes between East Asia, India and the Gulf of Arabia. It is the traders themselves that are believed to have been responsible for the promotion and distribution of weaving skills; the traders were usually Muslims and demanded only the best Islamic dress, so stimulating the production of appropriate textiles and their embellishment wherever they travelled.

Patronage

Throughout history, the labour and materials involved in producing lavish textiles has made them a perfect medium through which to express great wealth and status. Also, in their observation of religion the rich have demonstrated devotion in the form of commissioning elaborate, ornamented textiles. In Asia, traditional rituals often called for the most exquisite creations, and it was not unusual to find established guilds of embroiderers, weavers, dyers and painters settling around places of worship. Relatively poor villages often still possess beautiful painted textiles and magnificent ritual cloths to this day. The worth and importance of exquisite hand-crafted textiles within a society are measured by the value placed upon them by the community: they are treated with great respect and are handed down generation to generation. They form a significant part of the culture, they are described in the literature of the land and their patterns have found their way into books and onto ceramics. Due to the phenomenal fee the creation of these exquisite textiles commanded, normally the only way they could be afforded was by means of royal or aristocratic patronage, much as the aristocratic classes supported the arts during the 'Renaissance' in Italy. Textile patronage has existed throughout history and taken place all over the world, reflecting the key values that textile crafts have been able to embody, quality, preciousness and effort. This has enabled outstandingly talented textile craftspeople to practice their trade and produce splendid pieces of fabric.

In China, industry was influenced and regulated by individual aristocrats and the royal court. It was this moneyed class that cultivated Chinese textile crafts until the end of the nineteenth century. In India, ruling families became patrons to the brocade manufacturers of the Varansi region during the post-Mughal period (*c*.1700–1850). Royal patronage was also evident in Africa where fine luxury textiles were developed under the instruction of the court of King Njoya of Bamum (1876–1933) and the Asante court of Ghana (*c*.1700–1874), responsible for the traditional and famous 'kente' cloth. Although the 'kente' cloth is a mass-produced printed cloth today and considered to be an international symbol for Africa, it was actually developed as a richly coloured, textured and hand-woven silk fabric only to be worn once by Asante royalty. The wearing of this elaborate cloth – which displayed wealth, status and supremacy – reinforced the social hierarchy which existed in much of West Africa. Religion has often been a patron of textiles as well. In the Indian town of Kalahasti, under the patronage of local temples, the 'kalamkari' cloth was made, incorporating a narrative element where text from Hindu scriptures was interpreted and decoration was applied in the form of various gods and goddesses. The same cloth was also produced in Masulipatnam but the influence of Muslim rule led to a preference for Persian designs. Later under British rule new uses were found for 'kalamkari' cloth and there was a greater emphasis on the use of floral designs. The wax-resist dye method of producing this 'kalamkari' cloth is a process comparable to batik – the word 'kalamkari' literally means 'pen worked'. Still produced today, it is one of the most decorative and highly crafted forms of Indian textiles.

Ritual, Symbolism and Stories

In cultures throughout the world, textiles and their production have had strong and direct associations with magic, symbolism and storytelling, especially in the case of Asian and African and Native American textiles. Many of these ritual and magical functions that cloth once possessed have vanished, surviving only in countries such as Indonesia. In Western Indonesia, Sumatran women weave circular warps which are under no circumstance cut, since this symbolically ensures the continual cycle of life. In this community it is widely believed that simply hanging a textile in a specific location indicates a special place, or can actually make that place sacred. Also in Indonesia the threading of a loom takes place on an auspicious day and where a woven cloth possesses the power to protect its creator. This inextricable link between makers and the material they create is echoed in Navajo society where weavers habitually incorporated a flaw into the border of a rug. This 'spirit line' permitted the weaver's soul to flow out of the rug on completion.

The protective attributes of Indonesian textiles were also common to Japanese, Thai and Indian textiles. During the pre-Edo period in Japan, when the Samurai classes ruled the country, it was customary for Samurai to keep with them an image of Buddha embroidered on a piece of cloth. A similar practice took place in Thailand. Whenever a young man left his village in order to either seek work or perhaps serve his country, he would depart with a piece of silk cloth woven by his mother. This was intended to protect him from destructive spirits (Conway, 1992). In India, guardian power was assured by means of hanging an embroidered frieze above the doorway. The status of craft objects in many cultures has been closely linked to purposes of social distinction and symbolism, reflecting power structures in this or 'other' worlds. To the modern person, particularly when confronted by historical textiles, the strength of these associations are often lost. Textiles have often played fundamental roles in the psychic and political dimensions of communities. This is frequently a subject of academic study, such as in the recent 2001 symposium 'Textiles and the Negotiation of Power' organized by the Society for American Archaeology (www.saa.org/Membership/symposiums.htm).

Whereas Asian textile traditions have strong religious and ritual associations, many traditional African textiles have symbols and patterns. These are widely recognized and used to communicate stories and emotions as well as philosophical messages. For example, abstract cross symbols on genuine 'kente' cloth refer to a proverb that is translated as 'Every man carries his own mark', which means that we all have individual personalities. The Yoruba community of West Africa believed that the power within their woven beadwork connected earthly and spiritual worlds. The principle was that the colour and pattern contained in the beadwork could empower and influence the destiny of the individual (Jacobs, 2000: 46–9). Colour was an indicator of character and personality; meanwhile shapes, particularly geometric, had the ability to energize a surface.

Weave

Weave has evolved over thousands of years and numerous communities throughout the world have practised weaving. Plain weave evolved into simple bands of pattern and then became highly complex damask and brocade structures. It is very difficult to pinpoint the exact history and evolution of weaving, with it having been practised in countless regions scattered all over the world; but the view is widely held that weaving grew out of rope-, net-, basket- and mat-making. Before recorded history, through barter and the communications that developed with trade, knowledge of weaving must have been one of the earliest incidences of 'technology transfer'.

Almost all variations in patterned textiles are generally found to have existed originally, in some form, in China. The intricate and complex nature of Chinese woven textiles is a result of the narrative imagery chosen. Through weaving, fabric is turned into a canvas, covered in pattern and design. Examples of general motifs found all over the world include, flowers, stripes, scrolling vines, spirals, animals, birds, checks and swastika patterns. Images exclusive to China were perhaps rather more mythical, including the dragon, phoenix and other imaginary animals, as well as clouds and the inclusion of Chinese characters which were believed to emit magical powers. Japanese woven textiles were mainly influenced by Chinese textiles, but also by Indian and Southeast Asian textile traditions. Although Japan was enthused by and borrowed from Chinese advanced techniques in weaving, this also motivated the Japanese textile cultures to establish their own textile identity, moving from uncertainty to replication to eventually their own creativity. The manifestation of a Japanese weaving culture was founded in Nishijin which remains a centre of Japanese textiles (www.jgc.co.jp/waza/b2_nishijin/index.htm).

The traditional woven fabrics of China, India, Japan and South-east Asia certainly stand out as something special, first because of the luxury of silk fibre (a secret the Chinese guarded for so long), which was desired by the rich and noble classes everywhere, and secondly because of the complexities of the weaving methods they employed. Technically, weaving traditions in much of the rest of the world are somewhat overshadowed by those of the Far East; however, they are by no means less important. The main exception to this rule must be the fabulous and ancient weaving cultures of South America. Stretching back some 10,000 years, weaving grew to be the main art form of South American culture, a status that it and textiles in general have held nowhere else. We are fortunate that the climatic conditions of the Andean region, coupled with the use of woven articles in burial rituals (particularly mummification), has preserved many examples. Comprising some of the most startling and beautiful fabrics in the world, ponchos, tapestries, hats and tunics have been found which represent quite idiosyncratic civilizations, each having a distinctive style. The work of the Chancay, Paracas, Inca, Chimu, Nazca and many more reveal complex and highly artistic cultures, their expertise in weave amply supported by their skills in pottery and goldwork. There are now many collections of this pre-Columbian art in the United States, including woven items, for example those found at the Dumbarton Oaks Research Library and Collection (www.doaks.org). While many other craft practices in the Andean regions have ceased to exist, the weaving tradition has survived to this day.

We need to draw distinctions and judge the merits of weaving around the world relative to the purpose for which it was intended in various communities. In some parts of the world weaving was often much more practical in nature: for example, there is a history of nomadic communities producing woven blankets, rugs, tents and saddlebags. In the fifth century BC, the ancient nomadic tribes of the Central-Asian steppe, known to the Greek historian Herodotus as the Scythians, had a complex and artistic culture. They have left us the earliest known examples of felted textiles (2,500 years old), which were found in the Pazyryk tombs in Southern Siberia. Although nomadic communities are disappearing, their weaving traditions often remain and beautiful works, for example kilim and hambel rugs, continue to be produced to this day. The woven artefacts of modern nomads (such as the Berbers of Morocco) are now highly collectible. Examples of the woven goods of the tribes and nomads of the Middle East and Central Asia can be seen at www.marlamallett.com. Finally, it should be noted that as much as weaving has been for the rich and the powerful, it has also provided staple cloth for the poorest and the ordinary people. These humbler cloths are of no less importance in the history of our species but perhaps elude our attention by virtue of their simplicity.

Embroidery

It is difficult to specify the exact origin of the hundreds of stitch techniques termed as embroidery. Despite the conflicting opinions from one continent to another as to its origin, one of the earliest recorded thread embroideries was Chinese and dated 3500 BC. Embroidery has a history of being executed in many different ways to serve many different purposes. Ecclesiastical embroidery is common to many religious groups and royal courts. These devotional or commemorative textiles were meticulously stitched with precious metals detailing complex, illustrative designs and used to celebrate the glory of God or gods and to convey the superiority of the nobility. Although society generally associates the needle and thread with women, in the West it was originally men who were measured as masters of this craft and this was only after the completion of an eight-year apprenticeship. We often relate embroidery to a sophisticated culture; however, in contrast, embroidery also adorned plain peasant dwellings in the form of simply stitched samplers.

In each part of the world original, unusual and sometimes quirky embroidery techniques were concocted, and depicted a unique combination of style and stitch. An ornately detailed cutwork, 'reticella', was formulated in Italy; 'dresden work' was finely executed in Germany; England is credited with 'broderie anglaise'; the Danes originated 'hedebo' and the Netherlands created 'hardanger'. Both Chinese and Indian textiles incorporated a great deal of embroidery, and in many ways embroidery is as rich as the woven traditions in that there is a massive assortment of techniques to refer to. Many regions in India still employ the authentic traditional embroidery practice specific to their district: in Delhi it is 'zardosi', in Punjab we would find 'phulkari' and in Bengal is 'kantha'.

Oriental influences were very apparent throughout the world because of trade with the Far East, and traditional Chinese motifs such as exotic flowers and birds began appearing in Western Europe. Such designs were carried out in woollen-thread crewel work on cotton or linen rather than in silk on silk. In China silk fabric was treated as a canvas for embroidering narrative scenes as much as it was for painting and printing. The combination and exchange of textile cultures and traditions has lead to lots of hybrid and evolved solutions for embroidery. It is evident that embroidery has not necessarily been worked purely in thread; many cultures have used beads, precious metals, precious stones and jewels, and the Indians of North and South America continue to use whatever materials of natural extraction they can find from which to create beautiful embroideries.

Embroidery does not always have to be fabulous to charm; the work of many folk traditions commonly finds its way into the vernacular of contemporary design. The role of embroidery as a means of embellishment or adding beauty to a base fabric has in many ways been far more available to ordinary people than many other textile techniques. From Central and Eastern Europe to Africa and the Far East, embroidery styles have found their way into national costumes. In the Americas a tradition akin to modern 'multi-media textiles' has existed since time immemorial, for example the complex bead- or feather-work of the North American Indians (for a comprehensive overview of Native American crafts see www.native tech.org). These styles and resultant garments, while often lacking expensive materials, became valuable through the love, attention or labour paid to them, and thus they commonly became ideal to mark rites of passage, from birth to death.

Print and Dye

Some historians have traced the origins of block-printing and so textile printing in general to India: 'The export of printed fabric to China can be dated to the fourth century BC, where they were much used and admired, and later, imitated'

(Robinson, 1969). The craft of Indian block-printing varied from region to region in terms of designs which were generally based on scrolling foliage, geometric patterns and perhaps the occasional bird or animal. The workmanship of the intricately block-printed shrine fabric 'Mata-Ni-Pachedi' can be measured against 'kalamkari' and is by no means inferior. English chintz, Japanese 'Sarasa' and Indonesian batik reveal the inspiration and influence that Indian block-printed and 'kalamkari' fabrics must have had on textile craftsmen from South-east Asia to Japan and Europe, most probably as a consequence of trade. It is still common in India today for textile craftspeople to use wooden printing blocks to stamp designs onto fabric.

In the same way as all other traditional forms of cloth production, printing is prone to the influence of social and technological change. The application of image and colour on fabric by means of a variety of processes is an ancient art. Some of the earliest forms of textile printing take the form of stencil work cultivated in Japan and block printing, rooted in India. Printed and dyed textiles had a similar impact to that of their woven and embroidered counterparts. Their migration to various parts of the world resulted in a global transformation of the way in which colour and image on fabric were perceived. The artistic impact of textile trade between nations cannot be underestimated: for instance, the introduction of Indian chintz to England and France laid the foundations of modern textile design in the West.

Indian chintz incorporated imagery similar to that found in Indian block-printing: 'tree of life' patterns, animals, birds and geometries. As Japan exhausted imports of flower patterns from China, it introduced tiny Indian flower patterns and combined these with oriental motifs such as *karakusa* (scrolling vines), crests and folding fans. Chinese patterning also found its way to Indonesia, in the shape of embroidery and porcelain which provided a source for design ideas in the form of the Chinese lion and the cloud design (Gillow, 1992), the phoenix bird and the Chinese swastika emblem. Chinese patterning also drifted onto English textiles. In the eighteenth century the 'chinoiserie' pattern developed, which was a configuration of Chinese figures, birds, animals, pagodas and odd-shaped stones. As discussed earlier, Indonesia was a melting pot of religions and cultures, and as such it had a vocabulary of printed textile patterns descended from the Buddhist, Hindu, Chinese and Islamic communities. Due to the complex nature of textiles in general in this part of the world, there are countless references made to all manner of flora, fauna and various meticulous geometries.

The tie-dye, batik and paste-resist methods of textile design all involve manipulating, binding or treating fabric in order to avoid the saturation of dye. Many places around the world have devised their own ways of dyeing and preventing dyeing, including the techniques of using binding, wax-resist, paste-resist, alum and iron-salt. Tie-dyeing originated in China during the T'ang Dynasty

(AD 618–906) and traders whose merchandise included tie-dye cloths ensured its spread from the Far East to India and the rest of Asia. Gujarat is famed for its brilliantly coloured ikat and bandhani textiles. Though both fabrics utilize the tie-dye technique, there remains a substantial difference between the finished products. Ikat involves tie-dying silk yarn for weaving purposes and has a history of being demanded by the wealthy for ceremonial rituals, whereas bandhani is the tie-dying of a vast range of fabrics and is a relatively inexpensive method of production available to the masses. Tie-dye was also present in Indonesia and Peru, and it still prospers in West African countries such as Ghana, Nigeria and Cameroon. The spread of ikat in Asia led to its variation as it was adapted by other nations; Thai and Indonesian ikats for instance were far more colourful than Japanese ikat which was more abstract and incorporated a smaller scale of pattern.

Contemporary Uses of Traditional Textiles

When considering contemporary textile design styles, in many cases it is possible to trace their pictorial and geometric references to specific locations and perhaps times in the world. Given the evolution of textile traditions and the fact we have a rich heritage of textile exchange, it seems natural that the copying and swapping should continue to this day. There are ample examples of how the growth of modern industry simply accelerated this habit. For example, during the height of the Victorian British printed textile industry, designs were often conceived in response to textiles from overseas. These were interpreted with an English twist and hit their highest point when William Morris created an English version of the originally Indian chintz. Today, the fashion designer is as responsible as the textile designer for sustaining and reviving ailing traditional textile crafts the world over. Global textile heritage has become part of an international design vocabulary that leading couturiers such as Yves Saint-Laurent dip into occasionally in search of inspiration and direction. In the past, he has been influenced by, and based collections on, African, Moroccan and Indian themes, utilizing appropriate fabrics that honour the textile traditions of their cultures. It's probably safe to say that the elevation of these ethnic-inspired fabrics to catwalk status has stimulated renewed interest in the traditional textile crafts of the countries mentioned.

Contemporary designers utilizing the traditional textile skills of their countries are dotted throughout the world. An example of textile craft-revival is that provided by Kamaladevi Chattopadhyay, who set up the Crafts Council of India in 1965. In her endeavours to decorate her saris, she sought the assistance of textile craftspeople and started a trend in rediscovering the value of craft. Similarly, Ritu Kumar revived the tired 'zardozi' embroidery of Delhi, and design duo Mona-Pali based in Calcutta explored and applied the motifs of 'kantha' work on their saris. India's traditional textile craft continues to flourish through the patronage of fashion designers such

Figure 17. Indian Bandhani tie-dyed silk.

as these. Of the traditional hand-crafted textiles, Ritu Kumar says they do not '. . . exist in the rarefied atmosphere of a museum workshop in an artist's atelier . . . they survive in the vast weaving, printing, embroidery and dyeing belts of the country' (Kumar, 1999). There have been episodes in India's past where the survival of textile craft was at the mercy of social changes. For example, in the early twentieth century Indian nobility rejected traditional Indian dress in favour of Western attire, in so doing they also removed their royal patronage from textile crafts. Some textile craftspeople were also very secretive about their techniques, being careful not to reveal or share them. This had a detrimental effect on particular traditions which began disappearing with the passing of those individuals.

Africa has witnessed an increased interest in its hand-made fabrics, prolonging the survival of traditional textile crafts as art and as a feeder to fashion. Nigerian textile artists Nike Davis and Kekekomo Oladepo investigate and express modern themes via traditional textile methodologies such as indigo-dyed 'adire' cloth. Jose Rodriguez and Irene Blackwell are another two contemporary artists guided by spirituality and symbolism in their practice of hand-beading for the modern-day Yoruba society. In Thailand, Nagara is the only fashion designer who actually participates in the production of the traditional hand-woven ikat fabrics he requires for his garments (*Fiberarts*, 2000: 32–5). Hiroshi Jashiki from Japan is a designer for Calvin Klein: he assisted in the preservation and continuance of various Japanese weaving traditions through his efforts to update the practice for modern-day use. Japan's contemporary textiles are admired globally. However, Jashiki does not believe this to be so of the majority of current traditional textiles made for tourists in Okinawa. He is a firm believer of contemporizing traditional textile crafts to create a valuable product; he says, 'Don't just stick your foot in tradition and make ugly things . . . It's OK to preserve the skill, but not if it's preserved only for the tourists' (Oxygen Media, 2001). Jashiki identifies Toshiko Taira as a good example of both a traditional and a modern designer who understands and respects fabric.

Recent Textile Traditions

Some nations are seen in the eyes of the world, or sometimes in their own eyes, as 'new' or 'young'. Countries such as the United States and Australia fit this category. Of course they already had indigenous cultures, as ancient as any other, but these cultures have largely been overwhelmed by immigration and colonization. A particular feature of these nations is that they have been marked by successive waves of immigration, each bringing with it different cultural heritages. The result is a rootless, nascent national identity, waiting on history to establish centuries-old 'traditions'. Even in countries that see themselves as 'old', such as Great Britain, recent generations of immigrants start to establish a mythology of their origins: cultural snapshots based on 'home' that increasingly evolve to be something in their own right. The resultant anomalies between a pending national identity, a collection of old ones, and a collection of new ones are compounded by the fact that many older traditions had different social bases to them. In terms of textile traditions, the difference is often between a history of domestic or community craft textiles and the modern world. Personal craft is now generally abandoned in favour of consumerism, and the nature of domesticity and community is itself different. In these circumstances it is very difficult to attribute textile traditions (as opposed to textile history) to any modern nation, let alone to 'new' nations, but there is no harm in trying.

As highlighted at the beginning of this chapter, the United States is one of the few countries to have a relatively recently defined national textile history, and it is one often associated outside the United States with the pioneer, settler or immigrant. Textile traditions are deeply embedded in the cultural and social structure of a nation: its history shapes the textile traditions it conveys to others, be they of a domestic, commercial or spiritual nature. Upheavals – colonization, slavery, immigration, forced migration, social integration – relocate and redefine communities, but peoples' origins and experiences remain visible in a nation's culture, art and textiles. As the United States mythologizes its past and seeks to assert its cultural identity, textiles will find a particular role to play. Defined by the comparatively recent influx of a number of communities from Europe, Africa, Central and Southern America, Eastern Europe and South-east Asia, the widely held perception outside America is one of a nation that is relentlessly commercial, best suited to the strong and the ambitious, whatever their origin. This, however, seems balanced by some democratic, proletarian and domestic vision, 'the land of the free', 'the land of opportunity', 'the land of apple pie'. Many of the visible traditions of textiles seem to align with this softer, idealized vision of the United States; they are therefore derivative of domestic arts such as the creating of quilts, aprons and samplers – items which become symbolic of family sentiments or become heirlooms establishing dignity and continuity. Over the last fifty years, American textile traditions seem in a way to have mirrored media representation of the United States as homely, clean-cut or crisp; this is slightly counterbalanced by glitz, urban sophistication and sportswear, and finally peppered with indigenous and minority-group traditions. Only the Native Americans are in a position to call on a craft iconography which is identifiably historic and geographically 'true'. For the rest, they must follow the global principle of the exchange and development of textile culture. It will be interesting to see how demographic changes and social evolution may alter a future American aesthetic and cultural disposition toward textiles.

In a world of email and travel, logic would suggest that exchanges of textile cultures and information might become exhausted over time, and that a single global textile culture might result. However, textile traditions are still evolving and recently an example of this has occurred in Australia. The Aborigine community in Ernabella, South Australia, adopted textile practice purely as a medium for their decorative arts. By means of modern textile processes, they apply onto fabric ritual design, symbols and signs specific to their community. The introduction of textile practice to this modern tribal community in 1971 led to the development of a unique and distinct form of batik. Since then, cultural exchanges have taken place between Aboriginal Australia and Indonesia and, unexpectedly, it is now the Indonesian artists that are keen to adopt the techniques and designs which the Aborigines have originated (www.antiquesandart.com.au/ArticleAborig.htm). It is interesting to observe this modern-day version of the historical model of the migration and exchange of textile cultures by tribal groups around the world. The fact that nations are still exchanging textile ideas and techniques is an indication that an age-old tradition is still going strong, that textile traditions continue to evolve and develop.

Ecology

Of all the political issues that relate to textiles, ecology stands out because it isn't just an issue but a set of very practical problems which textiles contributes to. Any understanding of the relationship between textiles and ecology must therefore alternate between political analysis and plain practicality. For textiles the link to ecology is that, through manufacture, it is one of the greatest industrial perpetrators of pollution; through fashion and style it participates in the most wasteful and profligate aspects of consumerism; through design and science it often fails to take responsibility and be a guardian of the planet. If textiles could easily retreat from these misdemeanours, it surely would have done so by now; the truth is that, as with all major problems, the issues are complex and the way forward not clear. Manufacture will, implicitly, always use the world's resources; textiles will always exact a price for companies, workers, people and the planet. The moral challenge will never disappear or be solved. It is not that kind of problem: it is not a war to be won but a situation to be managed.

Pollution, Politics and Ecology

The concept of pollution starts with our perception that there is a balance in nature. When catastrophic events occur, even natural ones like volcanic eruption, pollution can be a consequence and we consider that nature's balance has been disrupted. Pollution caused by people is nothing new: wherever there have been large centres of population, waste of all kinds has been a problem. For example, by the end of the first century BC, ancient Rome had approximately one million inhabitants, with all the waste-disposal problems that would entail. In more recent times industry's need for a workforce has caused ecological problems. In this respect the textile industry has been no different from any other:

> New Bedford's population increased dramatically, from about 27,000 in 1880, when there were two mills, to about 121,000 in 1920 when there were 31 mills . . . increase in the population produced a dramatic increase in the amount of sewage . . . the local newspaper, *Morning Mercury*, reported . . .'water thick with slime and shores covered with filth from the sewers'. (EPA, 2001)

As well as the disposal of waste, large organized societies have always developed such destructive and polluting activities as mining and the processing of mineral ores. Even the basic cultivation of crops is an intervention in the natural landscape. The patterns of industry, consumerism and society we associate with modern pollution have historical precursors thousands of years old.

By the time of the Industrial Revolution the highly visible destruction of the environment and the social consequences of industrialization became the twin evils of industrial progress. Well before the beginning of the twentieth century there was strident opposition to the excesses of industry, its partner capitalism and the rise of the 'modern' city; there were, for example, groups and individuals such as William Morris who blended his aesthetics with politics

> The proper city to compare London with is Paris, which is now entirely modern, and like London is not a mere makeshift accessory to a set of workshops, an encampment of capitalists and their machines, as are Manchester, Glasgow, and Birmingham . . . It is difficult to express in words the feeling with which this 'cockney nightmare' burdens me . . . There are certainly smells which are more depressing and deadly to pleasure than those which are frankly the nastiest: the refuse of gasworks, the brickfields in the calm summer evening, the faint, sweet smell of a suspicious drain . . . the quality of London ugliness is just of this heart-sickening kind.
>
> (Morris, 1888)

The term ecology was originally a purely scientific term applied to a branch of biology. It was coined by Ernst Haeckel in 1873 and it rapidly became a popular and useful term for the scientific community, particularly botanists and zoologists (Bullock and Stallybrass, 1977). In the second half of the twentieth century the subject of ecology entered the public consciousness. The environment started to become a popular concept in the public imagination, triggered by the industrialization of farming, the political growth of the media, and an increasing sense of the planet (stimulated by travel, war and space exploration). The term ecology developed a political dimension. Ecology became as much about the human impact on the environment as about environments themselves. Various events and publications provided very clear indications of the consequences of pollution on the environment – for example, Rachel Carson's book *Silent Spring* (1962) dealt with the damage caused by pesticides, or the discovery of DDT in the bodies of Antarctic penguins a thousand miles from any possible source. As Stewart L. Udall, a former US Secretary of the Interior wrote:

> we grossly underestimated the power of technological man to alter and destroy the natural balances that support life . . . we also consistently misjudged the damage being done by the ever-widening wave of pollution and contamination. (Udall, 1970)

The broadened concept of ecology and its political aspects drew the subject of ecology into the old rhetorical and political arguments about industry, commerce and capitalism. While these older debates continue, ecology has also become identified with a new style of single-issue politics and the consequent political coalitions or 'rainbow' politics. It also became identified with new visions of social order and the way our societies and civilization should progress, such as that proposed by Schumacher in 1973 (Schumacher, 1999).

These many expressions of interest seem only to have made the politics and morality surrounding ecology fairly impenetrable. Some people are unmoved and find ecology boring. Others are emotionally drained to a point of utter despair, still others to anger and violent action. Yet more consider it not to be an issue at all. Some consider it part of another issue altogether, Marxism versus Capitalism, race versus race, poor versus rich, and throw it into the general arena of their arguments. Many consider ecological issues have embarrassing connotations of past subcultures, for example hippy sentimentality. Many consider the affiliations of green activists place ecology beyond the pale and find their own self-identity at odds with the rainbow politics of pressure groups and minorities. Some companies say they care and some patently don't. Some companies make very serious attempts at solving such issues as pollution, but some don't always do it for the noblest of reasons. Thus it has to be conceded that an interpretation of the role of textiles in ecology is on uncertain ground and played out against a backdrop of sometimes fierce politics, accusation and counter-accusation, of dissimulation, genuine concern, research, diplomacy and hard-nosed business.

The Role of Organizations and Agencies

Along with political parties and state environmental agencies, there are many organizations with an interest in ecology, including those that deal with sustainable development, third world development, ethical investment and ethical business. For example in 1975 the Federal Republic of Germany established The Deutsche Gesellschaft für Technische Zusammenarbeit (GTZ), a private-sector organization with a development policy mandate to 'make sustainable improvements to the living conditions of people in partner countries, and to conserve the natural resource base on which life depends' (www.gtz.de). Ecology is high on GTZ's agenda and the organization plays a substantial role in industrial development (including textiles) and technology transfer around the world. It has more than 10,000 employees in 122 countries drawn from Africa, Asia, Latin America and Eastern Europe. GTZ provides extensive information on its website about such matters as textile processes and pollution, developing textile industries in poorer countries, and consumer views of ecologically 'sound' textiles.

There are organizations which seek to lobby or campaign against what they see as adverse developments in the global political order, for example the Common Front on the World Trade Organization (CF-WTO). Its view of the World Trade Organization is that it will 'entrench the very patterns of economic development that have given rise to the ecological crises we confront' (www.sierraclub.ca/national/trade-env/env-guide-wto.html). Groups such as CF-WTO often have fairly clear political affiliations; many would be described as left-wing. Other types of group fall into the consumer protection and consumer rights categories. The rise of the internet has greatly enhanced the ability of industry watchdogs and ecology activists to spread their message. In the medium of the WWW their arguments and information often look as convincing as that of any company or state-run organization. Typical sites include those which draw together related organizations and begin to provide a sense of community, provide a forum, or create an information network for activists and enthusiasts, for example www.sustainable world.com or www.schumachersociety.org. Other sites such as that provided by Jon Rappoport engage in direct political attack on industrial giants – see http://home.earthlink.net/~alto/boycott.html. The development of public access to information, once very difficult to obtain, has been quite remarkable: for example, the Right to Know Network (RTK) in the United States provides access to a range of documents about housing, the environment and sustainable development. Users can look up information from their site (www.rtk.net) about safety at factories near where they live. Here, for example, is an extract from a policy document concerning the escape of chemical substances from a textile factory:

> The worst case scenario submitted for Program 2 and 3 toxic substances as a class involves a catastrophic release from chlorine storage and handling, in this scenario, 10,800 lb. of chlorine is released. The toxic liquid is assumed to form a 1cm deep pool from which evaporation takes place. The entire pool is estimated to evaporate over 10 minutes. At class F atmospheric stability and 1.5 m/s windspeed, the maximum distance of 11 miles is obtained.
>
> (Textile Chemical Company Inc., 1999)

A slightly different take is provided by the company *ility* who offer an up-to-date summary of major incidents reported in the oil, gas, energy and chemical industries at their site www.saunalahti.fi/ility

> Givet, north-east France. Workers protesting the closure of the Cellatex textile factory released a small quantity of sulphuric acid into the town's gutters. Fire-fighters had to work to stop the acid from leaking into the Meuse River, which flows into neighbouring Belgium. A police spokeswoman said authorities had not determined exactly how much acid had flowed from the open tank but that it was less than the 3,600 litres that some

workers claimed. The factory contains toxic materials including more than 40,000 litres of sulphuric acid and 54 tonnes of carbon disulphide.

(ility, 2000)

These two items provide an interesting window onto the chemical nature of much textile processing and its potential hazards. Kate Fletcher of the Britain-based Textile Environmental Network writes:

> Textile makers apply more than 700,000 tons of dyestuffs to 40 million tons of fabric each year. Besides consuming large amounts of chemicals, water, and energy, dyeing produces effluent. Though less toxic today, the inherently dirty nature of applying colour to fabric contributes to aesthetic pollution and puts dyers and finishers under increasing environmental scrutiny. (Fletcher, 2000)

Chemical hazards found in the textile industry can also cause problems for the work force: for example, the American government estimates that more than 80,000 workers drawn from the textile, paper and leather industries were exposed to benzidine dyes, a potential cause of bladder cancer. This association between factory pollution and the working environment provides a good example of the way in which many issues can politically converge. In an article for the International Labour Organization (ILO), Jean-Paul Sajhau discusses business ethics in the textile, clothing and footwear industries, in particular how non-governmental agencies can influence the ethical behaviour of companies. As he points out, it is not entirely a matter of preaching:

> the Interfaith Centre on Corporate Responsibility (ICCR) groups together throughout the United states almost 300 religious institutional investors which together hold a portfolio estimated at around 45 thousand million dollars and which are also consultants to major pension funds. This organization is therefore a significant pressure group . . . it takes a stand against militarism and violence and also tries to make public opinion aware of the role of enterprises in the deterioration of the environment. However, it is particularly concerned with the respect of basic human rights. (Sajhau, 1998)

Sajhau goes on to identify three types of association who bring pressure to bear on industry in slightly different ways: ecumenical associations who through their financial pressure can influence industry in developed countries, economic associations who seek to promote codes of conduct, and solidarity associations such as consumer-rights groups.

Not all environmental organizations deal with pollution from production: one important grouping deals with the final effects of textiles production, which is textile waste. Textile waste is classified as either pre-consumer or post-consumer depending on whether it is material discarded in manufacture or whether it is a product the consumer has finished with. The global volume of textile waste increases year on year and relates as much to emerging consumer economies as to established ones. A report from the 2000 Intertextile, a Chinese international trade fair for apparel, accessories and interiors, indicates that in some Chinese cities the purchase of goods for the home is rising by as much as 21 per cent per year, that there is an increased demand for 'stylish' goods and foreign products and that banks are financing consumer spending accordingly. Such growth in ordinary consumption as a result of both increasing wealth and fashion-led consumption directly contributes to the waste stream. Similar problems can arise in relation to pre-consumer waste. Textile industries can develop very rapidly; for example, in a few years the value of Bangladesh's textile exports has grown from a few million to more than four billion dollars and, of course, in such circumstances both anti-pollution and anti-waste issues arise.

Many organizations dealing with textile waste are actually straightforward businesses picking up on the opportunities presented. In the United States every year 750,000 tons of textile waste is recycled into raw materials to be used again. A 1988 study by the American Environmental Protection Agency (EPA) estimated that textiles accounted for 3.9 million tons of the solid waste stream. In Britain, textile waste is approximately 650,000 tonnes per year, of which about 25 per cent is recycled, and the majority of this annual turnover is from household waste. Two useful sources of information are the Council for Textile Recycling in the United States (www.textilerecycle.org) and Waste Watch in Britain (www.waste watch.org.uk). The waste-recovery and recycling sector is enormous, and for ecologists it plays a significant part in such issues as the use of landfill sites for refuse. Waste is also a significant concept when considering product life cycle and product longevity.

Government Policies and Organizations

Policies relating directly to the environment are generally initiated, developed and maintained by countries and textile manufacturers themselves. Most governments have different ways of intervening in industrial development, and so where the state ends and the private sector begins is sometimes ambiguous. Government activities include the funding of education and research, dealings with other agencies and countries and sustaining state environmental organizations. In many countries partially state-funded or state-initiated organizations play an active part in ecological issues and solutions, and such organizations are expected to generate revenues from their activities and collaborations, maintaining a practical edge to what they do.

Senses of regional identity, shared issues and trade zones often provide the *raison d'être* for ecological initiatives, as for example in the recent LOUHI project based at the University of Art and Design Helsinki, Finland. Funded by the European Union Structural Funds Community Initiative for small to medium-size enterprises, LOUHI offered nineteen small textile companies consultation services in design, design management and ecology in textile manufacturing. Projects such as this represent the growing trend in the strategic use of research-and-development funding in the higher education sector, using it to stimulate things such as economic regeneration or technology transfer. A similar, longer-term project, COST (Co-operation in Science and Technology) aims to develop an environmental index for textiles and to create a European network for textile research, bringing together industry and education. It involves partners from Finland, Denmark, Britain, Germany, France, Belgium and Spain and was initiated by the The Textile Research Centre CTF at the University College of Boras and the Tampere University of Technology.

The regional model of environmental research and development, such as the European one cited above, is mirrored by both a sector model based on product and a market model based on trade. A good example of all three is perhaps the relationship between India, Australia and wool. In Australia, CSIRO Wildlife and Ecology is a division of the Commonwealth Scientific and Industrial Research Organization, and it employs around 230 staff including 50 research scientists; part of its strategy is to 'draw on the expertise in other research organizations and other CSIRO divisions, building multi-disciplinary teams that enable us to address large-scale environmental issues'. CSIRO have an impressive research portfolio covering everything from the genetic improvement of wool to parasite control and insecticide use to the benefits of nutrition in wool production. Australia is the world's largest producer of wool and sheepskins, the second largest exporter of hides and the fourth largest exporter of raw cotton. Often mutual interest between developing industries and established industries can do much to benefit environmental issues, and research collaboration between Australia and India is one such example. Of various joint research projects managed by CSIRO, ACIAR (Australian Centre for International Agricultural Research) and India, Dr Brett Bateup, Chief of CSIRO Textile and Fibre Technology, said 'India is collaborating with us due to its developing industrial growth and use of Australian wool' while the Indian Minister for Textiles, Mr Rana, commented 'International cooperation involving textiles is becoming increasingly critical and mutually beneficial in this rapidly changing global textile market'. This kind of mutual economic development effectively paves the way for the application of quality environmental policies, so for example one project 'aims to reduce the environmental impacts of wool processing and improve economic outcomes in textile processing regions in India' (CSIRO, 2000).

In an article about the manufacture of eco-textiles (environmentally friendly textiles), Johannes Hummel considers this relationship between economic motivations and the ecological outcomes. He points out that although production is cheaper in poor countries, differences in national environmental protection laws have previously meant that ecologically sound manufacture could only really be guaranteed in an environment such as that of Western Europe. Developing his analysis, he goes on to indicate that economic stability in the supply chain can be just as effective a strategy as legislation, further highlighting the interdependence and benefits of collaboration between developed and developing nations:

> Secured sales outlets in cotton cultivation also greatly reduced environmental pollution. Only when the project has a secure buyer and thus a long-term perspective, can the project management invest in expansion (training farmers; creation of better framework conditions to motivate more farmers, etc.) . . . Considerable ecological improvements can be made if ecological aspects are included at an early stage in product development, or in the design. Moreover, large production runs make it easier to reduce environmental pollution. (Hummel, 1997)

It is within the power of individual organizations to create strategic alliances that are mutually beneficial:

> The company decided to no longer buy its organic cotton from several, changing producers on the market, but rather to work together with a single farmer and to give him a purchase guarantee. The organic cotton project involved was able to reduce its costs, increase the number of participating farmers and improve their training. (Ibid., 1997)

For the individual or company seeking advice or approval for their products and processes, the sheer multiplicity of agencies, their status and remit, can be quite confusing. Regional, national and international organizations abound, some industry-specific, most not, some with political affiliations, some not. On the one hand there are organizations such as the UK Environmental Technology Best Practice Programme (www.etbpp.gov.uk) that provides a wide variety of free publications relating to all industrial sectors (including textiles) and aims to generally improve business practice and environmental performance. This kind of agency deals largely with the dissemination of information. Then there are projects like the European Commission's eco-label, an extensive assessment scheme that looks at the environmental impact of a product at all stages of its life. In operation since 1993 it remains a voluntary exercise on the part of product manufacturers and its purpose is in the simplest sense no more than approval. The benefits of such approval are in the areas of consumer appeal or where there are legal constraints on products, for example import/export restrictions.

Government environment agencies can even be drawn into political whirlpools, particularly when their remit comes into conflict with that of other government agencies. In the United States the EPA has a simple slogan 'to protect human health and to safeguard the natural environment'; it has an extensive and lively website presence (www.epa.gov) and produces a comprehensive range of publications and information exclusive to the textiles industry, including pollution prevention opportunities, prevention incentives, waste management and so on. However, the story that follows is a typically ecological one where the cost of safeguarding the environment and political power can distort even the best intentions. In a fairly damning article, David Armstrong of the *Boston Globe* reports that the United States Government, which is supposed to protect the environment, is its own worst enemy: Federal agencies contaminated more than 60,000 sites throughout the United States with predicted clean-up costs of over $300 billion. Armstrong states that even the EPA itself was fined for violating toxic waste laws at its laboratories. His article goes on to recount the shameful tale of the reopening of the Avtex Fibers factory, which over a period of fifty years contaminated wells and ground water under the factory with carbon disulfide, phenol, sodium, lead, arsenic and cadmium. It was closed in 1988; however, the factory was the only producer of carbonized rayon used in NASA's space shuttle and in Air Force missiles. The National Security Council reopened it for another year and NASA and the military pushed for maximum production, considerably adding to the pollution problem. Virginia state officials said the EPA knew of the plan but stood by and did nothing. The final outcome is an acrimonious series of letters, statements and legal postures, rumbling into the following century (Armstrong, 1999).

Eco or Green Design

Against the enormous industrial and political background of ecology, it is often difficult for individual textile designers (or even a sizeable product-manufacturer) to comprehend how they can contribute to solving ecological problems, especially when arguments for and against particular 'environmentally sensitive' design solutions seem to muddy the waters. The pressures to develop a new kind of design philosophy (green or eco-design as it is now called) began, as much of the ecological movement did, in the 1960s. It is represented by seminal texts such as Victor Papanek's *Design for the Real World* first published in 1969 (Papanek, 1991) and his more recent *The Green Imperative: Ecology and Ethics in Design and Architecture* (1995). While the fortunes of green design have varied over the years and met with patchy success, the general consensus of much of the design world has been in favour.

Green design seems to have had particular successes in such areas as architecture where ecological solutions depend as much on new technology (like solar panels) as on old; green design can consequently look futuristic, avant-garde or cutting-edge. Although synthetic textiles account for some 45 per cent of the world's fibre demands, the fashionability of technological textiles does not seem to be about their ecological value. In textiles the sensitive issues are more traditionally about things like the origin and processing of raw materials and the choice of materials, for example 'ordinary' cotton. Cotton cultivation is a major source of pollution and environmental damage worldwide, consuming more pesticides than any other crop. The green-design community has therefore promoted interest in various alternatives such as 'organic' cotton and other traditional textile crops such as hemp. Typical websites include www.simplelife.com and its *Organic Cotton Directory*, The Society for Responsible Design at www.green.net.au/srd/ and Wendy Brawer's Modern World Design at www.greenmap.com.

Hemp is one of the most ancient, tough and versatile sources of fibre. As a pure fabric it is more resistant to rot than other natural fabrics, it is more prolific in its growth than cotton, and it does not deplete the soil or require crop rotation. All in all it sounds a very useful material; however, although once the world's largest agricultural crop and a mainstay of much historical fabric production, hemp has not generally been suitable to produce as modern high-quality fabric. Things may be changing – as Peter Styles says, 'The fabric already has friends high up in the fashion business', listing Calvin Klein and Armani among them. Most production takes place in China and Eastern Europe in limited quantities, but new technology may provide a solution for problems involved in the production and use of hemp:

> a new process devised in Germany involving the explosion of fibres with high pressure steam means that conventional machinery used for cotton can be used to produce cloth. Steam-exploded yarn also means that hemp can achieve the requirements of the textile industry in terms of fineness, homogeneity, flexibility and the distribution of fibre length. (Styles, 1999)

To some extent hemp itself and fabrics that include hemp fit the recent changes in taste for fabrics, with a focus on textural and surface qualities. Organic cotton on the other hand is indiscernible to the average consumer, and its future usage depends more on designers, manufacturers and environmental agencies. Nike provide an interesting case study into how corporate environmental policy can impact on the cotton issue. Nike's Sports Graphics Division produce 40 million cotton T-shirts a year. As part of their commitment to introduce organic cotton into their product range, they decided to blend three per cent organic cotton into their T-shirts, adding just two cents to the unit cost. To produce 100 per cent organic would have added 70 cents to the unit cost, and it would also have used up all the available standing supply of organic cotton! Nike hope to extend the practice throughout their cotton-based product range (www.sustainablecotton.org).

Waste textiles and the recycling of discarded fabrics, selvages and off-cuts is another area of attention for green design and an area for business potential. Recycling is often a popular design project in education but in reality the equations of sustainability and economy it raises are not always straightforward, the designer Luisa Cervese and her Italian label Riedizoni being a case in point. In the production of beautiful handbags from discarded scraps, off-cuts and end pieces, fabric is immersed in polyurethane (Jones, B., 2000c). Whether this is 'green' is open to debate: what is gained in terms of issues of disposal may be lost in terms of issues of manufacture. Another approach to fabric waste is to consider its life-cycle at the very beginning. For instance, architect William McDonough, the German environmental chemist Michael Braungart and New York City textile manufacturer DesignTex developed compostable upholstery fabrics. Made from wool-and-ramie-blend fibres they were designed to return to earth when worn out (Riley, 1995).

We don't always notice the effects of environmental exploitation, pollution and waste until they are upon us. Anticipation and planning to reduce effects are therefore very important. Design is just one such opportunity to intervene. Increasingly critical information is not so hard for the ordinary designer to find. For the textile industry, as for any industry, ecological issues are something that has to be addressed. For textile designers matters are a little more complex: education, conscience, fashion and work environment will all potentially influence their choice to be green or not.

Case Study: Corporate Environmental Policies

It would be unusual now to find a major textile manufacturer that does not have a corporate environmental policy. There are a number of reasons why this should be so, ranging from corporate leadership and vision to the basest expediency. For most major companies, factors include

- the legislative framework under which they have to conduct their business
- views of owners or shareholders
- media representation and corporate image
- views of consumers and the public about their products and practices
- views of the local communities at the sites of manufacture
- economic incentives, either as business opportunity, funding or subsidy

It is interesting to compare corporate environmental policy statements, which reveal a lot about company philosophy and management style. Two statements are compared here, those of Trevira and Coats Viyella. The companies are not chosen for any particular reason other than they make a good comparison and allow for observations about how, on environmental issues, the companies project themselves, expect employees to behave, and manage environmental problems and goals. It could be argued that the companies are not sufficiently alike for such a comparison, but it is not necessary that they should be so. Both statements can be viewed in full at their company websites www.trevira.de and www.coats-viyella. com respectively.

Trevira, a German company, strongly emphasize their commitment to environmental issues, stating that conservation of the environment and safety are central to their corporate activity:

> The maintenance of these principles . . . is seen as an absolute precondition for steering the company . . . we declare our support to the principles on Sustainable Development formulated at the Summit on the Environment in Rio in 1992 (the Earth Summit) and to the international initiative Responsible Care of the chemical industry.

The Rio Declaration is later explained, and Trevira states its commitment to the principle of sustainable development and its concern for future generations. Compare this with the nearest equivalent section of the Environmental Statement of Coats Viyella, where idealism gives way to the 'steady hand' of management approach:

> Our international businesses must operate under a variety of regulatory regimes and fulfil a range of stakeholder expectations. Accordingly, local management takes responsibility for environmental performance within the framework of the Group Environmental Policy, defined standards and procedures.

The two companies seem also to have a different view about accountability and the way in which environmental policies can be implemented. Coates Viyella emphasizes hierarchy, line management, communication and, perhaps ultimately, local more than central accountability:

> Environmental Management communication networks and action groups are in place across the Group to assist and co-ordinate the implementation of the policy, monitor issues and performance, and exchange information, including best practice . . . In each business a senior executive takes overall responsibility for environmental performance, supported by a site environmental management representative for local co-ordination.

Trevira imply a more holistic approach in the areas of conservation, recycling and waste disposal; Trevira state 'this latter can only be effective when every single employee plays an active part' and 'Each Trevira worker is expected to behave with a sense of duty, with commitment and responsibility, with management acting as models'. Trevira considers every worker has a responsibility to participate in

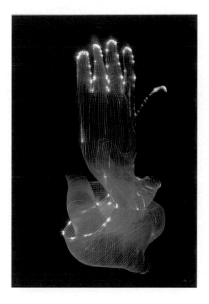

Plate 1. Woven fibre optics. Sarah Taylor.

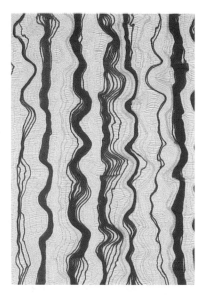

Plate 2a. 'Wandering Lines' a textile incorporating phosphorescent yarns, photographed in daylight. Sophie Roet 2001: Photographer Joe's Basement.

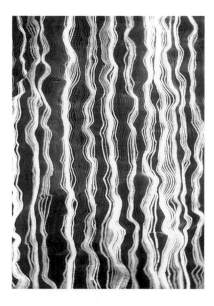

Plate 2b. 'Wandering Lines' photographed with UV light. Sophie Roet 2001: Photographer Margaret Proudfoot.

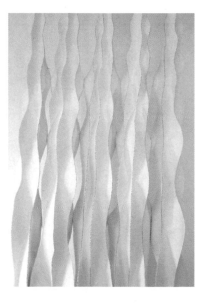

Plate 3. 'Felt White Wave'. Kei Ito.

Plate 4. Scarf. Rubber printed onto velvet. Isabel Dodd 1997.

pyramid,Stych.Cones.Dice,Venetian blind,Frisby,

Plate 5. Print samples. Bullen Pijja Design.

Plate 6. Printed synthetic fabric bonded with gold, silver and copper leaf. Sharon Ting.

Plate 7. Lit sculpture. Lindsay Bloxam.

Plate 8. Textile art. Chiyoka Tanaka. From the Textural Space exhibition. Photographer Gerry Diebel.

Plate 9. 'Woolgatherers' Basket', 1m diameter, willow struts. Anne Belgrave.

Plate 10. Festal Vestments. Hand painted/printed Duchesse satin. Coventry Cathedral commission. Victoria Richards.

Plate 11. Indian embroidery. A traditional Asian design.

Plate 12. Felt slippers. Miglena Kazaski.

Plate 13. 'Fragrance' Studio Sanderson's Essence Collection, Spring 2001. Courtesy Sanderson.

Plate 14. Woven Indian shawl.

Plate 15. Weave from the Jalq'a Textile Project, Southern Andes. Courtesy of ASUR.

improvements to air and noise pollution, reducing effluent and waste production and reducing energy and water consumption.

Slightly different strategies are used to measure the success of their respective policies. Trevira, as well as participating in the Responsible Care initiative, are also members of the Association of Chemical Industries in Germany, which has further environmental guidelines that all member companies must adhere to. They also voluntarily subscribe to the EU Eco-Audit Directive. Coats Viyella on the other hand have implemented an award-winning Environmental Auditing and Reporting System (EARS), and use the firm Deloitte and Touche to verify their internal auditing system. Both companies, it seems, do their best to implement their environmental policies positively and maintain a degree of objective control through collaboration with external agencies. The Coats Viyella report on the year 1999 shows no significant adverse environmental outcomes resulting in prosecution. It also reports having met a three-year target to reduce effluent, energy consumption and waste by 10 per cent. In general a company's environmental policy and the way they implement it is extremely important, and can have ramifications around the world. Coats Viyella for example have undertaken projects to improve effluent treatment in their units in Malaysia and China. For the world's textile industries and the professionals who run them, there can be few more responsible jobs.

–10–

Industry

In this chapter an overview of the textiles industry is provided. The industry is so large it is not possible to include all branches of it. Similarly there are many different categorizations that would lead to different types of analysis (for example by country, by company, by product, by sector and so on) and once again not all analyses can be covered here. The predominant analysis used is by country, followed closely by product sector. Together these two provide a good indication of the complexity and scale of the textiles industry, its role in politics and economics and its impact on the peoples of the world. The main focus is on fabric and yarn production rather than, for example, the trade in designs.

There is a general developmental or structural model that can be applied to the textile industry; the model starts with the cultivation or sourcing of raw materials then proceeds through subsequent stages of spinning and yarn production, through to cloth production, through to the making of fabric products such as clothing and eventually their sale. At each stage in the industrial process from raw material to consumer product, value is added. For example, cotton thread might be twice the price of beaten cotton, the making of cloth might add another 150 to 300 per cent, making up the final product might double or triple the value of the cloth. So the production of a ready-made suit for export can add 900 per cent to the value of the original beaten cotton (Alikhani, 1998).

All nations that develop textile industries normally do so as part of general industrialization, and they inevitably (in seeking greater profit) move toward the development of textile-product industries, such as furnishing or apparel. As countries develop industrially, so generally the standard of living increases and so too does the cost of local labour. This leads to a decline in the preliminary phases of industrialization, which tend to be labour intensive. By the time a country reaches the final stages of its industrial development, many aspects of textile production and manufacture become uneconomic and indigenous textile industry has a tendency to disappear. In the final phases, more often than not, successful textile companies in order to survive must have global rather than national strategies. While this is not the whole story, it is sufficient to begin to understand how and why textile industry shifts around the world.

The Industrial Story

The history of the British textile industry is a useful indicator of how industry impacts on societies. It also demonstrates how changes in industrial practices or global economics can make or break textile industries. Ultimately it is a reminder of the impermanence of industrial power. Brought about by the growth of mercantilism, liberal economic philosophy and advances in technology and science, the Industrial Revolution began in the British textiles industry. Starting in the middle of the eighteenth century, the next fifty years would see the introduction of steam-powered machines and the development of the factory system, replacing the manual and small-scale traditions of textile production that had existed since time immemorial. By the beginnings of the nineteenth century the innovations had spread to the rest of Europe and the New World. A good overview of the Industrial Revolution (and the role of the textile industry in it) can be found in *Compton's Interactive Encyclopaedia*.

The Industrial Revolution was to have a profound effect on the English psyche and social structure, drawing the population into industrial towns, provoking civil unrest, setting harsh and dangerous working conditions and creating a new identity for the working classes. The changes and growth in productivity in the textile industry were phenomenal, impacting on trade, transport and other sites of manufacture and production – for example, the American cotton industry. Printed cottons provide one such example of the effects

> Where it had been possible to print only six pieces a day on a single table, a steam-powered roller printing machine could print up to 500 pieces a day. Between 1796 and 1840, as a result of the introduction of these machines, the annual production of printed textiles in the United Kingdom increased from one million to sixteen million pieces. (Forty, 1986: 47)

Competition was fierce: 'each new season's patterns . . . were jealously guarded, and equally zealously spied upon' (Sykas, 2000), but it was not to last. From the dizzy heights of industrial success and economic power, the British textile industry could do little but decline, but not before establishing itself in the hearts and customs of generations and creating a dark but romantic mythology. In a preface to an elegiac collection of photographs (by Fay Godwin) and his own poetry, the poet-laureate Ted Hughes remarked of the Calder valley:

> Then in the early 1800s it became the cradle for the Industrial Revolution in textiles, and the upper Calder became 'the hardest-worked river in England' . . . Throughout my lifetime, since 1930, I have watched the mills of the region and their attendant chapels die. Within the last fifteen years the end has come. (Hughes and Godwin, 1979)

Between them Hughes and Godwin provide a melancholic memento of the decline of both English textile manufacturing and the community it created. By the next millennium the footnote reads:

> the rate of job losses is increasing with the move to offshore production . . . Between 1980 and 1999 a total of 360,000 jobs disappeared from the industry in the UK, reducing the workforce to 336,000 – an average of just under 19,000 jobs a year lost during the period . . . latest figures for the industry . . . show a dramatic leap. In the year September 1999 to September 2000 a total of 17,100 jobs disappeared in clothing and apparel trades and 9,600 in textiles and textile products. (Hinchliffe, 2001)

Such levels of catastrophe necessarily generate responses from government and industry. The independent British Textile and Clothing Strategy Group recently published an extensive report outlining recommendations and actions to be taken (TCSG, 2000) to sustain the industry. For the time being, with a few notable exceptions, textile design seems to be the main remnant and torch-bearer for the indigenous British textile industry; manufacturing declines apace. This story of the rise and fall of a national industry is not unusual: increasingly, with the global movement of capital, the power of multinationals and regional economic incentives, it feels like the norm. Whether textiles manufacturing is capable of firmly re-establishing itself in Britain is part of a broader economic equation about the balance between service-sector industries (such as finance, entertainment, tourism, software) and manufacturing industries. It is a question of whether the economics are right, whether the means and technology of manufacture changes or whether new processes or markets fundamentally change the equation.

Currently most other European countries find their industries under threat and seek to survive either through the use of new technology or by shifting the less profitable aspects of business to cheaper manufacturing locations. Paul Kiekens of Ghent University provides an interesting commentary on the problems facing the European textiles industry and a possible way forward. He strongly advocates a move away from textile products to advanced materials manufacture:

> in Europe one has to forget about commodities which are by far the majority of most textile (and clothing) products manufactured so far. One has to go to specialty materials, engineered products, technically advanced and research driven. By doing so, one can enter niche markets, explore markets where other materials were previously used and where quality and functionality at a reasonable cost are of utmost importance. (Kiekens, 2000)

Kiekens goes on to make some fierce criticisms of the textiles industry and the educational sector for failing to develop the new approaches needed. He particularly points out the low level of investment in research:

As research is critical to the survival of the textile industry in Europe, one must re-invent the actual research systems for textiles. Although the textile industry may claim that research and innovation is part of their activities, it is obvious that research in the textiles world has to be detected by a magnifying glass. Statistics reveal that less than 0.5% of the turnover in textiles is invested in research and development. This is the lowest figure from all industries. (Ibid.)

As the textile industry is so mobile the general struggle to develop, adapt or save textile industries is a commonplace story around the world. When the industry has been long established, tradition and sentiment can set in and a conservative dependency culture can arise. Richard A. Stanford, Professor of Economics at Furman University, South Carolina makes an important point about the role of textile industries as a preliminary phase of industrialization:

It must be recognized that the cotton textile industry has done something rather important for every region of the world which has been graced by its presence. It has induced a transformation of labor from agrarian pursuits to a first stage of industrial occupations. In doing so it acclimates and conditions the labor force to the discipline of industrial employment. Once it has done its work, it moves on to help another region to initiate industrialization. It leaves its former host in position to diversify into other industrial and post-industrial pursuits. (Stanford, 2000)

Stanford goes on rightly to observe the distress and political ramifications of industrial decline and also its inevitability, suggesting the United States should 'let go' of the cotton textile industry. He sums up the global perspective from the United States as:

China, the American textile industry's present devil, won't be able to retain the cotton textile industry any longer than Great Britain, New England, the South, Japan, or Korea have done. India likely will become the American textile industry's next devil. (Ibid.)

A climate of suspicion, resentment or panic tends to follow in the wake of the textiles industry as the more traditional forms of manufacturing move around the world looking for the lowest cost factors. In September 1999 representatives of the American Textile Manufacturers Institute (ATMI) told their senators that HR 434 the African Growth and Opportunity Act would:

open the door to illegal textile and apparel transhipments from China and other Asian countries, foreclose legitimate investment in Africa and jeopardize thousands of U.S. textile jobs.

(PR Newswire, 1999)

Against the broader picture of international trade and politics such concerns can look like the interests of a limited section of the business community. For example, trade agreements can demonstrate how textile industry is often linked to a much broader definition of industrial production, markets and competition. The well-being of American industry is underscored by agreements such as the recent US–Caribbean Basin Trade Partnership Act or the North American Free Trade Agreement. Both contributed in the year 2000 to the 12 per cent increase in exports of yarn, fabric and goods. During his Presidency, Bill Clinton championed the passing of the Trade and Development Act of 2000, an act designed to promote a trade-based rather than aid-based relationship with more than 70 African and Caribbean countries:

> From the start, White House officials were optimistic about the impact of the program, saying that the measure would boost the apparel trade by billions of dollars. African-made shipments of apparel could reach $4.2 billion by 2008 from the current $250 million. (*Jet*, 2000)

The health of textile industry can be assessed on a national basis or by sector, by trade bloc or as individual company performance. The performance of individual countries is a good indicator of the global pressures on the textile industry. The annual business review of the ATMI for the year 2000 showed various declines in American mill shipments, corporate sales and employment in spite of textile exports exceeding $10 billion for the first time. These declines more often than not represent growth elsewhere, such as in Mexico, which is now a major consumer of raw cotton from the United States; this in turn stimulates other industries and parts of the American economy.

The industrial story of cotton, which has had a significant Western dimension to it, is paralleled to some extent by the industrial story of silk in the East. Silk has a long and fascinating history, and during the earlier phases of the Industrial Revolution the rapid growth of international trade meant that various aspects of the silk industry, both in cultivation and manufacture, could be found all over the world. In 1865 for example, the value of silk manufactured in Britain was estimated at being over £17.6 million, and there were over 300 factories and 50,000 workers employed. Britain imported over 3,500 tons of raw silk, principally from China, the East Indies, the Levant, France and Italy. Exports were chiefly to the United States and the British Colonies but also extensively to South America, Germany, Belgium, India and France. During the 1930s Japan was the world's main silk producer. In 1934 Japan produced 45,352 tons of silk and exported 33,133 tons of it. Japan held over 80 per cent of the world trade and produced over three-quarters of the world's supply: silk accounted for 30 per cent of Japan's export revenues at this time. Although silk contributed significantly to Japan's economic recovery and industrial development after the Second World War, the economic success of

Japan gradually made silk production less and less tenable. By 1975 Japan had stopped exporting raw silk. By 1992 China was selling silk and silk products worth 218 million dollars to Japan, including 13.34 million metres of true silk. Interestingly, in the new millennium, the country that was once the greatest producer of silk, Japan, is most likely to be the greatest consumer of silk. Interestingly once again, the country that originated and kept the secret of silk for so long, China, is now the world's main producer with countries such as Brazil, Vietnam and India as its main competitors. China holds its position, for the time being, on the basis of either labour costs or quality (ChinaFace.net, 2000).

The location of textile manufacturing continues to be influenced by a pattern of sourcing cheap labour. The picture we gain from this can distort our view of the future and be misleading. It does not follow that future industrial practices will merely replicate or be minor modifications of existing models of manufacture. For example, new technologies and the consequent need for highly skilled workforces are a new factor in the industrial equation. The stories given so far are the stories of the industrial era, which evolved over two centuries or more; the epic stories of the post-industrial era are yet to unfold.

Power and Influence

The story of the growth and decline of textile manufacture in Britain, Japan and elsewhere reflects a standard pattern, that things come and go. It would be foolish to assume that those countries that currently do best in textiles manufacture do so simply because they have the money to invest in new technology or that they have the political or economic power to protect their industries or, more simply, that they have a cheap source of labour. All of these can be parts of the equation of success, but the economic efficiency and achievements of textile companies and countries with textile industries can be affected by many other factors, including global economics and environmental or political catastrophe. It is, however, undeniable that the factor of size can dampen the effects of change, slow it down or redirect it.

The size of the global textile industry is vast: Alikhani states that the trade of textile products in 1998 stood at $350 billion annually (Alikhani, 1998), while in a slightly more recent calculation Textrade.com figure it at $500 billion plus. Any industry of this size is heavily implicated in the relationship between economics and politics. In terms of the importance of zones or individual countries, to some extent these reflect standard perceptions of centres of economic power and international competition. So, for example, it is easy to make the assumption there is an East–West divide with various Asian countries, such as India or China, competing with such major Western powers as the United States or Europe, particularly on grounds of labour costs. A perception of that sort is not wholly true, as each economic or trade zone has its own internal conflicts over trade. For example, in the East, there is a developing competition in the silk trade between such countries as China, India and Vietnam. There is also competition in the area of synthetic yarns, for example between Taiwan, China and South Korea.

Another example of the way in which politics and economics entwine is the relationship between Taiwan and China. There are significant political tensions between Taiwan and China about Taiwan's status: whether it should be considered to be an independent nation or an independent province, or that it should have no independence at all. These tensions are played out against a complex background of economic relationships. In the year 2000 the global production of one type of synthetic alone, polyester fibre, reached 21,200,000 tons, with Taiwan producing 15.6 per cent of this figure and China, at 20.2 per cent, leading world production. The local competition between these two countries was further complicated by each wanting to enter the World Trade Organization (WTO), with China's entry in particular involving it in complex negotiations over synthetic fibre quotas with the United States. Being the world's largest producer of synthetic fibres, the American textiles industry has had a powerful say in the conditions set for entry. Although a substantial world economic power, Taiwan does not have the political and economic presence of China or the United States on the world stage. So Taiwan (where textiles is the third largest export industry after electronics and PCs) must wait to see how two superpowers, one of whom claims to be its master and both of whom happen to be its direct economic rivals, settle the future opportunities for its textile industry. (ITIS, 2000)

To give some impressions of scale in the textile world, the following statistics are provided for India and China. The sway that the textiles industry holds in India and its influence on the population is substantial. During the 1990s the textile industry accounted for almost 20 per cent of national industrial product, and it provided employment to more than 15 million people, delivered more than 30 per cent of exports and was the largest generator of foreign exchange (Dalmia, 1994). The Indian textile industry, in its own right, effectively has the workforce and economic performance of a small country. It is equally possible to consider the scale of a textile industry in terms of its production and productivity. For a country such as China, the figures are immense. According to the Textile Section of the State Economic and Trade Commission of China, throughout the year 2000, textile production and sales in China made substantial increases, chemical fibre output was up 16.3 per cent (6.9416 million tons), and yarn showed a similar increase. Chinese fabric production (19.105 billion metres) was up by 10.9 per cent, printed fabrics (17.095 billion metres) up 3 per cent, woollen fabrics (278 million metres) up just over 9 per cent and silk textiles (3.743 billion metres) up 17.6 per cent. There are almost 19,000 textile enterprises in China and their income increased by almost 21 per cent in 2000.

Figure 18. 'Express' DuPont Knitwear Trends Spring/Summer (2002). Vimar 1999 SRL (I) 100% polyester Bada SA (E) Lycra, polyamide.

When you start to analyse the textiles industry in other ways, for example in terms of companies instead of countries, the descriptions of the industry are equally complex and often quite different in character. The leading textile companies and names often have the economic resources of nation states; often they are part of a much larger organization with textiles being only one part of the corporate operations. A good example is DuPont, responsible for some of the most famous products in textiles and fibres (Lycra, Tyvek, Dacron). The textile and apparel element of DuPont's business provides revenues of only $3 billion (Gee, 2000) compared to its estimated overall revenue of $35 billion. It has many companies and interests, particularly in chemicals, ranging from drugs to fungicides, and also in such other areas as nuclear energy and firearms. DuPont is rightly famed for its innovations but, not unsurprisingly for a corporation of its size, it has had its critics too. Observing the nature and activities of large and powerful corporations is difficult: unlike many countries, their internal political processes and policies are not always available to public scrutiny. Their accountability also varies from country to country and often depends on the local legislative framework. The economic effects and impact of textile companies sometimes tip their activities directly into the world of politics. Texmaco is an Indonesian company that operates in the textiles and engineering sectors – it is a large manufacturer of polyester and made over $900 million between 1997 and 1999. Recently it has been involved in a scandal with accusations of impropriety in respect of a $1.5 billion loan from the Indonesian State Bank, Bank Negara Indonesia. The Indonesian State itself, at the highest level, became embroiled, with suggestions that former President Soeharto was involved. Finally the Indonesian Attorney General's Office halted investigations as there was not enough evidence that the state had suffered financially or had ever been at financial risk (*Jakarta Post*, 2000).

The textiles industry manages to span and be present in all stages of a country's industrial and political evolution. As modern textiles have developed alongside the chemical and engineering industries, these sometimes separate industries are often a natural commercial alliance or part of each other. Many large textile companies are thus part of much larger conglomerates. As a result, in various ways, the textiles industry blends and merges into the broader industrial, social and political landscape. For each industrial sub-sector of textiles, whether it is equipment manufacture or design, there are further stories to be told of their evolution, their structure and their impact in all spheres of life.

The Future

It would seem that countries develop textile industries, get wealthy and grow out of them. The simplest model that explains this is an evolution from early to advanced industrialization followed by post-industrialization. What does that really mean? The evolution from early to advanced industry is most easily understood. It is a decreasing use of labour and an increasing use of technology, perhaps too a shift to a more advanced range of products, such as synthetic yarn. An increasingly technological manufacture needs other sophisticated support industries and services; it will also need an increasingly knowledgeable workforce. In order to have the right workforce and support industries, all other aspects of a society will need to have developed along with industrialization – transport, education, the home market, consumer wealth, even culture. A country in a state of advanced industrialization is thus one with lots of very modern manufacturing plants and factories. It is at this point that we reach the evolution to post-industrialization and the question arises as to why factories close and industries disappear.

Some of the standard features of industrialization include the ability to look for cheap labour, having capital to invest in new factories, and using a management structure that can cope with the global stage. These features are really nothing new, they are almost pre-industrial. The post-industrial model of industry includes the same basic factors but they behave or are treated differently. For example the 'poor' of post-industrial societies (the 'cheap labour') are relatively wealthy (and costly) compared to the poor elsewhere. Companies can quickly move into a country or business sector supported by the speed of global finance and banking services. They can equally quickly withdraw. Finally, computing quickens business, management processes and communications. The signs of a post-industrial society are wealth and the acceleration of all its activities. Perhaps the disappearance of manufacturing industry is due to the broader transformation a post-industrial society undergoes. When it gets wealthy, like any individual, such societies start to play with stocks and shares, get others to do the menial work and pursue more rewarding activity. The loss of manufacturing industry is not simply on the grounds that others can manufacture more cheaply, it is also on the grounds that money can be made in either more lucrative or more pleasurable ways. The term 'post-industrial' implies an end-game, a finish to industry. The current reality is properly an industrial shift from manufacturing to service sectors. A more positive and directional future for the textiles industry is therefore most likely to be found in a closer inspection and analysis of 'advanced industrialization'.

For the textiles industry in general there remains, around the world, an almost unlimited resource for playing out conventional textile manufacture. For textile manufacturers with factories in the United States and Europe there are specific problems about survival. The options are either for companies to relocate their operations elsewhere in the world or to find a way through, using science and technology. In many senses the future of the textiles industry is more of the same: a fixed stage in industrial development, occurring where the conditions are right. However, the question arises as to whether manufacturing technology has more potential to evolve, whether advanced industrialization is, as yet, relatively undeveloped. Innovations in either product, process or technology have tended to stimulate changes in each other. The way in which computing and computer technology has changed all aspects of textiles from design to production is well documented. Computer-aided design (CAD), computer-aided manufacture (CAM) and computer-integrated manufacture (CIM) have been developed over the last few decades of the twentieth century and have become part of the industrial process. Advances in science, in such areas as bioengineering or genetics, may well impact on yarn or fabric production. Robotics, generally, are in an early stage and the full role of robots in manufacturing is yet to be realized. There may also be new and unexpected uses for textiles that demand new types of manufacturing.

While advanced industrialization may have further developments to make, 'conventional' textile manufacture can also be affected by technological change. In the space of just a few years, the internet has asserted a new area of business activity and development, the ramifications of which are not yet clear. One example is the growth in 'e-markets'. E-markets are internet sites where it is possible to post or buy goods and services. Various websites large and small such as textrade. com, tradetextile.com, texwatch.com, biz2biz.com and eGlobalTextile.com vie for market position as internet trading sites. They imply a change to something as fundamental as world trade, permitting the smallest of businesses to see and compare international opportunities very directly. Although there is nothing new in markets, the potential size, speed, reach and diversity of e-markets must change the future of textile trade. In other respects they offer all the usual facilities of modern commerce. Taking just one example, Textrade.com/Global Textile Network 'provides a secure online environment for sourcing, selling, logistics, and financial services for buyers and sellers of commodity fiber, yarn and unfinished fabric around the world', and its 'community' includes in excess of 5,000 companies in more than fifty countries. Recently textrade.com made an agreement with First International Bank to provide finance options for transactions up to $5 million for companies using its services (textrade.com, 2000).

Similar advances are being made in other areas. The role of visual communication (the portrayal of fabric or fabric products), as a tool in both selling and business management, has often been problematic for the industry, and so too the effects of globalization on production and production management. However, at the recent Seventh Osaka International Textile Machinery Show, the message was that sufficient advances were being made to integrate the visual representation of fabric and garments into the general business uses of computing and the internet:

> The progress of content creation technology these past few years has made possible the development of 3D movies, which can represent textile and apparel products, once thought to be characteristically difficult to digitise . . . At this 7th OTEMAS, we will blend image processing technology used for transmitting sensory information with management systems, integrating the marketing of apparel and other fabric products. (OTEMAS, 2001)

There remains plenty of healthy scepticism over issues such as how much you can close the gap between consumer demand and production and how well you can manage business (from design to sale) using virtual reality and websites. In a comprehensive article on these and other matters, after observing that only 1 per cent of clothing purchases are made online, Jules Abend writes:

> One key reason that's given for the chariness about shopping on the Web is concern about size and fit. According to a Pricewaterhouse Coopers survey, more than 80 per cent of Internet shoppers maintain that the biggest problem with shopping for clothing online is that they are unable to try on the items and don't trust the on-screen representations they see. (Abend, 2001)

Other areas of the developing use of the internet include an increasing number of 'portals' (which are gateways to all kinds of subject-related websites) and journalistic sites about textiles or textiles and apparel. These raise interesting opportunities and questions about the future use and flow of information among the textile community and also about the role of information as 'power'. Such sites range from the relatively personal, homepage projects, such as J.N. Vohra's collection of 700 categorized textile website links textilescan.com, to Hong Kong Polytechnic University's Apparel Product Development and Marketing website. The latter is a gateway to some very sophisticated materials brought together to serve the apparel industry of Hong Kong, and can be found at www.asd.polyu.edu.hk. While such sites often have an archiving, encyclopedic quality to them, other sites such as just-style.com follow journalistic models, providing breaking up-to-the-minute industry news. Today the small independent has almost as much access to market intelligence, trend information and new research as the largest of organizations. Depending on how much they want to spend on their website they can also appear as sophisticated as they like to an internet user on the other side of the world.

While the future of the textiles industry will no doubt be as complicated as its past, it is possible to see that a new phase is beginning. A phase brought about by, and dependent on, very sophisticated technology. Whether it is the impact of biotechnology on fabric, robotics and flexible manufacturing on production, or the internet on how business is conducted, there is the prospect of a different kind of industry. Textile industry in advanced nations would like to perceive this new future as a safeguard, a way of protecting manufacture though capital investment and sophistication, opening up new and niche markets. It may not prove to be the case; the technology may turn the world on its head, as it has done before. Only time will tell. Those who wish to succeed in this new environment will have to be prepared to engage with different cultures and attitudes, develop exceptional communication skills and be highly entrepreneurial.

–11–

The Role of Trends and Forecasting

Knowledge of trends and forecasting is vital to the 'textile chain' of industries – from yarn producer and textile manufacturer to retailer and designer. Companies are reluctant to take decisions independently about textile attributes, such as which specific colours to use. This is in marked comparison to their attitude toward technological developments and innovations. The adoption or use of technology or technique tends to be ongoing, often exclusive to a particular company and driven by forces within their sector. Although technology brings its own risks, the choice of textile attributes can be a crucial make-or-break decision for any company, so in a peculiar way they are regulated by the trends and forecasting world, removing responsibility from the manufacturer, the retailer and the designer. For example, most textile users and makers will make decisions on colour selection after seeking guidance from some sort of colour consultant. These consultants and consultancies play a crucial role in steering decisions made at one extreme by industry and at the other by consumers.

We cannot underestimate the impact and influence colour has on the whole spectrum of society, wielding its power over everything from industry to the individual and determining the atmosphere of a season. It is a key factor in consumer choice and is directional in everything from cosmetics to cars. We often make decisions to purchase based on colour selection. It is difficult to ignore those who make the decisions about the range of colour palettes we choose from. So who are the people that decide which colours will be fashionable? It is not usually the designers; textile designers choose from the same ranges that all other design professionals eventually use. It is actually a professional colourist's innate, instinctive foresight that determines what colour selections are made. Sometimes it seems that the colourist makes decisions based on a feeling or a hunch – or at least this is how the uninitiated must perceive it. In fact, these individuals are continually alert to the condition of the world, its cultures, societies, economies and innovations. Their knowledge enables them to speculate, hypothesize and foresee, generating an educated, informed opinion as to what will appeal to consumers in one or two years' time.

At the pinnacle of the colour-prediction world, supplying industry with information about commercial colour trends, is the International Colour Authority

(ICA). Having been dependable for more than thirty years, it is now renowned for its precision in delivering accurate colour predictions. Each season, consistently, it is the first prediction service to be published. The ICA panel is made up of the world's most accomplished colourists and, since it is international in its composition, a truly global outlook is assured. Congregating twice a year, for the spring/summer and autumn/winter seasons, they develop three principle colour collections which consist of menswear, womenswear and furnishing. The meetings allow the panel members to communicate and discuss their personal philosophies, reinforcing issues through presentations involving visual imagery and samples of appropriate materials. The motive for this exercise is to harmonize the focus of the group and begin forming a new colour palette, developing accent colours alongside the core range, and in addition to resolve issues of presentation. Timing is of the essence in trend prediction: most predicted colour palettes are ready to distribute to the textile and fashion industries anything from one to two years ahead of the retail selling period (*International Textiles*, 1999a).

Colour prediction is only one aspect of textile forecasting. Fabric trends are in constant transition: as soon as one set of ideals, colours, textures and thoughts hit the street, the powers that be, who work on concepts two years ahead, have already decided what we will desire next season. We, as consumers or spectators, eagerly await some indication of what will come next. Knowledge of what is to come, in some way, satisfies our innate curiosity and immediately puts us 'in the know'. This appears to render us all victims of a well-oiled prediction machine, for year upon year the prediction gurus know that industry and the public will 'need' some direction – the OK or nod from some authoritative figure or organization to say it's safe to go ahead with a specific colour palette, material or fibre. In dictating trends and colours, forecasting agencies create a workable and orchestrated system on which industry depends. Consequently for the media and the consumer, the agencies are rarely proved wrong in their 'guesses'.

Prediction agencies advise not only on colour but also on material effects, weights, textures, concepts and consumer markets. Although trends are sourced from prediction agencies and organizations, such as Trend Union, Nelly Rodin and Peclers (France), INDEX and The Bureau (Britain), and BrainReserve (United States), the prediction agencies actually source much of their information from within the textile industry. Usually, those at the start of the fabric-production process (that is, the fibre and material manufacturers) are the ones making the key decisions with regard to yarns, fabric 'looks' and concepts – so whom or what oracle do they consult in order to make their creative decisions and choices? There is a complicated chain of events that has to be unraveled in order to establish exactly who leads this series of decisions. The major fibre and yarn manufacturers, such as The Woolmark Company and DuPont, along with fabric trade fairs and the International Colour Authority dictate colours and tactile qualities. They suggest

Figure 19. Top by Mandarina Duck in Tactel. Courtesy DuPont.

colour and texture solutions, and also have a bearing on fashion direction, offering silhouette possibilities and shaping creativity.

As social individuals we want direction, reassurance or an indication of what we should wear, or have, and how we should behave. The need to know is a compelling human instinct which, when satisfied, allows us to fit into the right groups in society, or perhaps simply feel comfortable and accepted. For industry the needs are different: being in 'sync' with the rest of industry and the market is very important. Choosing the wrong colours can cost a company a lot of money, so any formula or collectively agreed opinion which reduces chance or guarantees success is worth paying for and following. Prediction agencies such as Li Edilkoort's Trend Union and Faith Popcorn's BrainReserve go some way to inform us and industry of imminent trends and so assure us of what is to come.

The Textile Industries and Forecasting

The role of the prediction agency or design consultancy is multifaceted. Other than the obvious trends and moods, clients often request specific information about everything from styling ideas to fabric sourcing and design, and even commercial marketing advice from agencies such as The Bureaux (in Great Britain). This inevitably holds the agencies involved answerable for the advice they supply. The value and importance of trend information cannot be taken too lightly in industry, where it can transform a company's performance. An example is the case of the Swiss textile firm, Schoeller Textil AG. The company reached a critical point in the 1980s, when it needed to make a profit or close down. With the appointment of a new managing director, Hans-Jurgen Hubner, the company was able to turn things around and to become synonymous with the highly innovative technical fabrics it offered. These fabrics had applications in performance wear as well as attracting the interest of fashion designers. This turnaround was largely because the managing director appointed a team of freelance researchers and trend spotters, constantly reporting back to the firm with new ideas (Langle, 1997).

Communication within the trends-forecasting world is of the utmost importance. To effectively convey an idea or concept, visually, takes skill and practice. Developments in communicating trends are the same as in communication in general; the internet is revolutionizing the way we organize our lives and seek information. It will be interesting to observe, in time, whether the introduction of technological mediums will ever replace the familiar tactile experience of opening and 'feeling' a huge trend book. Having said this, conveying trends by means of the super-highway has proven extremely effective for Britain-based WGSN (Worth Global Style Network). Their empire has escalated since they launched their website, whose greatest asset is the fact that it is able to deliver up-to-the-minute global information to clients in record time along with bringing like-minded individuals together from all over the world.

The practice of trend forecasting has its roots in the 1950s when trend offices were established and began to lead the way in advising the fashion industries about what the consumer would want in the future. Today's forecasting agency has a similar function to that of the mid-twentieth century; however, instead of advising merely on skirt lengths and trouser widths, it uses a rather more adaptable vocabulary of communication, with the intention to be useful to all categories of designers. The trends that agencies uncover these days are indicators of broad cultural patterns and, importantly, reveal the direction in which consumer tastes are moving. Current forecasting agencies are the business and marketing strategists of the twenty-first century: they use their insight on cultural and commercial trends to help businesses develop products, reposition established brands and define new areas of opportunity. Their consultancies identify consumer behaviour and anticipate future market needs, and they constantly deliver to us new buzzwords (such as 'nomadic') which describe envisaged future trends.

Trend books and catalogues together with trade publications and international yarn and fabric fairs inform us about prevailing trends. There is a range of formats through which trend information can be communicated, ranging from the two-dimensional visual display to the quirky three-dimensional tactile presentation. The trend book can be extravagantly illustrated and larger than life, informing clients through selected text, visuals, fabric and colour chips, fibres, yarns and material samples. All of these are organized into digestible themes. These representations act as a starting point of reference for the viewer, providing hints and signals on directions the individual user can interpret.

As far as trade journals are concerned, the universal and dominant professional publications within textiles, which circulate regularly among a wide audience of designers and industry, are *International Textiles* and *VIEW on Colour*. The first of these is long-established and provides global accounts of the textile world, covering everything from industrial and economic news through to design issues. The latter publication is rather more visionary and conceptual in nature, supplying information to all creative industries and professionals. Similar trend publications are found throughout the world, for example, North America's *Textiles International* and Africa's *Pursuit Magazine* which links businesses in the same sphere and informs the Southern African textile community of trends and commercial news. These magazines also benefit from the backing of professional textile organizations.

Trade fairs such as Premier Vision and Expofil (France), Pitti Filati (Italy), Interstoff (Germany), The Cloth Show and Cloth Plus (Britain) and The International Fashion Fabric Exhibition (United States) always incorporate a trend area. This is where visitors to the exhibition can obtain an overview or feel of what is to come. They can then act accordingly, making key business decisions based on what they see and hear. Within the trend area, selections of samples are made from exhibiting companies and shown as focal colour, texture and fabric directions for the coming season. Many buyers see this as a key part of the fair, critical in informing visitors about what they 'should' be buying. Complementary to this there is usually an audiovisual presentation, setting the ambience of the imminent mood (*International Textiles*, 1998: 92).

As stated earlier, technology is revolutionizing the distribution of information and the trend-forecasting world is by no means exempt from this. In fact it is difficult to ignore the success that the Worth Global Style Network has proven to be. With its headquarters in London and representational offices peppered across the globe, from New York to Paris to Tokyo, WGSN has transformed and revolutionized the distribution of trend information. Established in Britain in 1998 by brothers Julian and Marc Worth, they are currently the global on-line leaders in supplying commercial design industries such as Armani and Ralph Lauren, with 350,000 pages of news and information from around the world. Access to this indispensable well of information, featuring constantly updated data on trends, technology, resources and catwalk show reports, is generously provided free to all students on textile-, fashion- and design-related courses throughout the world for the duration of their study. Existing subscribers saw this radical move as a positive investment in the future of design. The educational site, www.wgsn-edu.com, is a mirror of the main site, www.wgsn.com, the only difference being a two-week lapse between subscribers and students receiving the information (*Textiles Magazine*, 2000: 5).

Key players in the textile and fashion worlds annually sign up to WGSN, which constantly feeds them global news, facts, reviews and inspiration. This enterprise has been hailed by industry as 'arguably one of the most dynamic Internet business-to-business ventures to emerge in recent times'. The operation has been greatly endorsed by its clients, and Robert Triefus, Corporate Vice-President, Giorgio Armani, says

> WGSN helps us to be wiser about the current industry trends and developments. It again underscores the power of the Internet today in providing real time information that in the past would have taken days if not weeks to obtain.

This view is supported by Alix Umen, Trend Director at The Gap Inc 'I use it mostly because I know that a lot of our competitors use it also. I want to know what everyone else knows. WGSN is incredibly comprehensive, it's one-stop shopping' (www.wgsn.com).

The Forecasting Gurus and their Roles

Two major internationally renowned futurists and trend professionals in the forecasting industry are Li Edelkoort of Trend Union (Paris) and Faith Popcorn of BrainReserve (New York). These prediction gurus both have impressive lists of clients: Popcorn's list includes IBM, American Express and McDonalds and Edelkoorts is equally impressive with Issey Miyake, Estée Lauder and Nissan. Their proven track records make them a very credible commodity in the business worlds. Although Popcorn specifically deals with lifestyle trends rather than with materials as Li Edelkoort does, there is still a crossover between them in that they both cater for industry, informing it of what the consumer is going to want. Their methods for seeking this information are very similar too – even to the extent that their organizations are almost identical models. Popcorn asked her fourteen best friends to join her TalentBank and Edelkoort gathered a few of her favourite designers to form her think tank. Since launching, both enterprises have matured to the point where Popcorn's TalentBank encompasses 7,500 experts, including an Indian chief, a rocket scientist and a microbiologist. In addition to this 4,000 people a year are interviewed and 300 journals and magazines are read each month. There is a lot of brainstorming, observing and collecting that goes on and essentially Popcorn and Edelkoort both do the same thing in the same way. Having said this, we note that there is a very real difference in the way they actually communicate their findings. For Popcorn, delivery is mostly verbal – whereas Edelkoort's in contrast is a more creative, tactile and visual experience.

As the world's leading trend forecaster, Faith Popcorn predicts up to ten years ahead and has a 95 per cent accuracy rate. According to Popcorn 'The thing about a trend is that you cannot look for it. It's like finding a wife or husband. They just appear' (Johnson, 2001). She defines trends in progress through – as she calls it – 'brailling the culture'. Via comprehending people and society she is able to make a calculated guess about the future. In response to being asked how much she relies on a personal gut feeling, Popcorn says

> Well you know we're analysing stuff and reading stuff, but then we jump off the roof. And what does that mean? Boom, there you go. I don't know if it's instinct, intuition or we're guided in some way, because we've been 95% correct. It sounds obnoxious but is true. Why would that be? You don't get that from content analysis. Our mission is to lift ourselves and others into their best futures. That's our mission. This is our path and this is how we're doing it.
>
> (*phenomeNEWS*, 1999)

Identifying the social trends of the future can be of as much significance within the textile industry as it is in all other industries. Popcorn's revelations about the way society is evolving, in the greater scheme of things, have implications for the industries involved with fabric, fashion design and manufacture. After all, she was right when in 1981 she documented the stay-at-home syndrome, calling it 'cocooning'. She informed industry that because of this we would buy more VCRs and babygrows. In her futuristic quest to chart impending trends and research her intuition, she has used psychics and regressed volunteers under hypnosis in order to reach the cultural subconscious pulse within society. She authenticates her predictions, recording them by writing books, and at the same time reaches a global audience that is able to measure her accuracy and benefit from her insights.

For Edelkoort, trends are very visual and material: she has already stressed that 50 per cent of what we buy is with the fingertips – she calls it the 'new tactility' and puts it down to a direct response in opposition to virtual reality. The way in which Li Edelkoort and her creative team fathom the future is similar to that of Faith Popcorn's BrainReserve. Edelkoort coaches her entourage to observe themselves 'observing', to be aware and alert to where their attention is lured, be it to a fragrance, a colour or an object. She believes that trends are divulged when incidents or experiences of the same type are repeated. In order to spot a trend in its initial stages it needs to be present on very different planes. For instance the same buzz could be circulating simultaneously in a fashion glossy as it is in some trade journal. This kind of lead is just the sort of indicator that is researched in greater depth, seeking confirmation for its long-term growth. Globally, there are many organizations which investigate and chart trends in demography, lifestyles, buying habits and retail structures. The leading players in this field are Roper Starch Worldwide Inc and Yankelvich in the United States and Kurt Salmon Associates and Gallup in Great Britain. Spotting an up-and-coming trend is not just a case of invention but a matter of reading the clues which indicate that it's already out there. Edelkoort explains this in relation to the medium of textiles:

> textiles are ahead of fashion – they're more immediate, closer to the body . . . The diagonal was the dominant weave in the 80's, and the diagonal is a weave that makes things look more beautiful than they are . . . It's very much a facade weave, and the 80's was very much about facade. In the 90's we suddenly went to this square weave, which is one-up, one-down. You can't really cheat, because you can't hide the threads . . . You may think this honest weave is sort of boring, but it's not – you can paint it, embroider it, leave threads out to create transparency and, most importantly, you can cut it on the bias . . . The honest weave announced a new period in which we're shifting from a profit-driven to a value-driven society.
>
> (Baude, 2000)

In summary, the world of trend forecasting can encompass a diversity of roles: statistical, demographic or materials researcher; commercial marketing adviser; studio photographer; creative journalist; professional speaker; art director; colourist; stylist; cultural observer and interpreter. This listing is by no means comprehensive. There are major skills a forecaster requires in order to recognize trends and profit from them. It seems that entrepreneurial skills and understanding are essential, as trends present real business opportunities. On attempting to enter the world of the creative clairvoyant, the predictor has to skim through all sorts of journals and magazines, so it looks as if a fascination with information is also a fundamental prerequisite. Finally, it is essential to talk about, listen to and look at everything that the world is involved with and interested in.

Both Edelkoort and Popcorn profess the necessity for trend prediction. In suggesting what colours, materials and concepts will be fashionable two or more years ahead, Edelkoort says 'there is no creation without advance knowledge, and without design, a product cannot exist' (Mode . . . information, 1999). We could interpret this to mean that trends and predictions are self-fulfilling prophecies. We are given this advance knowledge of which Edelkoort speaks in various forms by the media, and thus we are told what will be 'in'. Industry is the first to react to the trend-forecasting information and, in acting on the guidance given, physically takes steps to make it a reality. Once the wheels are in motion, it is just a matter of time before the media tell us what we should desire in the coming season. Quite simply and willingly, then, we want exactly what we are told we should want. It is possible to be sceptical about the 'predictive' quality of forecasting, but let us end with what the experts say about what they do. Popcorn states:

> If you knew what was going to happen tomorrow, wouldn't you know what to do today? You look at your talents, you look at the future and you say, 'I'm moving this way' . . . Understanding the trends is like getting the newspaper in the morning and instead of it saying 1999, it says 2009. (*phenomeNEWS*, 1999)

Li Edelkoort says of her role:

> What I do is really 'archaeology of the future.' I uncover bits and pieces, little fragments – I never find the whole vase . . . the more I work at my job . . . the less cement I need to put all the pieces together and understand the forces behind it. (Baude, 2000)

Part IV
Related Disciplines and Studies

–12–

The Buyer

There are many different types of buyer working in the textile industry; this chapter focuses on textile buyers who work in the retail sector. Most of the material is based on interviews with two buyers, Peta-Gene Goodman, Office Manager, Agal Limited, London and Johan Verbruggen, Haberdashery, Needlecraft and Fabric Buyer, Liberty, London. Various comparisons are drawn between their businesses. There seems no typical route by which individuals enter the textile-buying profession – it is often a role that employees evolve into as they accumulate professional experience in the retail sector. Companies seek different qualities in buyers. Some may insist that an individual has a background in design, business or marketing for the job role, for others it may not be a concern. Formal design training can be a prerequisite for buyers who have creative roles within industry, for example the buyer seeking fabric for garment manufacture. In this case it is probably an asset to be aware of the various characteristics of different fabric types. On the other hand, it is not unusual to find individuals who have worked their way through various roles within the same firm or in a variety of companies, eventually reaching the position of buyer. It seems that on-the-job training is just as valid as a design education background. A case in point is Johan Verbruggen who, after working in various capacities for Liberty, landed the role of buying fabrics:

> Technically, I have no design degree, but this is not a hindrance, you learn on the job all the time, and I think from our point of view here, it's probably an advantage, because if you know an awful lot about the technical side of fabrics you tend to buy a specific sort of material which may be complicated and difficult for customers to understand and use, whereas I go for probably quite easy fabrics to work with which probably makes it a bit more commercial.

The Buyer's Role

Within buying there are many roles ranging from the buyer's assistant or clerk, whose jobs include receiving and marking goods, through to operating as a buying agent on behalf of a number of stores or organizations. The latter generally involves sourcing and researching for the clients and perhaps dealing with the export of goods, often working within critical time frames. Within organizations, buyers are separated into different divisions and so buy for different departments. When buyers travel abroad for a buying trip they may well use a buying office or representative in the host country of their visit. This is the case with Neiman Marcus from the United States who use the services of Agal in Britain: the latter act as an export-buying office. Before the Neiman Marcus buyer is to come to Britain, perhaps for a trade fair or during fashion week, the company inform Agal. The buyer's visit is usually for anything from one to five days, and during this time a schedule of all his or her appointments is arranged with established and possible new suppliers. Agal don't actually do the buying, but source goods right from their origin, which could be from a start-up company or similar business, and then they introduce that company's agent to the buyer. In sourcing items, Agal anticipate what the buyers may want. They also pick out items they believe to be new and of possible interest to the buyers. The final decision as to whether to buy lies with the buyer, who then places the order through the buying office. In effect, such buying offices as Agal act as intermediaries between the suppliers and Neiman Marcus, seeing the buying process right through from beginning to end.

The widespread belief that buyers have glamorous lifestyles is by and large a fallacy, and the degree of travel involved in the job can vary greatly. The more prestigious stores such as Liberty are lucky in that fabric suppliers go to them. Liberty are in quite a unique position, given that people recognize their store for its textiles. Whenever suppliers have new designs, they want them showcased at this particular store. At the other end of the spectrum there are those buyers who travel constantly, which can be taxing and exhausting. It can be a lot of hard work, as over the years the 'season' seems to have got longer and longer, and there are more and more trade fairs and fashion shows to attend. In the United States for instance, the fashion cycle operates on four seasons instead of two, as is commonly the case in Europe.

Issues Affecting Buying Decisions

Trend and prediction information governs and guides buying decisions. However, this is not simply a case of using a trend and prediction agency to provide all the required information. Textile trade fairs such as 'Première Vision' in Paris provide directions to industry, indicating colour, texture and mood choices for the coming season. It is from such sources that in-house studios gather, interpret and organize information for use by their organization's buyers. In contrast to this, there are those organizations which do not consult any commercial trend and forecasting material. Instead, every season they observe what's happening around them, looking through periodicals, newspapers, journals, and generally reading signs within society in order to interpret trends in-house. They then buy based on their own judgements. Peta-Gene Goodman expresses the accuracy of this method of working:

We pretty much find we're in tune with general trends and prediction … If a particular store feels that we need specific buying direction, they'll send us a guide as to colour selection and so on, this happens more in the accessories world than in fashion.

The buyer's or the buyer's agent's highest priority is to meet the needs of his or her client or client's client, which is ultimately the public at large. In addition to buyers' agents perhaps concocting their own particular buying directions, they may also receive some loose parameters to work with. Buyers will send the agent an idea of what they require and what groups they are looking to buy for. The agent then works in relation to those groups. These boundaries are only set as a rough guide so that the agent's selections aren't totally out of sync with the sort of items that the buyer is looking for. As the boundaries can still be quite fuzzy, the agent is able to keep an open mind. Peta-Gene Goodman cites an example of this idea – if they come up with a great item that is not on the trend list they still add it on because they intuitively think that their buyer should have it:

If they think its an item too, then it goes. For instance there was a crazy bag-maker, she made bags out of the tops of jeans and then decorated the denim with all kinds of bits, they were really 'crazy item' bags for real 'Hollywood types'. The buyers came, and said 'We haven't got a lot of money to spend, we're only doing leather bags this season, we're not buying any textile bags'. We said 'We think you should see these'. They saw the bags and said 'fantastic, we'll order them right away'. They know. You get an eye after a while and you know what will sell.

Johan Verbruggen at Liberty reinforces the importance of considering the needs of the client when deciding what sort of textiles to buy:

Our customers don't necessarily have the skills to work with very complicated fabrics. For this reason, it's probably more commercial to keep the fabrics quite simple and user friendly. On balance, my primary consideration is whether it's fit for the purpose it's intended for.

This, in the end, is the reasoning behind why particular fabrics or fabric ranges are continued or discontinued. For example, Liberty in the past have stocked many luxuriously embellished fabrics and complex constructed fabrics, such as Schlaepfer (Langle, 1996: XI–XIII) and Nuno respectively. Problems can arise when fabrics like these become perhaps too technical for ordinary customers to understand and use, so their inclusion as Liberty stock has to be reassessed.

For buyers, profiling the customer and being aware of market changes is extremely important as an indicator to buying habits. A proportion of the Liberty customer base, for instance, demands the classic Liberty print; for the most part, this is the more loyal traditional customer, as opposed to the tourist market. In contrast to this, there is great interest in signature Liberty prints for fashion applications. The stamp of approval from a designer, in itself, stimulates interest in these fabrics for fashion, which is the market that Liberty are aiming for. Endorsements such as these encourage the development of the expensive but exclusive designer end of the market. Their fabric area is already quite design-orientated, stocking Armani and Christian Lacroix fabrics. In fact, though it is not widely known, many of the couturiers, such as Versace, Yves Saint Laurent and Krizia, all do their own fabric by the metre, and more designers are starting to produce fabrics now.

Buyers are sensitive to changes within the market and when they buy, they do so appropriately. They are constantly in touch with what the customer wants. Johan Verbruggen emphasizes this:

> I think people will always want quality and exclusivity: now, what is more exclusive than buying a piece of fabric and having it made to measure by a dressmaker? There is a trend for this now and this is also the reason for developing the designer fabric market. All things considered, if you buy a piece of Armani fabric you are wearing Armani – but it's not widely available. It's not so much about being label-orientated – people want to be quite unique in what they wear. Though they might not make their own garments, they are still very creative in their views as to what they want and how they want to look.

This view is very reflective of current media which focus on how people look and feel; it's about being special, and from the actions of stores such as Liberty, it is a sentiment that is being encouraged. This trend is not unique to Britain; it is typical of advanced consumer societies everywhere. Given this, it appears that for the foreseeable future there will be a need for exclusive fabric departments. When we consider that the fabric areas of large department stores are shrinking, it is perhaps a sign that buyers realize that offering a wide spread of 'normal' fabrics with no exclusive qualities doesn't reflect the shift in what the customer is looking for.

Buying Textiles and Design-Led Textile Products

Both Liberty and Agal are lucky in that sellers approach them quite often. Of the two, the Liberty fabric buyer actually only attends the Première Vision trade fair. He is approached throughout the rest of the year by suppliers from abroad, who have quite a lot of business in Europe and frequently visit with new fabric ranges. As well as this, buying is also done through London-based textile agents who source most of their fabrics from the Middle East or the Far East. Having a constant stream of suppliers from overseas works to Liberty's advantage as they save on buying trips, so increasing their profitability. This is a very different approach to that of perhaps a textile buyer for a fashion chain; in this instance, we can imagine that because of the huge volumes of fabric being considered, these larger chains would probably have working relationships with textile mills throughout the world. Agal have a very different approach to both of the above, since they source a lot of design-led textile products, which involves visiting all sorts of exhibitions and trade fairs, for example 100% Design, Top Drawer, London Fashion Week and Chelsea Craft Fair. They also attend previews and openings at such venues as the Clerkenwell Green Association and Cockpit, both in London. Possibly in Agal's view the only prerequisite for a product is that it is suitable for the top end of the market.

Buyers need a good eye for commercial items and their buying choices are tested by how well their selected items sell in the stores. The job can involve a lot of risk-taking and pressure, and a great deal of responsibility, since buyers are held accountable for decisions that they make. 'Buyers need physical stamina to keep up with the fast-paced nature of their work' (Bureau of Labor Statistics, 2000). The role can be very target-driven, as figures are set for buyers to reach. Sometimes buyers have to make very difficult decisions. For example, as the 'look' of a store changes, and is updated, it is almost inevitable that there will be a product that happens to be a great seller, but is looking tired in the store environment. At this point, buyers would be faced with the difficult task of looking for something to replace that item. It is a huge risk to take and a dilemma that faces buyers. Sometimes it takes a change of buyer to carry the risk and assume the responsibility of such a major decision. The main reason buyers would cease to buy from specific suppliers would be that their goods failed to sell during the previous season. Buyers' product and material choices have to hit the right buttons every time; their choices, when spot on, allow the basic mechanics of the store to operate and make the all-important profit.

When seeking goods for the top end of the market, exclusive rights to a product is one of the main concerns for a store buyer. Therefore, when a new designer is sought, exclusivity is required, in order that the same product is not found within a rival's store. Many buyers and companies are more than willing to work with young or new designers, providing them with opportunities to bring in and discuss their wares. According to the buyers' remit, their expectations in terms of product prototype or fabric samples will vary. In turn designers need to bear in mind that a textile-product buyer will have a very different set of concerns to those of a fabric buyer.

For the most part, a product buyer is interested in seeing quality, finished, items – a range of actual, finalized, product prototypes, rather than drawings or concepts. Having said this, we know that there are also those organizations that develop their own range of design-led textile products in-house. This sort of company is perhaps a little more amenable to viewing proposals and conceptual ideas which a designer may have ahead of producing a prototype, perhaps in collaboration with the company. If showing a product, it is up to the individual designer-maker to complete thorough preparation and research in order to 'sell' the item. This 'theatre of retail' counts as much for producers trying to supply things as for stores trying to sell things. The romance of business has a great deal to do with personality and efficiency: sincerity, confidence, presentation, having prices for what is shown, knowing the product really well, quantities and delivery all count. A buyer may be interested in how the item was made, what the future plans are for the product and the business, how it can be developed, how the product was created and enthusiasm for the work.

The Supplier's Concerns

Research and preparation are of the utmost importance for the manufacturer or maker when meeting a buyer. It is only through research of different market levels that the supplier becomes aware of the position of its product in the retail environment and so is able to gauge its status and viability in the world. It is only after these issues have been considered that the supplier can arrive at a realistic price. If selling an item at the top end of the market, it has to have 'perceived value', which is the price that the customer would most likely pay for the item: if an item looks expensive or luxurious, it can demand a higher price. Pricing concerns are further complicated when considering selling goods abroad. In this scenario, the cost price of an item would have to have any imposed freight costs and duties built in and then an assessment has to be made as to whether the item is still competitive with its somewhat inflated price. Also there are special considerations that may affect cost; for example, some items must conform to importation requirements regarding safety or information labels. Guidelines for prices are generally aligned to what the customer will pay for the goods, and limits are based on that premise: the Liberty customer, for instance, will pay up to £300–£400 per metre for the most luxurious and exclusive of fabrics.

As stated, some organizations encourage and support the concept of working with new designers who do not necessarily have a proven track record. By and large, new independent textile designers are strong in terms of creativity but, sadly, they may lack an awareness of the practicalities involved in manufacturing, production and price points. In considering the retailing of fabric there is much for both the buyer and the supplier to consider. Business sense is extremely important, especially when it comes to resolving the commercial viability of producing fabrics. Pricing is always a sensitive detail to deal with, and to a large degree the volume and method of fabric production both govern the price that is attached to it. As well as knowing whether it is possible for the fabric samples to be produced commercially, the fabric buyer would have to have some information about costings, price points for volume production, suitability of the fabric and colour for inclusion within a range. Then there are all the mundane, general technical criteria for a supplier to contemplate, such as whether the widths produced meet standard industry dimensions and what is a viable 'minimum run' within industry for various sorts of textile production. It is only when suppliers are armed with this information that they can weigh up whether it is cost-effective to produce and supply. In a similar way, only when buyers are convinced of suppliers' information can they begin to weigh up their own financial issues.

International Issues

Each nation has its own views about textiles and textile products. Also, each nation is seen to represent a particular approach to design that results in products having a national identity. Not only do buyers bear these in mind when making their selections from different nations, but they also have to be sensitive to the tastes in the country for which they are buying. National preferences for fabric colour and decoration can vary widely. For example, Malay women will wear amazingly bright, hot-coloured florals that are unseen in Europe. Also, from Turkey to China modern urban and business clothes are sometimes decorated with patterns and embroidery in a style totally unfamiliar to that found in the West. Britain, as representative of the West, is quite sophisticated in its tastes. This probably has something to do with its geographical size, the density of its population and the proximity of its citizens to major towns and cities. All this makes trends and movements more obvious for everyone to see and follow. Moreover, perhaps the sophistication is indicative of the general multicultural nature of British society.

On the textile-supply side in Britain, there is the benefit of a coveted art college tradition. With reference to this, Peta-Gene Goodman points out 'Though it produces not very commercially minded students, it does produce lots of talent. It is very unusual what we have here and we should guard it'. The various associations mentioned are precisely why buyers go to Britain – in order to find mainly British-made items that tend to be interesting, unusual and sometimes classic. On an international level, the products are perhaps more expensive, but there are customers scattered around the world who understand or want this type of item. Alternatively, the appeal of what Britain stands for can add value to a product. The story is different for each nation as to what its products represent culturally, a factor which can be underestimated or overlooked by designers and manufacturers. In the increasingly competitive international market, this appeal can be a valuable asset, adding a further dimension to branding.

For those buying from around the globe, quality assurance is of paramount importance and expectations about quality and standards are universal, no matter where in the world fabric is sourced. The last thing a buyer wants is materials or products that will fall apart after a couple of washes. After buyers have worked for a number of years with specific mills and suppliers, a trusted and effective relationship is formed where standards are set and terms of delivery are established, and before long it becomes quite easy for these parties to work together. Buyers are assured of the service they will receive and suppliers are aware of the quality the buyers desire. The suppliers therefore know they should not allow sub-standard production. It is difficult to escape the issue of money here, as buyers are in the business to make money, hence price point and discount negotiations are an unavoidable part of the buying process. In this context all suppliers must know their lowest price point, that point at which they can still make a comfortable margin of profit.

Economics, politics, trends, the media and ethics all affect buying decisions to some degree. These days it is a worry that the search always seems to be on for the next cheapest place for production, which brings with it fears of workforce exploitation including that of child labour. In an effort to protect themselves from association with such elements, companies such as Neiman Marcus distribute a letter with their shipping instructions, informing their suppliers that they expect the highest standards from the factories where their goods are made, which means that the use of child labour is prohibited. It is a very sensitive issue and manufacturers are aware that such companies as Neiman Marcus can go and check the supply chain at any time they wish. Whenever the tabloids profile a nation in an unfavourable light, perhaps for ethical reasons, the general public by and large will accordingly behave in a politically correct manner, so that people generally won't buy fabric from countries with those associations. Economic and political disruptions within a country are also just as damaging, and trade suffers as a direct consequence.

The Future

As we consider what will shape the future of buying, we cannot ignore the effect of the internet revolution. This has enabled us all to select and consume from any place in the world, so in a sense we can all take on the role of the buyer. But what of its place as a tool for the buyer? Both Peta-Gene Goodman and Johan Verbruggen agree that when it comes to the internet, it is great for initial research, sourcing and reordering. The latter works as long as people *know* already how a product feels, its quality and how it behaves. However, neither Goodman nor Verbruggen believes that there is a substitute for touching and feeling the quality, weight and texture of material, and viewing it in the context of everything else around it. Johan Verbruggen summarizes his view

As a buyer, [I feel that] buying fabric off the internet really wouldn't work at all; the only thing I think it would work for is perhaps buying our own Liberty fabrics. That's the only thing I would consider, but even so, I think people have to be able to feel and drape it over themselves and see what its like before they buy. Internet doesn't work for our business.

One imagines that half the decision to buy textiles and textile products lies in 'feel'. After all, a fabric could look absolutely exquisite, but perhaps feel uncomfortable. Consequently the internet is not yet seen as a serious threat to the business and practices of buying in any way; instead, it is seen as a platform for introducing the profile of a company. Over time the internet will no doubt change the way in which buyers are introduced to (or seek out) potential suppliers. There is an increasing number of internet markets and websites aimed at the professional buyer, including such as www.italianmoda.com/buyers.cfm and www.textileweb. com/buyersguide/.

In a broad sense the future of buying is synonymous with that of retailing. The buyer, representing the retailer, stands in the middle of the cycle of supply and demand, the relationship between manufacturer and consumer. Much of buyers' power is premised on their ability to identify and choose the right product, and their skill is both subjective and experiential. Any changes in the future of retailing that do away with this personal subjectivity and experience will therefore diminish or alter the role of the buyer. There are various reasons to believe such changes are already happening. At the moment buyers have two key roles, one being to sustain or support a retailer's public identity or brand name. They have to buy products that conform to the retailer's image and what we, as customers, would expect to see in their shops or catalogues. The second role of a buyer is to act as a kind of 'pre-shopper': when we buy, *our* choice has been preceded by someone else's choice. In a way, through these roles, the buyer becomes an obstacle to what we might call 'direct consumption', the ability of customers to buy whatever they want from the range of choices they want.

The twentieth century saw significant changes both in the way manufacturers respond to demand and in the way consumers respond to supply. Consumers' 'freedoms' to buy what they want coincide with the wish of manufacturers and retailers to match consumer taste and spending habits more closely. The way in which this can be achieved is through product customization and consumer profiling. These two areas are those most likely to affect the future role of buyers. Customization is about bridging the gap between manufacturer and consumer and, in the process, possibly cutting out the retailer. There are three prerequisites to customization: flexible and short-run manufacturing, good communication, and trading facilities. In the United States the American Textile Partnership (AMTEX) is undertaking a research and development programme aimed at providing a blueprint for the future of the American textile industry, and the notion of flexible manufacturing plays a key role:

> Flexible manufacturing – the ability to rapidly switch from one product to another without sacrificing quality or increasing cost – will enable companies to respond to the short-lived market opportunities created by the electronic marketplace.

> One goal of the flexible manufacturing initiative is to produce custom-ordered, made-to-measure apparel at the cost of mass-produced items and deliver them to the customer within seven days.

(AMTEX, 2001)

There already exist manufacturers who can customize their product and use the internet to sell directly, for example the American towel manufacturer McArthur Professional (www.mcarthur-towels.com), who can incorporate customers' artwork requirements into their products.

Increasingly retailers have needed to increase efficiency in order to remain competitive; they have needed to ensure and increase sales. This has resulted in various initiatives in retail practice, all of which impact on the buyer: for example, more frequent changes of stock in retail premises, warehousing and economies of scale, the increased use of sales and discounting. All of these either increase the number of choices buyers have to make and the volumes they have to buy or expose buyers to a greater chance of failure. In contrast to the hazards of retailing based on buyers' choices and general fashion, consumer profiling is an area that promises guarantees of sales and repeat purchases. The use of computers, databases, credit cards and loyalty cards point to a future of consumer profiles, where our personal tastes are known through our recorded spending habits. Marketing becomes more direct, targeting the individual. There are greater opportunities for niche markets through being able to identify groups of consumers that share idiosyncratic tastes. Overall, by using consumer profiling, retailing shifts from guessing what will sell to knowing what will sell and to whom. While buyers' guesses may prove better than statistical records, for some retailers buyers may become little more than stock controllers.

The politics and technology of shopping are becoming increasingly complex. Tomorrow's buyer may have to deal with new manufacturing and consumer issues as part of their remit. As stated, the conditions of manufacturing workforces now concern many consumers. The internet provides a forum for such concerns and there are growing trends toward organized boycotts of goods or retailers, for example the campaign to support outworkers in Australia organized by the Textile Clothing and Footwear Union of Australia (TCFUA) which has gradually accumulated support (www.green.net.au/textiles). Similarly, consumer profiling may be set to become a major political issue. In the United States the Federal Trade

Commission (FTC) has been asked to consider the data privacy and the consumer affairs aspects of profiling:

> The upcoming workshop also comes in the wake of letters that were sent to the FTC and other government officials in December by U.S. Sen. Richard C. Shelby (R-Ala.), who expressed concern about the Customer Profile Exchange Network, a group of 70-plus companies that has proposed a standard method of pooling and exchanging data on consumer buying habits and other personal information.
>
> (Thibodeau, 2001)

Whatever the future, there will always be shops and stores. We associate shops and retail companies with the type and level of products they sell. These retail identities are important to their marketing success and market visibility. Someone, somewhere, has to choose and develop the concept of what a retailer represents in the marketplace. More than anyone, this is the buyer. There is a broad spectrum within the buying profession: at its best it is highly creative, stimulating business, opening new markets, spotting new talent or new products. Even if the methods and nature of textile buying change, the more creative attributes of buying are indispensable.

–13–

Journalism

For the textile world journalists and journalism represent a key professional group and practice, providing exposure for products, dealing with industry issues and stimulating markets for textiles. Like most modern professions, journalism is experiencing considerable changes in how it is done, where it is done and by whom. Textiles journalism appears in a number of guises. There are specialist textile publications, which can generally be divided into contemporary, historical, craft and industrial categories. There are consumer magazines dealing with homes or fashion, areas also dealt with by television 'magazine' and lifestyle formats. Many of the examples cited will have an internet presence, and there is also an increasing number of web-based and internet 'e-zines' and news services. As well as the consumer and professional interest markets, there is a strong business information sector, both in print and video, which informs the public, shareholders and other journalists about company activities, performance and products. Most sizeable textile companies develop a public-relations wing especially to deal with press releases, creating or protecting company image, or dealing with media and public enquiries.

The Media Industry

Popular textile journalism is stimulated by the public desire for information and entertainment. Textiles are something everybody has to buy and the media and the shopping experience inform their choices. Where there is advanced consumerism, even the thought of spending money and possessing goods become entertainment and vicarious possession is almost as good as the real thing. It is worth remembering this, as – from the media industry point of view – it is the pictures and stories of textiles that make money, not the textiles themselves. The relationship between the textile industry and the media industry is therefore one of symbiosis. Magazines are probably the sector of the media industries that currently most influence textiles and this sector has seen tremendous growth during the last decade. In Britain during the 1990s, reader expenditure on magazines increased 64 per cent in real terms and advertising revenues increased by 30 per cent. Circulation increased by 67 million, indicating a 5 per cent growth and there was a 45 per cent increase in consumer titles. By the year 2000 the British business information sector in total was worth more than £8 billion with 94 per cent of business professionals reading publications regularly and 70 per cent seeing them as essential reading (PPA, 2001). This pattern is repeated variously around the world, and the huge economic returns in the media industry have created a cut-throat climate of mergers, takeovers and expansion.

Emap is a typical example of a major media corporation. Operating in more than nine countries it has more than 6,000 employees, has more than 400 products and holds many of the titles found on magazine racks throughout the world, such as *Arena*, *The Face*, *Minx*, *Elle Decoration* and *New Woman*. In 1996 it abandoned its background in newspaper publishing to concentrate solely on magazines, radio and exhibitions, and has rapidly entered into digital markets and ventured into television. It has consolidated its international activities through purchasing other companies and properties. In 1997 it established Emap Australia, when it acquired thirty or so titles from another publishing company; in 1998 it purchased Petersen Publishing Inc. for nearly £1 billion creating the American Emap Petersen, later known as Emap USA. Most interestingly, in 1999 Emap completely reorganized its British business, reflecting perhaps a new perception of how the magazine and publishing industry was changing. Emap's traditional divisions of Consumer Magazines, Business Communications and Radio were disbanded and replaced by Automotive (cars and bikes), Performance (music), Elan (lifestyle) and Esprit (health) (Emap, 2001).

The rapid growth of much of the media market and the reason for many mergers and buyouts is partly to do with the straight profits from sales. It is also to do with establishing control over information and content and the means of access to it. The media needs information in the form of pictures, stories and so on, since this is what it needs to fill the package whether it is a magazine, CD or website. On the basis of content there is a natural synergy between one kind of media sector and another, so primary ownership of material permits its use in different products and product sectors; hence many media companies will buy out other media companies not only for their holdings but also for their 'archives'. This said, for many publications the 'stories' stay the same but the content changes with the fashions. This can be particularly true for those general consumer publications that deal with textiles, such as the home, interiors and fashion magazines. Stories such as furnishing the first apartment, the first house, the first business suit, the dress 'to die for', 'new talent on the block', are perennial stories and each demographic group has a set and recurrent menu. However, public tastes can change, particularly when there are significant factors such as changes in age, wealth and work. The Japan Magazine Publishers Association has identified seven factors which have influenced magazine publication in the last decade or so: generational change, increase in leisure time, the participation of women in public affairs, developments in internationalization, the blending of genders, from the matcrial age to the spiritual age, the development of multimedia. They also state that their magazine market has concentrated on titles with strong themes liable to ensure a viable readership (JMPA, 2001).

It seems likely that the findings of the Japanese assessment are broadly applicable to the rest of the world, and it is interesting to conjecture what the implications of their analysis for textiles in the coming decades might be. Certainly the increasing independence and empowerment of women, coupled with their increasing financial power, will have some bearing on the nature of women's magazines and those publications which represent idealizations of the home. While such gender issues suggest a harder portrayal of textiles, more designerly, status driven, the other factor of spiritual escape or nourishment seems to suggest the opposite, something less assertive, more personal. Perhaps we will have very serene and beautiful but terribly expensive and exclusive textiles as a result, meeting spirituality and status halfway. This would suit the craft and high-tech ends of the textile market.

Lifestyle and Textile Journalism

The textile professional has access to a wide range of media publications, and the journalistic approaches vary according to the nature of the publication. The technical-, business- and specialist-related aspects of textile journalism tend to be information-rich serving a fixed purpose, and they are sometimes published in the context of other media and information services such as industrial reports and market assessments. Specialist publications can be found for all areas of textile activity: science, design, craft, retail, manufacturing and so on. There are also more generic titles where textiles is just one topic among many. Lifestyle journalism embraces a number of dominant themes connecting fashion and interiors, food and health, life and work. Journalism in magazines such as *Red* and *Living Etc* covers everything from the food we eat to the way our homes should look to the way we should dress. Through cleverly styled photographic shoots and gossipy copy, these magazines incorporate objects such as ceramics and glass, fashion, furniture and textiles. They depict a media image of the way our lives could 'look'. In bringing many disparate strands of design together in a broader context they provide a cultural snapshot useful to maker, seller and buyer. This journalistic model begins to reflect directly the diffusion and fragmentation of the retail marketplace where diversification and 'just in time' retail create 'mall world', a shopping buffet that has everything, but nothing for very long.

Popular lifestyle journalism obviously has a key role to play in relation to public awareness of products but, along with specialist publications, it is also often the basis on which textile designers interpret the market and changes in style. In this kind of publication the role of photography cannot be underestimated, nor can that of styling and art direction in terms of defining image and trends. Many designers seek inspiration from what are already journalists', stylists' and photographers' creative visions although these may in turn simply be recycled approaches: ethnic, bohemian, pure, savage, sexy, romantic and so on. The journalists' lexicon is almost identical with that of the designer's moodboard and the forecasters' predictions. The utilization of past or pre-packaged, media-ready concepts swiftens the pace of the industry and assists in the mechanical synchronization of what are faintly portrayed as the monthly revelations of some mysterious design oracle or muse. Most likely, it is only possible to see significant shifts in fashions and tastes decade by decade, but we desire that our magazines maintain a tone of surprise and excitement, as if each month the design world was reborn. Journalism can entertain through this excitement, which in turn naturally blends with the excitement of design and shopping. The journalist, the creative, the manufacturer, the retailer and the consumer mutually benefit in the publishing environment. It enables designers or companies to gain coverage and promotion while journalists find an almost endless stream of copy to turn into publishing product for their industry.

Throughout this book we have referred to magazines and journals which represent possibly the best and main source of discourse in the world of contemporary textiles. Increasingly the speed and global nature of business may mean that most business textile journalism and information-related services move to the internet. Also many companies now seem to view their corporate websites as a journalistic opportunity. The consumer market, operating on different principles, has no such direct need to abandon paper, although the synergy between journalism, marketing and retail will no doubt find its way into internet shopping. For the ordinary consumer the increasing number of titles is only evident through the shops but there are now also listing sites such as publist.com which describes itself as 'the premier online global resource for information about print and electronic publications'. For the textile professional there are now many textile websites which, as well as often being journalism in their own right, provide leads to specialist publications and publishers, such as Textiles Intelligence (www.textiles intelligence.com) responsible for *Textile Outlook International* and *Technical Textile Markets*.

In order to seek maximum opportunity and remain competitive, the individual involved in the world of textiles needs to recognize and keep abreast of transformations in the material, technological, industrial and creative culture. They need to liaise directly with the media to promote their products and, while they need to be able to identify information or ideas themselves, they will often benefit from journalists' researches and their filtering and summarization of what can often be disparate sources. Publishers also need to have their finger on the pulse, and magazines will have journalists sending in stories from all over the world.

Sometimes people believe that the press and journalists hold power, that they influence choices and directions – this may be so in the political arena: however, the media's main coverage of textiles is as business information or as consumer commodity. The journalist who specializes in or covers textiles is therefore far more likely to simply reflect the interests of the textile community or the public at large. The dependency of this type of journalism on the willing participation of the textile industry and culture is absolute. In turn textiles as a modern industry and culture cannot survive without communication in every sphere and of every type.

The nature of journalism is to reflect circumstances, while the effect of journalism can be far more elusive. Each nation and geographical region has its own demographic and logistical issues which impact on consumer choice, retailing techniques and cultural developments. While certain titles may travel internationally, their content may change to reflect local circumstances; others are bound by national borders and considerations. Necessarily journalists, editors and publishers develop a keen professional eye for the prevailing climate. As Donna Warner, Editor of the American magazine *Metropolitan Home* says:

> We report on what's happening, what's new and thereby hope to encourage and promote awareness of interiors. This interest magazines arouse then stimulates the growth of the home interior industry. And, of course, our readers use the magazine as a personal resource. The designer-maker community in the US is very small and select, perhaps due to the size of the country. Because of the nature of designer-makers and their small production, there would be problems of satisfying demand from the readership of a magazine with our circulation (over 2 million readers). We do feature designers regularly – but not usually textile designers. We feature manufactured designer fabrics. (Warner, 2001)

This sensitivity to national circumstances brings into question the notion that e-zines automatically have a transnational viability. It also raises the question as to what types of information and journalism are truly of international value. The debate reflects an older one raised when comparing regional media with national media. Obviously the jury is out for the verdict. Successful internet information and news services such as just-style.com have a kind of abbreviated journalism appropriate to industry news; to what extent cultural content or shopping needs fit the global internet model is a moot point. Finally there is the pleasure factor, as Donna Warner says of e-zines, 'I don't think they will replace the tactile nature of the magazine'.

Courting Fame

As the media has grown, so has the idea of its manipulation. Simultaneously as the public become more sophisticated about media products, so the communicators try new devices and styles to catch their interest. The result is an elaborate courtship between those who seek to use the media in some way, the media who seek to allure and interest their audience and finally the public who want what they want. For the makers of textile products, whether they are established or new, the hope must always be for good press – the objective is working out how to get it. Marketing is now a sophisticated art, but can still fail miserably. Paying for advertising is a straightforward solution and publishers welcome the revenues, but advertising alone won't guarantee sales. There remains the Holy Grail of becoming a well-known name, inspiring consumer confidence and standing for something. The concept of branding is now well established, and the 'household name' has been with us for well over a century; most modern corporations are sensitive to product and/or company identity. Buying, developing, sustaining or extending the value of brand names is a normal part of modern business. In the design world increasingly, individual designers' names become the brands. Sometimes a 'name' can become so successful it can be used to market other products. Sometimes the 'name' becomes owned and is still in use long after it's original owner lost the right to use it in trading. The media play a key role in maintaining both brands and 'names', having a natural interest in the familiar and celebrity.

Part of running any textile enterprise is developing the press release or the press pack, something to hand over to journalists that clearly describes and illustrates products and highlights any particular features about them. A more sophisticated approach to dealing with the media involves establishing a very strong identity for an individual or a company and their associated products. This type of identity needs to have been thought through as part of a longer-term marketing and development strategy. As forecasting, journalism and design share a common language, company identities, individual designers and products must play the same rhetorical game. The trick that design companies must play is to catch the eye and entice the mind of the sage journalist. While this depends on product it also depends on the 'story' a product or its origin affords. In a sense, in dealing with textile consumer products, the journalist's role is to act as both a guide and as a filter for the general public, to empathize with their interests and contextualize their decision-making. From the maker's point of view it is about gaining the attention of this sophisticated journalist 'consumer'.

Branding can act as a huge asset, as we all identify with and are conscious of labels. Informed textile designers and makers have readily taken advantage of this, and their company names have become synonymous with a definitive house style. Two British design partnerships maximizing their business opportunities through using branding and successfully operating in this way are Bullen Pijja and Eley Kishimoto (Jones, B., 1999a: 52–3); both comprise two designers who have found benefits in joining forces. All started with a background in textile design. The two

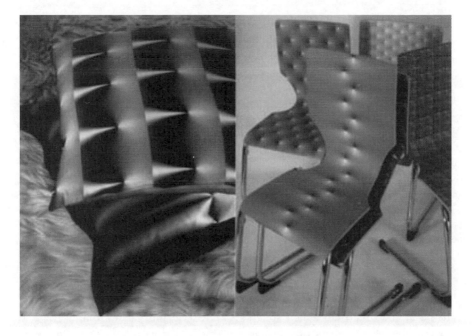

Figure 20. Product shots. Bullen Pijja.

partnerships have since established themselves in the worlds of fashion and interiors, optimizing the return on their names – both as individuals and as a team – branding their design identity which smoothly moves from one medium to another. Bullen Pijja's original technique involved digitally printing computer-generated imagery onto fabric. The direct adaptation of the versatile imagery has been applied to both apparel and interiors, in the form of fashion collections and furniture ranges as well as accessories in the form of scarves to jewellery. The duo's fusion of design histories and theories formulate a distinct style:

> Bullen Pijja are a rare example of real innovation in a market place filled with unsuccessful attempts to jump on the lifestyle design bandwagon. The key to their success lies in the importance of retaining a strong visual image throughout their separate ranges, from kitchen worktops to high fashion, without compromising their originality and edgy style. (*International Textiles*, 2000: 76–8)

Neisha Crossland is another example of a designer who crosses boundaries. Having begun her career as a textile designer, making printed fashion accessories, she now also produces a range of interior products including wallpaper. This type of versatility points toward a general move by many young designers to a more holistic approach which is defined by design 'signatures'. Recognizable signatures, identified with a single designer or small company are ideal for what we might call 'micro-branding'. To the general public, and if successful in the media, a micro-brand can do as much for a small enterprise as a major brand can do for a large enterprise. Exploiting a design ethos and identity for marketing purposes is not a new way of thinking and is not exclusive to young, new design practices, but spans the length and breadth of industry too. For instance, Mikel Folcarelli, International Creative Services, Polo, Ralph Lauren, has stressed:

> Lauren's desire to create 'the climate dream, the best environment imaginable'. Lauren realised the potential of lifestyle shopping and rapidly demonstrated its success all over the world . . . The modern consumer is readily bored by old shop floors and is eager to embrace a new, tailored shopping culture. Design is the all-important factor and to stay ahead of the game companies are looking to adding that personal touch.
>
> (*International Textiles*, 1997a: 30)

The modern textile professional not only needs to keep up with advances in other areas, such as product design, in order to remain competitive but also needs to be alert to the interrelated spheres of lifestyle journalism, marketing and promotion. While much of the material covered here relates to mainstream commercial textile design it is equally applicable to all types of textile work: for example, almost identical circumstances prevail in the relationship between the textile artist and the art press. Increasingly, persons wishing to succeed in promoting themselves or their products must have a clear and compelling story ready to tell, backed up by the goods themselves.

The Internet

As has already been acknowledged, the effects of the internet on journalism are yet to be resolved. What is certain is that the introduction of computers and computing has a tendency to subvert and modify old forms. The changes are not always immediate because technology, while fast, still develops at the rate at which people change their habits. One thing which is quite evident is that currently the Web can create an even playing field where relatively small design outfits can look as substantive as the largest company. Similarly the authoritative voice of the journalist now has to compete with any articulate Webmaster. Journalists and publishing have been gatekeepers and intermediaries between the provider and the public, and while much of their business is based on being a channel through which advertising takes place, another part has been their role in telling us about other people's business. Logically the internet creates a new channel, directly linking business to customer, person to person. Over the next few decades we can expect a gradual expansion of direct representation on the Web, people creating their own stories, selling their own product, perhaps even taking their own advertising. As word processors created new typographers so the internet might create new journalists.

It would be a mistake to conclude that the internet represents the impending doom of such forms as magazines, but it may mean a change in them or in journalism. What is certain is that journalism and its role in relation to textiles will not get simpler, since it cannot retreat to a pre-lifestyle, pre-internet innocence. Contemporary textiles are sold into a market as much defined by the stories of journalism as by the environment of retail, and they will continue to be so. Currently, it seems for many magazine manufacturers that the Web presents an opportunity for an extended advertisement of their product, often offering a free sample or taster as a prelude to inviting subscriptions. These taster sites, such as those provided by *Bobbin*, *Textile Forum*, *Textile Month* and *Textile Industries*, already suggest the possibility that a fully electronic version of their product is not far off. Rather than a commitment to preserving the aesthetic of magazines, it is perhaps only the problem of generating advertising revenues and ensuring subscriptions that restrains magazine publishers from taking the full and final plunge.

(*For more information about journalism and magazines there are various national professional publishing organizations, of which examples include the Magazine Publishers of America (www.magazine.org) whose website includes advertised internships and job vacancies, The Periodical Publishers Association in Britain (www.ppa.co.uk) and The Japan Magazine Publishers Association (www.j-magazine.or.jp). Most nations and most media sectors will have similar organizations.*)

–14–

Science

There are a number of ways in which science and the scientist deal with textiles, ranging from forensics to archaeology; in this chapter the main emphasis is given over to what is often called 'textile science' and how science is involved in the development and manufacture of yarns and fabrics. Modern science is fundamental to the production of both fabric and fabric designs – it is involved in all the traditional textile processes of dying and finishing and the testing and care of yarns and fabrics. Science is also involved in the development of the machinery and equipment used in contemporary textile design and manufacture, including in such areas as aftercare and storage. Finally, science is involved in textile innovation, creating new markets and products and providing new opportunities for business, research and industry. At the level of dyes, yarns and fabrics, science is virtually inseparable from any type of textile activity, whether for art or mass production.

The role of textile science is likely to increase. Many of the future circumstances within the textiles industry will be decided by the substantive impact that science is beginning to have on the absolute basics of textiles. The very idea of what a fabric is and what it can do is beginning to change in a manner without precedent. In a time when fabrics can act as a communication device or as a healing cloth, when weaving and knitting may be replaced by new industrial processes, textiles science presents some breathtaking challenges to the broader textile community. These kinds of change will not only impact on major manufacturers, they will have repercussions throughout the educational sector and throughout the professions that have traditionally been the guardians of textiles.

A Scientific History

The history of science has been closely intertwined with the historical development of textiles. It is worth noting that when we speak of science, we are often referring to the model of science established in the last 500 years. In the popular imagination this recent science has been marked by experimental procedure, hypothesis, a pursuit for accuracy and knowledge as truth. It is also true to say that in the latter half of the twentieth century science increasingly became understood as in various ways fallible or subject to the same broad social issues and influences that affect every other sphere of life (Mulkay, 1979). The relationship between textiles and science reflects this broader role of science in all our social, cultural and industrial activities. In many ways science is both a culprit and a benefactor of textiles. This mature view of science now finds its way into the ethics and politics of contemporary textile design and manufacture. At the same time science leads the way in textiles, establishing new functions and aesthetics.

The history of science in textiles, as some of the following short stories show, includes tales of vision, experiment, observation and pure accident. In 1665, during the great philosophical and scientific era of the Enlightenment, Robert Hooke – using the new techniques of microscopy – studied cells in plants (and indeed coined the term 'cell'), and he suggested the cell walls of plants could be used to make artificial silk; it was to be some 220 years before his vision became a reality. Today artificial man-made fibres are among the staple products of the world's textile industry, produced in all corners of the globe: in the year 2000, the global production of polyester fibre alone exceeded 21 million tons. While vision and methodical science have played their part in the development of textiles, so too have chance and accident. For example in 1856 the eighteen-year-old William Henry Perkins was working in his garden shed, trying to synthesize the anti-malarial drug quinine, and by accident he created the dye aniline purple (mauveine), which subsequently led to a fashion for purple clothing. Again, when Jean-Baptiste Jolly spilt camphene on to a gown in Paris in 1855, the consequent effect (it made the gown cleaner, not dirtier) led him to form the world's first dry-cleaning company. What is certain is that over the centuries thousands of people have played their part in the scientific advancement of textiles, whether by tinkering, observation or deliberate experimental method. The cumulative effect is that now textile science constitutes a significant repertoire of applied science, one that has been put to good effect in the pursuit of textile applications so diverse that they range from aerospace to building to surgery.

The various chemical and physical processes used in the development of textiles obviously predate the era of modern science by some millennia. Dyes such as indigo were used in ancient Egypt as long ago as 3000 BC, and a variety of plants, animals and minerals were known to be sources of fabric dyes. Although expertise was developed to a high level, little change took place until the middle of the nineteenth century when chromium salts were introduced, permitting dyes more resistant to fading. From that time on there were significant developments in the chemistry of dyestuffs. Although the late nineteenth century is famous for the introduction of synthetic dyes such as the mainly yellow or red azo-dyes and the synthesis of such natural dyes as madder and indigo, it is important to remember that chemistry already played a role in conjunction with more traditional dyes. This extract from a practical and vocational encyclopedia of the Victorian era shows how the natural world, labour, international trade, industry and science all contributed to the production of textiles.

The culture of the cochineal insect has extended from the New to the Old World, and it is now produced in India, Java, Algiers, and many parts of Europe. The cochineal insect is small, rugose, and of a deep mulberry colour. It feeds on several species of cacti. These insects are scraped from the plants into bags, killed by boiling water, and then dried in the sun. Those are preferred which are plump, of a silver appearance, and which yield when rubbed to powder a brilliant crimson. It is estimated that 70,000 of these minute insects are necessary to make a single pound of cochineal. In 1868 we imported 35,375 cwt. of cochineal, valued at £588,691.

The red colouring matters known by the names of *carmine* and *lake* are made from cochineal. Cochineal is used for dyeing scarlet, and is employed chiefly for woolen goods. The dye is obtained by fixing the colouring matter of the insect by a mordant of alumina and oxide of tin, and exalting the colour by the action of super-tartrate of potash.

(*The Technical Educator*, 1870)

The Industrial Revolution gave a great impetus to textile manufacturing, stimulating demand for both textile design and science. In the same way the effect of the growth in manufacture and markets in the nineteenth century was to stimulate the application of science around the world. Cellulose (a natural polymer) is found in traditional textile crops such as cotton, flax and hemp; it is also found in wood with another polymer called lignin. In the nineteenth century it was discovered how the components of wood could be chemically separated and then the cellulose be reconstituted to make a fibre and a plastic. The fibre later came to be known as rayon but was initially manufactured under the name Chardonnet silk (after Louis-Marie-Hilaire Bernigaud, Comte de Chardonnet); it was the first commercially produced man-made fibre. The process used gives a good indication of how machines and manufacturing technology were coming to be used in conjunction with fundamental chemistry. Nitrocellulose solution (created by mixing cellulose and nitric acid) was pushed through spinnerettes to create threads, air dried, then chemically reconverted to cellulose (Britannica.com, 2001 (*for the non-scientist this is a useful website; it currently provides an excellent history, overview and explanation of various man-made fibres and industrial polymers including polyamides and cellulosics*)).

The Basics

Market demands apart, the engine that drives the development of new textiles is a combination of chemistry, physics and engineering applied over a series of stages and steps in the construction of textile goods. The stages, simply divided, are the production of a raw material, the creation of yarn, the creation of fabric and, finally, the manipulation and embellishment of fabric.

At the level of raw material, the role of atoms and molecules is key in defining certain basic performance properties. Rather like one of those children's toys where small plastic polygons can be locked and fitted together, the extended molecular structure of materials used in yarns can vary from rigid to floppy and, where there is available space, molecules can combine momentarily or permanently with other molecules or molecular structures of the same or different sorts. The function of this underlying structure influences whether, for example, a raw material is bendy, stretchy or brittle. It can affect the way it responds to heat and light, perhaps making it an excellent thermal or electrical conductor or changing its flexibility if temperatures change. The physics and chemistry mean that energy in the form of heat or light, or chemical presences such as gas, can change the performance or appearance of a material.

The next stage is the creation of yarn. Building on the properties of the raw material used, yarn construction introduces another range of processes that influence the final appearance of textiles. At this stage, chemical and physical properties and appearance are altered by, on the one hand, constructional and engineering processes and, on the other, secondary chemical processes such as dyeing. Contemporary yarn development and manufacture can be a highly scientific, technical and industrial process. Industrial techniques of drawing or pushing out yarns can be used to produce various type of filament, a replacement of historical spinning. Yarns can be coated with other materials such as ceramics or metal to provide new properties such as the ability to survive extreme heat. Sometimes coatings are used to permit the weaving of a special fabric: after weaving, the coating is removed to produce an effect such as a previously impossible super lightweight fabric. Yarns combining different raw materials or combinations of yarns can also be spun, allowing sometimes apparently contra-dictory combinations of properties such as delicacy and toughness.

The relationship between yarn production and fabric production is sometimes planned and explicit in the industrial process, sometimes not. The physical properties of yarn shape and texture will affect the nature of the final fabric. Fabric production may also involve a variety of interim or finishing processes which are dependent on the physical properties of a yarn, such as its tendency to shrink or stiffen or soften. Similarly properties such as adherence to other materials, a property required in bonding fabrics, or the ability of a yarn to react to different dye types or retain colour, become design issues. Yarns can also be altered by the application of chemical or biochemical processes such as the use of enzymes. These types of alteration are often undertaken for design purposes.

The fundamentals of fabric production and construction draw heavily on what is essentially an engineering process, whether it is the traditional techniques of weaving and knitting or techniques which, in the past, we would more readily have associated with the plastics and laminates industries such as rolling and pressing. Creating fabric introduces a whole new range of issues, whether as the production of sheet or planar material, typically lengths of cloth, or as more complex, preformed, industrial components, such as those used in architecture or the aerospace industry. The rich history of cloth, particularly weaving, has left a record and insight into a world of permutations and effects so complex it is almost surprising we would wish to do more. However in a world of new materials and chemicals the traditional repertoire of surface variety, including crinkles, bobbles, crease, stretch and drape, are revisited and played out in a million new ways. The ability of industry to pre- and post-process fabric is brought together with the experimentation of the fabric designer or engineer to introduce sequences of physical or chemical operations on fabric, the sole objective of which is to find new appearance or performance characteristics.

The potential aesthetic and functional variety achievable during the three developmental stages of raw material, yarn and fabric production is immense. However there remain two further stages that traditionally we associate perhaps more with textile design than with science, namely fabric manipulation and fabric embellishment. The traditions of fabric manipulation and embellishment include further craft or industrial processes, for example printing or embroidery, and these too have their own repertoires of scientific and engineering developments. To some extent where these processes begin and end in the overall sequence of fabric production is variable. They may for example involve a working into the fabric, deconstructing it, taking away, 'distressing' (damaging or wearing down) or material substitution. Direct physical interventions in the structure of fabric are primarily derivations of the constructional traditions of embroidery, tapestry and weaving, although chemical processes such as dévoré (a process whereby one yarn is dissolved away and one stays behind), because they deal with liquids, are essentially print techniques. A further advance is in the development of special printing materials and techniques that allow various rubbery or metallic substances to be deposited on the surface of fabrics. In these last stages, having set the scene, science finally gives way to art, craft and design.

The Science–Design Gap

There is a potential gap between textile science and textile design which reflects a famous debate about a growing cultural divide between the scientific and non-scientific communities. In 1959 C.P. Snow, a novelist and scientist, gave the Rede lecture *The Two Cultures* and published two books relating to it (Snow, 1993); in them he argued that practitioners from the scientific and literary worlds knew little about each other and that communication between them was almost impossible. His thesis, though widely argued and contested, has developed into broader debates about divisions between the arts and humanities on one side and the sciences on the other. The kinds of issue which have arisen include the inadequacies and limitations of science and the dismissive arrogance of the arts. For those who work in and with textiles, where both the sciences and the arts are omnipresent, it is a pertinent debate rarely addressed.

Science is an important creative resource in the development of textiles. Science can span and influence the artistic, engineering and manufacturing aspects of textiles; but how can designers participate in the creativity science affords? The answers become increasingly difficult for the non-scientist to understand. Much of the future progress of textiles will depend on techniques, knowledge and methods well beyond the traditional craft origin and scope of textile design and construction. Both the way fabric is designed and the way it is used may require scientific knowledge. Many future textile products will require specialized engineering knowledge to make them. For example, the future design and production of clothes may become as complex a process as automotive design, requiring a design approach much more like that of industrial design or engineering.

Education, and collaboration between industry and education, may prove fundamental to resolving a science–design gap. Around the world the scientific aspect of textiles is given varying weight in the educational sector: in some institutions it is an essential and fundamental part of the textiles curriculum, in others it is not present at all. In some countries textile science and textile design are treated as quite separate subjects taught on specialist courses. There are various potential solutions for the future, such as increasing teamwork approaches to design and manufacture or perhaps the emergence of intermediaries whose role is to 'translate' and communicate between the different professional communities involved. The science–design gap may provoke a radical rethink of textiles education; as the science of textiles grows more complex there will undoubtedly arise different perceptions and definitions of what a textile 'designer' is, and in some instances terms drawn from engineering and science will be just as pertinent as terms drawn from art and design. Some textile designers may ultimately prefer to abandon the term 'designer' altogether, seeing it as a misrepresentation of their work or having the wrong connotations.

Whatever the outcome, textile users and product developers, whether for clothing, interiors or any other sector, will need to develop strategies to cope with increasingly complex performance- and construction-related issues. Market analysts, buyers and journalists will have similar problems interpreting the special characteristics and value of new textile products. For anyone who underestimates the science–design gap they are advised to look at a project currently being undertaken at Hong Kong Polytechnic University to develop intelligent thermal-management apparel (Li, 1999). On their website some seventy relevant publications are listed covering a breathtaking range of practices and knowledge, from ergonomics to consumer analysis to physical sciences. In such projects the relationship between science and the creative nature of design are not mapped out, and there is no simple clue for non-scientists spelling out how they might intervene in, or interpret, such advanced and technological projects.

The Stuff of Fiction

Modern fabric has certain basic potentials, and can for example be strong in one dimension and weak and giving in another; it can be a skin-like membrane or as open as a net; it can be permeable or impermeable; it can be saturated with chemical or other agents; in its construction other materials such as metals can be incorporated adding their properties to the fabric. As the field of science and technology has developed and found application in all spheres of human endeavour, fabric and textiles are always present as a possible solution to a problem. Hence modern textiles find a place in disciplines as diverse as medicine, architecture and building, electronics, agriculture, aerospace, clothing of all kinds, furnishing, the military, manufacture and industrial processes. The list is fairly endless and the result is, perhaps, that fabric becomes a tool, a raw and intermediate resource, for many disciplines. Two conclusions can be drawn from this. The first is that textiles is as much about these new spheres of application as it is about its traditional uses in clothing and interiors. The second is that areas such as fashion and soft furnishings are increasingly influenced by the textile discoveries in these newer technological and scientific spheres of application.

The website www.technical-textiles.net provides an index to articles from the journals *High Performance Textiles*, *Technical Textiles* and *Medical Textiles*, and the index itself contains more than seventy categories on textiles from abrasion-resistant materials to wound dressings; it outlines hundreds of textile innovations. Some of these innovations seem logical developments of the types of aspiration so often revealed in science fiction, so for example 'a music keyboard that can be rolled up'. Others are practical developments of or substitutes for products which already exist, for example a fabric hinge which is 'inherently corrosion resistant, unlike its conventional counterparts'. On occasion (and out of context) some entries are even amusing: 'inventors have developed a bra lining which they claim provides a therapeutic massage'. An overall appraisal of the entries shows how miraculous and transforming many modern uses of textiles are: 'using embroidery technology, Swiss researchers have developed textile scaffold structures for tissue engineering'. Other example applications and inventions are as diverse as antibacterial and antiviral fabrics; biodegradable cigarette filters; the use of shape-memory materials in clothing; and new tensioned textile structures in architecture.

There are now worldwide a number of websites which provide this kind of technical and scientific information, some interpretable only by specialists. Some are related to professional organizations or state agencies, for example http://

nvl.nist.gov the National Institute of Standards and Technology website, part of the United States Commerce Department's Technology Administration. Others are provided by companies as part of their corporate web presence. Sometimes these have been specifically created to easily communicate what the company does or the nature of its product: for example, Trevira offer a downloadable PDF data file about chemical fibres, including their chemistry, their structure, how they are made and their aftercare, from www.trevira.de. Cognis is another such example and provides other services from its website such as sample or literature ordering, www.cognis-us.com.

The WWW and the internet seem, in various ways, to have radically altered the availability of scientific knowledge about textiles, making it both increasingly accessible and comprehensible. Partly this seems to be a consequence of the fact that information industries and service companies need to have a lot of information available to be a plausible contender in the volatile internet market. As a result, such companies as About.com can provide websites that combine sophistication with broad mass appeal, no doubt hoping to satisfy the school student, the browser and the businessperson, in fact the broad middle ground of information needs. An article by Bruzel demonstrates how a little potted history about textiles can be combined with a popular commodity such as stonewashed denim blue jeans (and how to fade them without using stones) and finally some hard-nosed science:

> The enzyme used is cellulase, which is obtained from several species of fungi, although bacterial cellulase is also available. The beta-(1-4)-glucosidic linkages of cellulose are randomly hydrolyzed by this enzyme. Cellulases from different biological sources are capable of additionally hydrolyzing other linkages in cellulose, for example, the beta-(1-3) and beta-(1-6) bonds.
>
> (Bruzel, 1999)

Similarly, the internet provides scope for the relatively anonymous (or at least non-corporate) presence, or uncertain origin, of individual websites which provide authoritative and incisive delivery of scientific history, textile chemistry and textile physics, for example that provided by Gernot Stangl at http://xarch.tu-graz.ac.at/home/gernot/skin – at Stangl's website everything from an explanation of gore-tex to a genealogy of textiles to the tensile strength of kevlar can be found. The general change in the availability and visibility of textile science is bound to have some influence upon the cultural perception of it and on the community with potentially both a stake and an interest in it.

Kiekens makes the point that within a decade, up to 90 per cent of textile products currently made in Europe will be made more cheaply elsewhere. He particularly expresses concern about what should replace the current output, the nature of textiles education, and the dwindling appeal for European youth of textiles manufacturing (Kiekens, 2000). He goes on to state that 'The textile future in Europe is for engineered, multifunctional textile materials' and proceeds to list what amount to the textile sectors founded on high technology and science, such as interactive textiles, biomaterials, space textiles and so on. This relationship between 'scientific textiles' and the identification of niche markets as a survival strategy finds echoes elsewhere, in fact wherever conventional textile manufacture has moved to 'off-shore production'. For some commentators science is not so much a weapon of industrial survival as a positive spur for new business and economic growth. Keynote speaker at the Eighty-First World Conference of The Textile Institute, Dr Ann Whitaker from NASA, predicts that research into space textiles will boost the textile industry in the twenty-first century and beyond, providing solutions for space travel and spin-offs to the military and others.

For the individual consumer the effects of textile science may be rather more subtle and low-key than space colonization or global economics, but nonetheless beneficial. In a paper for the 1998 Institute of Physics Annual Congress in Brighton, England, John Chubb reports on the development of a test protocol to stop or reduce electric shocks when getting out of an automobile. The cause, it seems, is dependent on the choice of seat fabric and the way it interacts with clothing:

> Getting out of a car can easily create body voltages of up to 15kV and give a very noticeable shock when the car or earth is touched . . . body voltage can be effectively limited to below shock levels by choice of seat material. (Chubb, 1998)

By appropriate use of scientific method it is hoped that the most reliable and economic solution (one to deal with all the variables of what people wear) can be found.

While we are used to the portrayal of science as being at the vanguard of our culture and industry, it is best to remember that many of its applications are in the sphere of everyday life, aimed at very practical solutions of ordinary problems both great and small. It is also the case that in spite of the complexities of science and its application, individuals can still make their mark. So for example the work of Dr Sally Hasselbrack, the first woman to achieve the Boeing Corporation's highest technical engineering award and become a Boeing technical fellow: from a background in textile science and competing in the world of the 'glass ceiling' (or as Hasselbrack calls it a 'male bastion') she went on to make major changes in the use of textiles, changes which have contributed to air passenger safety throughout the world:

> Dr Hasselbrack set up Boeing's textile and flammability lab. Initial research reduced the weight of airline textiles without compromising service life, which decreased industry costs. Further research identified a less toxic flame-retardant finish leading to FAA fire

safety compliance. Hailed as a landmark fire safety initiative, Sally pioneered textiles used as fire barriers on passenger seats. These findings were used to retrofit the US airplane fleet in 1984 with seats required by the FAA.

(Minnesota, 2000)

Future Issues

The effect of science on textiles is to push it into a much broader modern category of meshes, nets, membranes and skins. Increasingly the traditional roles for textiles, for clothing or for interiors, only represent one part of their potential applications. More recent markets such as those in medicine, architecture, engineering and electronic goods represent growth sectors for the textiles industry. This does not mean that the clothing and interior markets will diminish, but simply that these newer markets have considerable potential for development through exploring new products, techniques and applications. As a result of this new research, the nature and performance of textiles and fabrics will also develop (Black, C., 2000b: 58). We can expect to see new aesthetic and functional properties. It is also possible that techniques of product fabrication and construction used in other disciplines find their way into fashion or interiors. In a way we are already used to the fact that developments in one area of textiles can affect those in another. For example, fabric developed for industrial clothing or sportswear is now a hunting ground for the fashion designer. Special performance-fabrics such as those which are heat-resistant, water-tight, air-tight, luminous or fluorescent have, in general, not been developed initially for cosmetic purposes but can be adopted and adapted. New developments may affect traditional manufacturing and design processes. Cutting, stitching and tailoring may give way to the increasing use of robot welding or preformed products. Weaving, knitting and embroidery may give way to genetically engineered or chemically 'grown' fabric. We cannot forecast the future entirely but from what we already know of the past of textiles, we know that it will have roles in soft engineering, in reinforcement and in protection, some of the most basic ways we intervene in our material environment.

Many of the technological and scientific developments in textiles point the way to increasing fusions within our constructed 'world' of consumer goods. As much as textiles start to become integral parts of household electronic appliances or building construction, so many electronic goods and their functions will find their way into the traditional arenas of clothing and furniture. The incorporation of the mobile or cell phone into clothes and furniture is already nothing remarkable; soon perhaps, through our clothing, we will carry a second identity with us wherever we go, our clothes becoming a means of integration into a 'smart' urban or interior environment. For example the recent Echarpe Communicante (Communicating Scarf) developed by Naziha Mestaoui, Yacine Ait Kaci and Christophe Beaujays with France Telecom R&D/Studio Creatif, or the collaboration between Philips and Levi's to produce the 'Industrial Clothing Design' (ICD+) range (www.pcc. philips.fr). Such thoughts and possibilities and the research for them have been around for some time (Tebbutt, 1991). What is pointed to is a future of hybrid products, where the base functions of conventional electronic-product archetypes, sound, vision or computing, are mapped onto the world of fabric products or vice versa where the weight, flexibility, strength or comfort of fabric is incorporated into consumer or other goods. In the longer term such developments raise interesting questions, for example about what kinds of communication or information-content develop (Amidon, 1999: 38–43) when they are potentially omnipresent in our clothes and in our furniture, and indeed wherever we are?

At the level of the mass market, and perhaps in other sectors too, these changes and innovations will increasingly blur the distinction between the professions of textile designer, clothing designer, product designer, industrial designer, engineer and scientist. The conclusion is that the era of post-industrial design is upon us already, stimulated by science, technology and a cultural hunger for its benefits. There will also be significant pressures for new techniques of managing the design process and its role in industry and commerce. Multidisciplinary teamwork and interdisciplinary knowledge are key requirements in the task of creating new products and new markets, which in themselves are seen as a key to economic survival and development. Against this background, what constitutes a textile specialist is no longer as clear as it was even half a century ago. The potential for uncertainty that textile science and research stimulates, coupled with an already shifting industry, creates issues about training, skill sets and career paths for those involved with textiles.

The final observation of the scientific future of textiles brings us full circle, back to the original and intimate relationship between textiles and the body. We might first reflect on the correspondence and coincidence of many of the aspects and fantasies of modern culture: the use of clothing as expression of identity, fetishism, body modification, cosmetic surgery, cyborgs, androids, the pursuit of youth and longevity. These all in some way represent arenas of intervention in our bodies, their appearance and even their performance. Each in its own way is culturally significant or culturally central. When they are considered in conjunction with various developments in textiles, particularly medical textiles, textiles for therapeutic purposes and hybrid electronic/textile products, it is possible to see that there is a future role for the subject of textiles as potentially disturbing or optimistic as, for instance, the future role for genetics and genetic engineering. The natural consequence of new technology and scientific discovery must be in the end to extend the influence of textiles, making them increasingly pervasive at both a micro and a macro level. The intimacy that has traditionally existed between people and textiles may enter a new order, a further outcome of our scientific evolution.

–15–

Research

Research forms a part of any modern professional practice. Each of the textile disciplines, from textile art to textile science, undertakes research of one kind or another, looking for inspiration, techniques or new products and markets. It isn't feasible in this book to cover each category of textile-related research, so in this chapter special focus is given to a range of professions which are, in a way, outside and looking in on textiles. These professions provide us with insights into the value and history of the textile industry and they do much to promote textiles culturally. Some of the professions and industries outlined also represent alternative career routes for those who start with a more practical interest in textiles. Covering academic disciplines such as archaeology, history, anthropology and cultural studies, this chapter also includes such related industries and professions as tourism, entertainment, museology and curatorship. Each area provides different insights about textiles and the people who use and make them. Together these areas, industries and professions form a significant and influential group who, much like journalists and buyers, have vested interests in textiles but are not engaged directly in its production. They affect textile practitioners and industry, in terms both of practice and ideas and of their influence on the economic environment surrounding textile production.

Archaeology and Anthropology

Two academic disciplines that play a very special part in our knowledge of textiles are archaeology and anthropology. In the study of historical textiles they often go together and to the non-specialist it can sometimes be confusing as to where one begins and the other ends. The *Concise Oxford Dictionary* (Sykes, 1976) defines archaeology as the 'Study of human antiquities, especially of the prehistoric period and usually by excavation'. Anthropology is a somewhat more recent and complex discipline concerned with the 'biological, prehistoric, linguistic, technological, social, and cultural origins and development of mankind' (Bullock and Stallybrass, 1977). Anthropology, in concerning itself with early models of society, and dealing with tribes and peoples, has much in common with sociology. What archaeology and anthropology permit is the opportunity to unearth, preserve or record textiles, which are historical either by virtue of their age or by their form. They also allow for the investigation of textiles technology and practices, the lives of those who made textiles and the cultural roles and significance of textiles. Most of our knowledge of ancient textiles is based on painstaking and methodical research, sometimes using advanced scientific techniques such as radiocarbon-dating to accurately measure how old something is, or electron microscopy to study and identify the fibres used. The design and symbols employed in fabric can also be interpreted by listening to local folktales and beliefs; sometimes the cloth itself can provide knowledge about an early society's customs and beliefs.

One interesting area of research concerns the origins and age of textile practices. There is roughly some 10,000 years of evidence of the existence of textiles, although there is no reason to believe that it might not be considerably older still. Archaeology and anthropology show us that during the period of the Upper Palaeolithic, some 35,000 to 17,000 years ago, there was an explosion in human technology and cultural activity. Apart from tools for hunting, scraping and grinding, there is evidence throughout the world that ancient peoples practised body adornment using beads and shells, and also had knowledge of such colouring materials as ochre and hematite (Jurmain and Nelson, 1994: 484–5). Some finds are of particular interest to the textiles community, for example what appear to be bone needles found at Upper Cave, Zhoukoudian in China (Ibid.: 485–6). When and how fabric first made its appearance is lost in the past, since in general textiles have not been sufficiently robust to survive great lengths of time. Certainly though, 10,000 years ago materials for spinning had been identified and many great and ancient civilizations later came to be associated with a main fibre, Egypt with flax, India and Peru with cotton, China with silk and Mesopotamia with wool (STNews, 1998).

The use of animal skins for warmth, a practice so old its start cannot be dated, in some way logically precludes the idea that the first cloth was made for items of clothing. Basketry, twining and rope-making on the other hand have much in common with weaving and it might be that the first weaving was to make containers and holders. Mozaffar Alikhani claims that spinning and knitting activities in Iran date back to the eighth or tenth millennium BC, and among various evidence he provides:

> The objects found in Kamarbandi cave in Behshahr (Mazandaran Province) which belong to the sixth millennium BC indicate that spinning thread out of sheep wool and goat hair was common at that time (Alikhani, 1998)

He goes on to state that pieces of knitted fabric from the fourth millennium BC have been found in the city of Shush and explains that ancient Iranian books and poems indicate the Parthians were the first people to weave, knit and spin in that region. Similarly, finds have been made in Anatolia in Turkey in the ruins of a large prehistoric settlement at Chatal Huyuk, where the archaeologist James Mallaart found pieces of charred cloth dated back to the sixth millennium BC.

What remains today are various samples resembling fragile wrapping canvas. The experts who analysed these fragments discovered that the threads had been carefully and regularly woven and that the fibres had been meticulously prepared before spinning. The well and evenly woven cloths showed no signs of hasty preparation or inadequate techniques, and had no less than 30 threads per inch in the weft, and 38 in the warp, directions.

(DuPont, 2000)

Such research, as well as telling us about when textiles started, also reveals something of the people who made them and how widespread such practices were. There is an implication that fine weaving indicates settled and established societies with well-organized routines. Finds such as those found in North Africa and the Middle East are not restricted to any particular part of the world; one example from North America also demonstrates the impact of new technologies on archaeological practice. For almost sixty years a mummy excavated from caves in Nevada's Churchill County was believed to be only 2000 years old, but radiocarbon dating finally revealed its origin to be nearer to 7420 BC. Various artefacts were found in the caves, including textiles:

The style of weaving used in the textiles, known as diamond-plaited matting, marks the earliest stage in North American weaving technology. 'People were more settled than we thought', says Dansie, noting the time it must have taken to gather the fibers and weave them into mats. (Asher, 1996)

By the second and first millennium BC, textile production had become a highly sophisticated process and art form in various parts of the world. It is a period when, in many cultures, textiles reached a high cultural status rarely, if ever, achieved since:

The textiles of ancient Peru . . . represent the acme of their culture's artistic achievement . . . just as painting and sculpture . . . are considered to be the most potent expression of modern Western aesthetic systems . . . so were textiles the pinnacle of aesthetic production in pre-Columbian Peru. (Rovine, 1997)

Deeply implicated in the social, political and religious lives and rituals of communities, the artistry of textiles is also a sign of the labour involved in its production, while ownership of elaborate textiles is a sign of power, wealth and status:

People of high status were buried wearing richly embroidered mantles, lace-like woven tunics, shirts bordered with bands of brilliantly patterned fabrics . . . The labor force required to produce textiles was immense, each step in the process being performed by experts. (Ibid., 1997)

There is a great deal of material to be found on ancient and pre-historic textiles, much of it in specialist journals and books for the anthropologist and archaeologist. While for some the facts and discoveries are exciting enough on their own, it would be foolish to presume that *the study of the old* is somehow locked in the past itself. The detective stories of archaeology, for example, make compelling television shows. Through anthropology, history is revisited, and the debates of our times are turned to meet and re-evaluate the historical record, no more so than in Elizabeth Wayland Barber's compelling account of the interplay between the status of women, textiles and our cultural and industrial evolution (Barber, 1991 and 1994). Nowadays commercial data agencies such as STN and public and private textile organizations and museums offer online access to large amounts of historical information, allowing researchers of all kinds to glean practical clues and information from past textile knowledge.

Textiles, Cultural Identity and the Culture Industry

As time has progressed, the historical record of textiles (the number of artefacts and documents) has increased, and so have the continuities and connections to our own times. We can identify with the textile artefacts, through the manner in which they were made, the location of their making, and the type of imagery they employ. They speak to us of our cultures, our heritage and our identities. This relationship between textile history, contemporary culture and contemporary identity strongly lends itself to the requirements of some very modern industries – tourism, entertainment, design and marketing. It also means that textiles history becomes part of broader industrial and social equations such as regional and national identity, cultural policy and education. This has stimulated extensive research activities involving the study of past and existing textile industries and crafts, attempts at regenerating or developing new textile businesses, and finally finding new social and industrial roles for textiles. In such research, textiles may only constitute a part of the overall picture, being grouped with other crafts or creative industries. The varieties of research involved can be quite complex, combining economic analysis and evaluation of markets with broad reflections on the role of culture. Equally, research can be very focused on solving particular regional problems or assisting disadvantaged groups to help themselves.

Throughout history there has always been a complex relationship between international power, trading between nations and cultural identity and values. The economic development of Asia and the resultant shift in global economics have forced many Asian commentators to consider the value of their indigenous culture, both as something to be sold overseas and also, perhaps, as something to be preserved during a period of rapid modernization:

> On the one hand, the diversity of cultures should be respected and the equality of cultures should be accepted. On the other hand, the general trend of the integration of global economy is also to be recognized. Interdependence and interrelatedness are a trend of the times. The globalization of the economy may promote the fusion, cooperation and development of different cultures but it should not and could not eradicate completely the differences in cultures.
>
> (Gong, *c*.1995)

In parts of the world such as Western Europe, much indigenous culture has long since given way to the power of consumerism, the service sector industries and the media. People look to buy whatever they respond to, or what is in fashion. In general, craft traditions are no longer practised and regional communities that might have sustained them have dispersed. Local culture becomes replaced by the output of new creative industries. For example, the British government identifies creative industries as the fastest-growing industrial sector with revenues of almost £60 billion and employing almost one and half million people. Increasingly, around the world, textile and design styles are not in step with geography or language: through new media, the cultures of the world are all on offer.

Ironically, at the same time, the culture industries become an increasingly important part of national economies, the cultural heritage of regions playing a key part in tourism and the branding or reputation of their creative industries. Consequently people attempt to create fictions of artistic continuity or to keep a hold on the marketable past. Against the background of this complex and unfathomable set of social and economic changes, human nature often reacts in a very ordinary way, creating sentimental associations with the past, with the lives of our parents, our grandparents and our forebears. As nations and international organizations react to the onset of what looks like a new and uncertain world order, tension is indicated between an adherence to the past and the prospect of the future. This has stimulated much research into the area of cultural policy and its formation, with most countries developing explicit policies about such issues as state funding. Funding is seen both as a stimulus for creative work and as a way of increasing the cultural life of communities, but it is also seen as a way of protecting indigenous art forms. Latvia, which identifies textiles in its cultural policies, adopts such approaches:

> ensure diversity of cultural life, supporting those branches and manifestations of culture, which cannot be ensured by the free market, but without which sound spiritual life of society is impossible (Latvian Ministry of Culture, 2001)

In 1998, Sweden hosted a UNESCO conference *The Power of Culture* with some 2,400 participants representing 149 governments, 23 inter-governmental organizations and 135 other agencies:

> Its point of departure was the new light on the interactions between culture and development shed by the World Commission on Culture and Development in the report entitled *Our Creative Diversity* which it submitted to UNESCO and the United Nations in November 1995. The Commission underlined that '*when culture is understood as the basis of development the very notion of cultural policy has to be considerably broadened*'. (UNESCO, 1998)

Professor Nestor Canclini, in an extensive and fascinating paper, points out many of the complexities and sensitivities involved when individuals or the state attempt to rationalize their 'culture' and see it as something in which they can trivially intervene. Speaking of some African, Asian and Latin American artists, their desire to be modern, and their sense of national identity, he remarks:

> Some of them were confident that international avant-garde innovations could be integrated into local cultures; others considered that symbolic 'customs' mechanisms should be set up to block foreign encroachment, and that the resources of each nation should be invested in strengthening their independent progress. Taken to extremes, these options proved unworkable for the technological, economic and symbolic restructuring of cultural markets. (Canclini, 1998)

For textiles, the ramifications of issues such as these are in such areas as the preservation of indigenous craft traditions, which increasingly come under economic pressure and disappear. Alternatively they have a bearing on the ownership of 'ethnic' textiles and their appropriation by modern designers and manufacturers – for example, the way in which some Australian aboriginal artists have protested over the use of aboriginal motifs and design by other countries and races. However, sometimes the outcomes can be more positive in bringing new life and opportunities to hard-pressed communities. In Bolivia some remarkable work has been undertaken by ASUR (Antropólogos del Surandino), The Foundation for Anthropological Investigation and Ethno Development. Its mission is to encourage the indigenous artistic and handicraft production of the peoples of the Southern Andes with a view to generating employment, revitalizing their cultures and strengthening tourism. Most of their projects involve weaving and tapestry, drawing on ancient local traditions. Practical business projects, such as those undertaken in Potolo, exploit the availability of museum resources and research expertise:

Figure 21. Weave from the Tarabuco Textile Project, Southern Andes. Courtesy of ASUR.

Weaving techniques recovered from the pre-Columbian era are being used. These tapestry-makers are the only ones in the Andean region who are reviving and continuing the practice of these ancient techniques. The group is composed of 16 weavers whose success in this enterprise is inspiring others to undergo training. These weavers are passing these techniques to weavers in other communities within Tarabuco. (ASUR, 2001)

The policy of ASUR is that local economic development is inseparable from local cultural context, and that craft production and craft values will prove a key element in stimulating other developmental opportunities. The projects undertaken by ASUR demonstrate how textiles, cultural policy, anthropology, business and economics can be interdependent when it comes to real world problems.

Museums and Collections

One particular section of the cultural industries brings together such institutions as textile museums and galleries and such research disciplines as history, critical and cultural studies, and museum studies or museology. The practice of history and the nature and purpose of museums both underwent significant changes during the twentieth century. There were shifts in how history should be perceived and portrayed, and shifts in why and how museums are created and sustained. For textiles these changes have made a difference to the public's perception of the subject. In earlier times and in particular during the nineteenth century, museums were often a matter of civic pride, company pride or personal aggrandizement. The practices of collecting and classification informed the way in which collections of artefacts were displayed and exhibited. Nowadays, for a whole host of reasons, textiles are often exhibited in context, portrayed as part of some social routine or moment in time. The study of history has changed too, reflecting the evolution of political thought and the social concerns of our times.

While ancient textiles might be in short supply, there is an abundance of historical and world textiles, providing ample opportunity for their study (Harris, 1993, Schoeser and Rufey, 1989, Welters, 1999). In most countries there are organizations and interest groups that study historical textiles (often by discipline or medium or period, sometimes textiles in general). Such studies are part of the remit of the Textile Society of America (TSA). It has about 500 members, many being major museums and universities (http://char.txa.cornell.edu/zbs/webdocs/tsa/tsahome.htm). There is also a sufficient turnover and interest in textiles to stimulate a small but thriving network of specialist, commercial, textile galleries throughout the world. For example the *Textile Gallery* in London stages exhibitions of historical textiles, primarily from East, Central and Southern Asia but some European too. Gallery activities are run alongside a publishing operation and consultancy work (www.textile-art.com). Specialist commercial enterprises often use scholarly knowledge and examples of textiles as part of their promotional and sales activities, incidentally providing rich sources of information or inspiration for browsers, the company *Tapestries and More* being an excellent example (www.tapestries.cc). Computing, the internet, and virtual reality are having a substantive impact on the commercial, educational and organizational aspects of museums, galleries and their collections. New technologies permit levels of access to museum holdings not possible before, and they also create demands for more information and more sophisticated techniques of presentation. Finally, they provide access to research activities and materials, create greater links with education and create links to new audiences which could not be physically reached before.

The 'virtual' presence of museums can be a great leveller, creating some parity between small focused museums and galleries and much larger national institutions and textile collections. One such example of a smaller museum is the old jute mill *Verdant Works* in Dundee, Scotland. The museum, part of the Dundee Heritage Trust, is an example of how, as the textile industry has moved around the world, it has left remnants of its existence in the shape of factories, mill towns, machinery and folk memories. Graced with a well designed website (www.verdant-works.co.uk) and a compelling, sometimes harrowing story to tell, *Verdant Works* fulfils both tourist and local educational functions as well as reaching a worldwide audience. Such museums employ the more recent research disciplines of industrial archaeology and industrial history and often benefit from the availability of a photographic record. A combination of sensitive restoration, reconstruction and historical documentation retrieves textile history and puts it to a new economic and cultural use. Britain has a number of such sites from the Industrial Revolution and before, but their past grimness has given way to an archaeological variety of beauty,

Figure 22. Sack sewing flat. Photographer Soutar. Courtesy Dundee Heritage Trust, Verdant Works.

entertainment and education. It will be interesting to see if the often charmless factories of modern textile production find a comparable destiny.

Another example of a specialized textile museum, but this time based around a collection, is *The Calico Museum of Textiles* in Ahmedabad, which holds one of the finest and most extensive collections of hand-made textiles in India. Founded in 1949, it contains examples of rare and exquisite woven, painted, printed and embroidered fabrics (Morrell, 1999). In a telling narrative about the aesthetic sensibility of the museum, B.N. Goswamy describes it as a peculiarly Indian museum 'and embodies ways of seeing, and of establishing relationships, that are most appropriately rooted in the culture from which the objects it houses come'. The *Calico Museum* provides a good example of how the physicality and sensations of an actual museum visit will continue to defy a virtual one. This is something that will most likely always remain true of textile collections, the presence of which can range from the drama aroused by strong use of colour and imagery, to the almost imperceptible realms of texture best experienced through touch

> The display suddenly bursts upon one, the riches taking one's breath away, and we are close to having what explorers and archaeologists refer to as 'the cave experience'. Once the eyes adjust to the light inside the galleries, all that one has to do is to stand there and soak in the sensation, allow oneself to be laved in colour and pattern and honest texture, while those wonderful tents and awnings, saris and patkas, pichhavais and 'Palampores', phulkaris and soznis and rumals, whisper softly about the past and keep picking up resonances from one another. (Goswamy, 1998)

As well as exclusively textile museums, there are of course some truly great collections of textiles, based in major international museums and benefiting from all the resources that large organizations can provide. Such collections are often a great source of inspiration to contemporary textile designers and manufacturers. The link between the past and the present is nowhere better exemplified than in the work of the Antonio Ratti Foundation, which originates in the founder's desire to harmonize the artistic, cultural, economic, and industrial components of the textile field. The Ratti group designs and produces seven collections of womenswear a year, originating over 3000 designs and 9 million metres of fabric. During the 1960s Antonio Ratti started collecting ancient fabrics, and from this start the Foundation has developed to become a major player in textiles research and conservation, its activities now extending to textiles publications, conferences and training. It also encourages avant-garde and innovative research in the visual arts. Two of the major projects supported are the Antonio Ratti Textile Centre at the Metropolitan Museum of Art in New York and the Textile Museum located in Como, Italy. One example of the benefits of larger organizations is the way in which these collections benefit from excellent multimedia and internet documentation and world-class curatorship, conservation and study facilities. The New York collection can be viewed online via the museum's website (www.metmuseum.org); the Foundation also publishes *The Antonio Ratti Book Collection* highlighting significant pieces.

Contemporary Textiles and Critical Studies

As a footnote to this chapter on research it is worth considering the study of modern textiles. In a sense, whether we speak of textiles in the last century or those of the last decade, it remains a relatively small part of textile history and the textile record. However, critical and academic commentary on contemporary textiles has its own particular problems. These take the form of a narrow range of academic commentary coupled with limited 'third-party' interest in textiles. Much of what there is, is to be found in magazines, exhibition catalogues and what is still a relative scarcity of worthy books. In comparison, contemporary fashion has fared much better attracting the attentions of psychology, sociology and cultural studies. There is no shortage of books looking at subcultures, styles and the social and personal significance of fashion. They range from perspectives on Parisian fashion and style (Steele, 1998) to dress as a global aspect of religion and tradition (Arthur, 2001). There are of course many excellent titles dealing with textile techniques, textile history, textile industry and so on, and the Textile Institute in conjunction with bookseller Blackwell's maintains a superb list. However, the social place and the aesthetic issues of contemporary textile design, craft and art are more often played out in lifestyle magazines than in academic books.

In academic discourse and research there are generally two approaches, one of which is called *hermeneutic*, a chatty, discursive and expressive form, the other *empirical*, a thoughtful, planned and exact form. In the study of textiles (as opposed to textile industry), as the studies begin to deal with more recent fabrics and designs, the bias is toward the hermeneutic variety of research, in essence, a sort of reflective commentary. The kinds of discipline involved shift from archaeology, anthropology, art history and so on, to design history, cultural studies and critical studies. A particular problem facing these disciplines when studying contemporary textiles is that what is popular is not necessarily equivalent to what, in time, will prove significant. However, in a way, what will prove to be the historical importance of textiles is not so much at issue. Contemporary discourse can articulate and stimulate the living relationship between our current culture and our cultural industries. Much as the historical remains of textiles create opportunities for the museum, tourist and educational sectors, so contemporary textiles can play into the postmodern milieu that is the blurring of high and low culture, where shopping and entertainment can join with the form of the art gallery or theatrical performance, in somewhere as trivial and transient as a window display. In this arena the curator, the academic and the journalist can play key roles in establishing context and opportunity for the creative and the entrepreneur.

During the twentieth century the academic disciplines that saw most growth and developed most influence were those that dealt with language, sign and symbol, and perhaps this was appropriate to an era in which mass communications developed so inexorably. The effect was that such subjects as fashion, film and visual communication – subjects naturally full of signs and signing – drew the attention of sociologists, psychologists and the like. For these subjects and in that time, the historical separation of the functional arts and high art was broken. However, for textiles, its transcendent virtues such as touch and warmth and its powers beyond speech such as colour and rhythm have gone, once again, largely unnoticed except to those that love it. In many situations around the world this has placed textiles at a disadvantage, unable to argue for a seat at the table, whether the table is politics, education, cultural policy or funding opportunities. It is just as well we can rest assured that textiles itself is hardly likely to disappear, but the question remains for many as to whether there will continue to be a textile culture where they live and how much that textile culture will reflect them and their community.

The challenge is, for those who are absorbed in contemporary textiles, to see the cultural and industrial merits of language and research, and to establish the breadth of discourse that the subject deserves. In modern societies, power, funding and opportunity are increasingly brokered by the 'professional' and the professional is marked by the presence of codes, standards and philosophy readily to hand. The complexity of textiles industry and culture has often militated against the idea that it constitutes a clear 'profession'. The ability of the textiles community to talk about the cultural value of contemporary textiles, perhaps even more than about its industrial value, will play a key political role in the subject's future. In the absence of a significant interest from the chattier academic disciplines, the task of establishing such a discourse rests quite clearly with the textile community itself.

Bibliography

Abend, J. (2001), 'E-commerce in the Apparel Industry: Tapping into a Virtual World', *Bobbin Magazine*, February, 1.

Alikhani, M. (1998), 'A Glance at Textile Industry in Iran', *Letter of Chamber of Commerce*, March, 1, Chamber of Commerce, Industries and Mines of the Islamic Republic of Iran.

Amidon, C. (1999), 'Using Textiles to Navigate Our Way to the Next Century', *Fiberarts*, September/October.

AMTEX (2001), 'R&D Road Map to the Future', at http://amtex.sandia.gov/roadmap.html, The American Textile Partnership.

Argyle, M. (1996), *The Social Psychology of Leisure*, Harmondsworth: Penguin.

Armstrong, D. (1999), 'Even as the EPA pursues . . .', *Boston Globe*, at www.boston.com/globe/nation/packages/pollution/day1.htm

Arthur, L. (ed.) (2001), *Commitment and Conversion from a Cross-Cultural Perspective*, Oxford: Berg.

Asher, L. (1996), 'Oldest North American Mummy', *Archaeology*, 49(5), Archaeological Institute of America.

ASUR (2001), 'Description of ASUR's Activities, Programs and Projects', at www.bolivianet.com/asur/textilin.htm, The Foundation for Anthropological Investigation and Ethno development, 'Anthropologists of the Southern Andes'.

Barber, E. (1991), *Prehistoric Textiles*, Princeton: Princeton University Press.

—— (1994), *Women's Work: The First 20,000 Years: Women, Cloth, and Society in Early Times*, W.W. Norton & Co.

Barthes, R. (1983), *A Barthes Reader*, S. Sontag (ed.), New York: Hill & Wang.

Baude, D. (2000), 'Trendgame: The Hues, Moods, and Truths We Will Desire', *France Today*, at www.francentral.com/features/culture/cu126_02.shtml

Baudrillard, J. (1994), *Simulacra and Simulation*, S.F. Glaser (trans.), Ann Arbor: University of Michigan Press.

Baurley, S. (1997), 'Some Aspects of Contemporary Japanese Textiles', *Textile Forum*, 1.

BBC (2000), 'Dressed for Success', at www.bbc.co.uk/worldservice/sci_tech/features/science_of_sport/dressed_swimwear.shtml, British Broadcasting Corporation.

Black, C. (2000a), 'Making the Right Connexions', *International Textiles*, March, 811.

—— (2000b), 'Prince of Plastics', *International Textiles*, April, 812.

Black, S. (2000), 'The New Knitting', *International Textiles*, July, 815.

Brandt, B. (1999), 'Carol Eckert: The Power of the Small', *American Craft*, April/May, 58–61.

Brennand-Wood, M. (2000), 'Charting Influences', *Fiberarts*, September/October.

Britannica.com (2001), 'Industrial Polymers, Major Heterochain Polymers', *Encyclopedia Britannica* at www.Britannica.com

Bruzel, A. (1999), 'Cellulase Treatment of Textiles', at http://chemistry.about.com/science, September 27.

Buckley, C. (1989), 'Made in Patriarchy: Toward a Feminist Analysis of Women and Design', in V. Margolin (ed.), *Design Discourse*, Chicago: University of Chicago Press.

Bullivant, L. (2001), 'Curtain Call', *Interiors for Architects and Designers*, March/April.

Bullock, A. and Stallybrass, O. (1977), *The Fontana Dictionary of Modern Thought*, London: Fontana.

Bureau of Labor Statistics (2000), 'Purchasing Managers, Buyers, and Purchasing Agents', *Occupational Outlook Handbook*, at http://stats.bls.gov/oco/ocos023.htm, US Department of Labor.

Canclini, N. (1998), 'Policies for Cultural Creativity', *The Power of Culture*, at www.unesco-sweden.org/Conference/Papers/garcia.htm, Stockholm: UNESCO.

Carson, R. (1962), *Silent Spring*, Boston: Houghton Mifflin Company.

Cassalle, T. (2000), 'Tricks of the Light', *International Textiles*, May, 813.

Chenevix (1799), *A Visit to Germany: 1799, 1800*, The Dean of Westminster (ed.), London: privately published (1861).

ChinaFace.net (2000), 'Chinese silk', ChinaFace.net.

Chubb, J. (1998), 'The control of body voltages getting out of a car', Abstract for 'Static and Textiles' Meeting, Institute of Physics Annual Congress, Brighton.

Coatts, M. (2000), 'Commissions: New Craftwork for Coventry Cathedral', *Crafts*, January/February, 162.

Colchester, C. (1991), *The New Textiles*, London: Thames and Hudson.

Colette (1974), 'Bel Gazou', in *Colette: Earthly Paradise*, R. Phelps (ed.), Harmondsworth: Penguin, 225–41.

Conway, S. (1992), *Thai Textiles*, London: British Museum Press.

Cotton Incorporated (2001a), 'Fashion Designers Come Home', at www.cottoninc.com/MediaServices, Cotton Incorporated.

—— (2001b), 'Living in the Fast Lane', *Lifestyle Monitor*, June 7, at www.cottoninc.com/wwd, Cotton Incorporated.

Csikszentmihalyi, M. (1991), *Flow: The Psychology of Optimal Experience*, New York: Perennial (HarperCollins).

CSIRO (2000), 'Australia and India: mutual benefits from research', *CSIRO Media Release*, at www.csiro.au: Commonwealth Scientific and Industrial Research Organization.

Dalmia, R. (1994), 'Indian Fabric Industry in Global Competition', in M. Teli (ed.), *Integrating Indian Textile Industry into the World Economy: The Golden Textile Conference*, Mumbai: The Textile Association of India.

Danziger, P. (2001), 'Consumers' Spending Spree on the Home Continues', press release, Unity Marketing.

Dawney, S. (2000), 'Britain's Great Emerging Talent at The Craze Gallery, London', *Textile Forum*, 2.

Defoe, D. (1725), 'The Cloth-market at Leeds', in *Tour through Great Britain, 1724–1725*.

de Oliveira, N., Oxley, N. and Petry, M. (1994), *Installation Art*, London: Thames and Hudson.

Dormer, P. (1997), *The Culture of Craft*, New York: St Martin's Press.

DuPont (2000), 'Where east meets west', *DuPont Magazine Online*, at www.dupont.com/corp/products/dupontmag/00/article49.html, DuPont.

Durie, C. (1998), 'A Giant Slims Down to Fight Another Day', in *International Textiles*, October, 797.

Emap (2001), 'who are emap: the big picture', at www.emap.com, Emap plc.

Emmanuel, J. (2000), 'The Body and the Cloth: Ultrasonic Pleats', *World of Embroidery*.

EPA (2001), 'Imprint of the Past: The Ecological History of New Bedford Harbor', at www.epa.gov/nbh/html/textile.html: US Environmental Protection Agency.

Fiberarts (2000), 'Fashion Asia', *Fiberarts*, March/April.

Fletcher, K. (2000), 'Textile Architecture: More with Less', at www.greendesign.net/greenclips, Manchester: Textile Environmental Network.

Fong, H. (1932), 'Cotton Industry and Trade in China', in J. Gentzler (ed.) (1977), *Changing China: Readings in the History of China from the Opium War to the Present*, New York: Praeger, 208–10.

Ford, S. (1994), 'On the Destruction of the Institution of Avant-Gardism', *Variant*, 16, Winter/Spring.

Forty, A. (1986), Objects of Desire: Design and Society 1750–1980, London: Thames and Hudson.

Gamewell, M. (1916), 'The Gateway to China: Pictures of Shanghai', in J. Gentzler (ed.) (1977), *Changing China: Readings in the History of China from the Opium War to the Present*, New York: Praeger, 162–3.

Gee, C. (2000), 'DuPont Combines Apparel and Textile Businesses into New $3 Billion Global Unit', News Release, 30 October, E.I. du Pont de Nemours and Company.

Gillow, J. (1992), *Traditional Indonesian Textiles*, London: Thames and Hudson.

―― and Barnard, N. (1993), *Traditional Indian Textiles*, London: Thames and Hudson.

Gong, F. (*c*.1995), 'Cultural Fusion or Conflict', *Lock Haven International Review*, 9, Lock Haven University of Pennsylvania.

Goswamy, B. (1998), 'Introduction', in *Experiencing a Museum: A Photographic Essay by Dashrath Patel through the Galleries of the Calico Museum of Textiles and the Sarabhai Foundation, Ahmedabad*, Ahmedabad: Sarabhai Foundation.

Guth, C. (1999), 'Structure and Surface', *American Craft*, June/July.

Guy, J. (1998), *Woven Cargoes: Indian Textiles in the East*, London: Thames and Hudson.

Harris, J. (ed.) (1993), *Five Thousand Years of Textiles*, London: British Museum.

Harris, P. and Lyon, D. (1998), 'Linda Behar', *American Craft*, June/July, 42–5.

Harvey, J. (1996), *Traditional Textiles of Central Asia*, London: Thames and Hudson.

Hermes Lab and Associazione Tessile Italiana (2000), 'An International Growth Scenario for Home Textiles and Furnishing Accessories', *Pitti Immagine Casa* at www.pittimmagine.com/eng/fiere/press/casa/sept2000/economicocasa_eng.htm, Pitti Immagine.

Higginson, S. (1997), 'The Art of Textiles: Joseph Otten reinterprets Delaunay and the Constructivists', *International Textiles*, October, 787: XXXI–XXXII.

Hinchliffe, C. (2001), 'UK: Textile and Apparel Job Losses Speed Up', 23 February, at www.just-style.com

Hoggard, L. (1998), 'Lookout: Anne Belgrave', *Crafts*, November/December, 155.

―― (2000), 'The Perfect Mistake', *Crafts*, November/December, 167.

―― and Coatts, M. (2000), 'Lookout: Miglena Kazaski', *Crafts*, June/July, 163.

Holinshed, R. (1577), *England in the Sixteenth Century*.

Hughes, T. and Godwin, F. (1979), *Remains of Elmet*, London: Faber and Faber.

Hummel, J. (1997), 'Integrating economy and ecology: Eco-textiles on the way from a niche market to a mass market', *Gate*, 97/1, GTZ.

ility (2000), Disaster Incident Monitoring, Process Incident, France at www.saunalahti.fi/ility/PI0007.htm

International Textiles (1997a), 'Staying ahead, Retail Trends and Consumer Attitudes', *International Textiles*, May, 783.

―― (1997b), 'Innovations: Future Fantastic', *International Textiles*, July, 785.

―― (1998), 'The Cloth Show and Cloth Plus: London's Key to the International Collection', *International Textiles*, October, 797.

―― (1999a), 'The Century of Colour: The Birth of a Colour Card: Behind the Scenes at the International Colour Authority's Trend Meetings', *International Textiles*, July, 805.

—— (1999b), 'Abstracts: An International Overview', *International Textiles*, July, 805.

—— (2000), 'Optical Illusion', *International Textiles*, February, 810.

ITIS (2000), 'Synthetic Fiber & Textile Industry', Taiwan: Industrial Technology Information Service (ITIS), Technology Department of the Ministry of Economic Affairs.

Jacobs, P. (2000), 'Beads, Body and Soul', *Fiberarts*, March/April.

Jakarta Post (2000), 'Investigation into Texmaco scandal halted', *Jakarta Post*, 20 May.

Jenko, M. (2000), ' Textile and Fashion Design and Textile art in Slovenia', *Textilforum*, 2.

Jet (2000), 'African, Caribbean Clothing Market in U.S. to Expand Thanks to New Trade Act. (Trade and Development Act of 2000)', *Jet*, 5 June, Johnson Publishing Co.

JMPA (2001), 'A Profile of Japanese Magazine Publication: Current Trends in Magazine Publication', at www.j-magazine.or.jp/FIPP/FIPPE/mokuji.html, The Japan Magazine Publishers Association.

Johnson, R. (2001), 'Guessing Dame', at www.rjsj.demon.co.uk/pieces/faithpop corn.htm

Jones, B. (1997), 'The Scarf Reinvents Itself', *International Textiles*, July, 785.

—— (1999a), 'Small Wonders', *International Textiles*, February, 800.

—— (1999b), 'Let There be Light', *International Textiles*, July, 805.

—— (1999c), 'Bags of Character', *International Textiles*, September, 806.

—— (1999d), 'Cutting Edge Textiles', *International Textiles*, October, 807.

—— (2000a), 'Maglia Magic', *International Textiles*, June, 814.

—— (2000b), 'Kei Ito: Neat Pleats', *International Textiles*, July, 815.

—— (2000c), 'Creative Salvage', *International Textiles*, October, 817.

Jones, S. (1997), 'Ph2 Textile Research Project', at www.csm.u-net.com, London: Central Saint Martins.

Jurmain, R. and Nelson, H. (1994), *Introduction to Physical Anthropology*, St. Paul: West Publishing Company.

Kettle, A. (1999), 'Transition: A time of change', *World of Embroidery*, January, 50(1): 52–4.

Kiekens, P. (2000), 'Textiles and Clothing in the Next Millennium: Quo Vadis?', at http://textiles.rug.ac.be

Kirk, V. (2001), email to Jasbir Kaur.

Kumar, R. (1999), *Costumes and Textiles of Royal India*, London: Christies.

Langle, E. (1996), 'Dancing Between Creativity and Commerce', *International Textiles*, July, 775.

—— (1997), 'Fashion Follows Function', *International Textiles*, October, 787: XXIV–XXIX.

Bibliography

Latvian Ministry of Culture (2001), *The Infrastructure of Culture. Propagation of Culture and its Accessibility*, at http://vip.latent.lv/culture/English/access.htm

Li, Y. (1999), 'Development of Intelligent Thermal Management Apparel Technology', at www.asd.polyu.edu.hk/aoe/asd/ITFC/ITFM.htm

Lippard, L. (1976), *Eva Hesse*, New York: New York University Press.

Mahoney, M. (2000a), 'Nuno: In Search of Elements Past and Present', *International Textiles*, August/September, 816: XXVI–XXVIII.

—— (2000b), 'Sophie Roet: Stages of Development', *International Textiles*, October, 817: XLV–XLVIII.

Marchetti, E. (2001), recorded interview with Jasbir Kaur.

Marx, K. and Engels, F. (1888), *The Communist Manifesto*, S. Moore (trans.), Harmondsworth: Penguin.

Maslow, F. (1970), *Motivation and Personality*, New York: Harper and Row.

McCluhan, M and Fiore, Q. (2001), *The Medium is the Massage*, Hamburg: Ginko Press.

Metcalf, B. (2000), 'The Hand at the Heart of Craft', *American Craft*, August/September.

Millar, L. (2001), 'Textile Art in Japan and the UK', email to Dr. Colin Gale.

Minnesota (2000), 'Making a Material Difference', at www.che.umn.edu/centennial/hasselbrack.htm, College of Human Ecology, University of Minnesota.

Mode . . . information (1999), 'Li Edelkoort', at http://musterion.com/musterion/pages/edelkoort.html, Musterion.

Morrell, A. (1999), *Indian Embroidery Techniques at the Calico Museum of Textiles*, Ahmedabad: Sarabhai Foundation.

Morris, W. (1888), 'Ugly London', *Pall Mall Gazette*, September 4: 1–2, at www.marxists.org/archive/morris/works/ugly.htm

Mulkay, M. (1979), *Science and the Sociology of Knowledge*, London:George Allen & Unwin.

Nath, G. (1999), 'The Art of Craft', at www.hindustantimes.com/nonfram/201099/SUN08.htm

Negroponte, N. (1990), 'Hospital Corners', in B. Laurel (ed.), *The Art of Human Computer Interface Design*, New York: Addison-Wesley.

Olmsted, F. (1996), *The Cotton Kingdom: A Traveller's Observations on Cotton and Slavery in the American Slave States*, A. Schlesinger (ed.), New York: Da Capo Press.

OTEMAS (2001), 'Background and Toward Solution', OTEMAS IT Pavilion greeting, Seventh Osaka International Textiles Machinery Show.

Oxygen Media (2001), 'Japanese Textile Design by Hiroshi Jashiki', at http://womenshands.oxygen.com/artisans/japan/related_textile.htm

Papanek, V. (1991), *Design for the Real World*, London: Thames and Hudson.

—— (1995), *The Green Imperative: Ecology and Ethics in Design and Architecture*, London: Thames and Hudson.

Parker, C. (2000), Catalogue *Cornelia Parker*, Boston: Institute of Contemporary Art.

Parker, R. and Pollock, G. (1981), *Old Mistresses: Women, Art and Ideology*, London: Routledge & Kegan Paul.

People's Daily (2000), 'China's Consumer Spending Rebounds', at http://english.peopledaily.com.cn/200007/20/eng20000720_46005.html

phenomeNEWS (1999), Excerpt from a 'phenomeNEWS on the air' interview with Cindy and Gerri, at www.phenomenews.com/archives/feb99/popcorn.html

Postan, M. (1939), *Economic History Review*, May, 165.

PPA (2001), 'Data and Trends: Summary', at www.ppa.co.uk/dataandtrends, The Periodical Publishers Association.

PR Newswire (1999), 'Textile Industry Employees Blast African Growth and Opportunity Act During Capitol Hill Visits', 17 September, PR Newswire Association Inc.

Riley, L. (1995), 'Compostable Upholstery Fabrics', *Metropolis*, September, at www.greendesign.net/greenclips

Robbins, F. (1999), 'The K-G of Knitting: An individual viewpoint from UK conceptual textile artist Freddie Robins', *International Textiles*, July, 805.

Robinson, S. (1969), *A History of Printed Textiles*, Cambridge, Mass.: MIT Press.

Rovine, V. (1997), 'Ancient Andean Textiles from the Schnell Collection', Iowa City: The University of Iowa Museum of Art.

Sajhau, J. (1998), 'Role played by non-governmental organizations in the promotion of codes of conduct', *Business Ethics in the Textile, Clothing and Footwear Industries (TCF)*, 3, at www.ilo.org/public/english/dialogue/sector/papers/bzethics/bthics3.htm, ILO (International Labour Organization).

Schoeser, M. and Rufey, C. (1989), *English and American Textiles*, London: Thames and Hudson

Schumacher, E. (1999), *Small is Beautiful: Economics as if People Mattered*, Vancouver: Hartley and Marks.

Seeling, W. (2000), 'Peter Collingwood: Master Weaver', *American Craft*, February/March, 74–7.

Shepley, C. (1999), 'Innovations in Textile Art', *Fiberarts*, November/December.

Snow, C. (1993), *The Two Cultures*, Cambridge: Cambridge University Press

Sorrell, T. (1991), *Scientism: Philosophy and the Infatuation with Science*, London: Routledge.

Stanford, R. (2000), 'Let the Textile Industry Go!', at www.furman.edu/~stanford/textile.htm

Steele, V. (1998), *Paris Fashion: A Cultural History*, Oxford: Berg.

STNews (1998), 'Textiles – ancient history to current trends', at www.cas.org/ STNEWS/OCTOBER98/textiles.html

Styles, P. (1999), 'Hemp is Hip', *International Textiles*, July, 805.

Sumner, B. (1966), *Survey of Russian History*, London: Methuen.

Sykas, P. (2000), 'Material Evidence: Nineteenth Century Calico Printers' Pattern Books', PhD Thesis, Manchester Metropolitan University.

Sykes, J. (ed.) (1976), *The Concise Oxford Dictionary of current English*, 6th edition, Oxford: Oxford University Press.

Takeda, S. (1999), 'Textile Innovation: Form and Antiform. Makiko Minagawa', *American Craft*, June/July: 61–3.

Tanaka, Y. (1995), 'A comparative study of textile production and trading from the beginning of the 16th century to the end of the 19th century', in *The Hosei University Bulletin*, February, at www.lian.com/TANAKA/englishpapers/ comtext.htm

TCFoz (2000), 'Consumer Lifestyle Trends to 2005', at http://202.139.232.101/ browse/Information%2FBriefing, Australian Commonwealth Department of Industry, Science and Resources.

TCSG (2000), *A National Strategy for the UK Textile and Clothing Industry*, Textile and Clothing Strategy Group.

Tebbutt, D. (1991), 'Inside Pandora's Box', *BYTE*, 116IS, November, 59–66.

Textile Chemical Company Inc. (1999), 'Environmental Protection Agency Risk Management Plan 3613 Pennsylvania: Executive Summary', Reading, PA: Textile Chemical Company Inc. and at http://db.rtknet.org/E34940T1115

Textiles Magazine (2000), 'Student Access to the Worth Global Style Network', *Textiles Magazine*, 1.

textrade.com (2000), 'Global Textile Network, First International Bank Form Strategic Alliance', textrade press release, 31 May.

The Queen (1935), 'Our Royal Needlewomen', *The Queen*, Jubilee Issues, 2: 33.

The Technical Educator (1870), 'Animal Commercial Products, 15: Products of the Sub-Kingdom Annulosa', *The Technical Educator: An Encyclopedia of Technical Education*, 1, London: Cassell, Petter and Galpin.

The Woolmark Company (1999), 'Apparel consumption, distribution and fibre trends into the third millennium', at http://melpub.wool.com, The Woolmark Company.

Thibodeau, P. (2001), 'FTC to focus on consumer profiling at privacy workshop', at www.computerworld.com/cwi/story/0,1199,NAV47_STO57460,00.html, Computerworld Inc.

Tradepartners UK (2001a), 'Clothing, Footwear & Fashion Market in Germany', at www.tradepartners.gov.uk/clothing/germany/profile/overview.shtml, UK Government.

——— (2001b), 'Textiles, Interior Textiles & Carpets Market in Japan', at www.trade
partners.gov.uk/textiles/japan/profile/characteristics.shtml, UK Government.

Trevelyan, G. (1942), *English Social History*, London: Longmans, Green and Co.

Udall, S. (1970), 'Paradise in Peril', in HRH The Prince Phillip, Duke of Edinburgh
and J. Fisher, *Wildlife Crisis*, London: Hamish Hamilton.

UNESCO (1998), 'The Conference', *The Power of Culture*, at www.unesco-
sweden.org/Conference/programme.htm, Stockholm: UNESCO.

Walvin, J. (1993), *Black Ivory*, London: Fontana Press.

Warner, D. (2001), Excerpts from telephone conversation with Jasbir Kaur, April.

Welters, L. (ed.) (1999), *Folk Dress in Europe and Anatolia: Beliefs about
Protection and Fertility*, Oxford: Berg.

Weltge, S. (1998), *Bauhaus Textiles: Women Artists and the Weaving Workshop*,
London: Thames and Hudson.

——— (1999), 'Helena Hernmarck', *American Craft*, December/January.

Woodham, J. (1997), *Twentieth-Century Design*, Oxford: Oxford University Press.

Index

Index